Sociology and the Stereotype
of the Criminal

SOCIOLOGY AND THE STEREOTYPE
OF THE CRIMINAL

Dennis Chapman
PH.D., B.SC. ECON. LOND.

TAVISTOCK PUBLICATIONS
London · New York · Sydney · Toronto · Wellington

First published in 1968
by Tavistock Publications Limited
11 New Fetter Lane, London E.C.4
Printed in Great Britain
in 11 pt Modern Series 7
by T. & A. Constable Ltd. Edinburgh
© Dennis Chapman 1968

SBN 422 72720 2

Distributed in the United States of America
by Barnes & Noble, Inc.

TO PAULINE AND TERENCE MORRIS

Contents

Preface

The object of this essay is to present a study of a matter of great public and professional concern, using the methods of functional analysis.

The products of the essay are hypotheses and *not* conclusions. This is inevitable from the anecdotal nature of the evidence. It is, however, important to assert that many of the works in this field that have the appearance of system are in fact no more substantial, since they fail to take account of the social determination of, rather than the scientific discrimination in, the selection of the evidence.

Much of the data employed comes from newspapers. This method has been chosen not only for its obvious convenience, but to display the function of newspaper reporting in creating the stereotypes which control our thinking about crime.

The substance of the essay is an argument that much of the work done by social scientists in the field of Criminology has been unprofitable because it has begun with definitions – stereotypes – which have determined the course of the inquiry and the conclusions that have emerged. The result of this has been the production of a vast and complex literature, but no substantial progress in social change. Lack of progress has begun to lead to a reconsideration of fundamentals, especially in the U.S.A., but the commonest reaction in Britain is to argue that lack of success is evidence of the need of more studies for the same kind as those that have been made in the past. It would be arrogant to suggest that the literature is valueless, for not only has it provided much new information about such behaviours as shop-lifting or thefts from employers, but methods have been steadily refined, sampling methods have been improved, statistical significance recognized as important – if albeit a trifle reluctantly – and the values of objective tests and the necessity of replicability are now appreciated by many scholars.

The next step, the author would argue, is to establish by

empirical inquiry the extent to which behaviours that are disapproved or illegal are normal in the culture, and the extent to which they are functional or dysfunctional. This may well prove to be a great act of human liberation, such as the studies of Kinsey and his colleagues are slowly becoming recognized as being.

If this could be achieved, then a datum would exist for a critical examination of the institutions of social control and for their modification without further delaying for the diffusion of awareness to create what is called 'public opinion'.

The selection of the stereotype of the criminal for discussion was largely accidental – in that it had its origin in the author's childhood reading of Oscar Wilde's 'Soul of Man Under Socialism' and his 'Ballad of Reading Gaol' and was not fundamental to the main theoretical purpose of the essay, which is to show the consequences in society of the stereotype in determining social behaviour. Many other stereotypes await analysis, those, for example, of women, the poor, the rich, the coloured, and the Jew.

Acknowledgements

The author wishes to record his debt to a criminal organization, which, to its obvious advantage, served during the war as a unit of the National Fire Service, and as such was organized as a university extra-mural class, to which the author was a tutor. The members of this class, with their extensive knowledge of crime, their pride of craftsmanship, and their personal experience of the prison system and the police force, combined with a remarkable intellectual detachment, were largely responsible for reorientating the author's thinking on the subjects dealt with in the following pages.

The author must also acknowledge the help and forbearance of his colleagues, especially Mrs Carol Owen, Mr J. A. Banks, Dr Olive Banks, Mr Derek Jehu, Miss E. Gittus, Dr A. H.

Hudson, and Mr Norman Wilson, all of whom have helped in discussion and criticism.

Thanks are due to the individuals and publishers concerned for permission to quote passages from the following books and journals:

The Editor of *The Howard Journal*: 'A Behavioural Theory of Drug Taking' by L. T. Wilkins. George Allen & Unwin Ltd.: *Social Science and Social Pathology* by Barbara Wootton. Routledge & Kegan Paul Ltd.: *Authority and Delinquency in the Modern State* by Alex Comfort; *The Criminal Area* by T. Morris (published in the United States by Humanities Press Inc.); *Pentonville* by T. Morris and P. Morris, with B. Barer (published in the United States by Humanities Press Inc.). The Institute for the Study & Treatment of Delinquency and the Editor of the *British Journal of Criminology*: 'Delinquency Areas – A Re-assessment' by J. B. Mays; 'The Effects of Imprisonment' by A. J. W. Taylor. Liverpool University Press: *Growing up in the City* by J. B. Mays. John Wiley & Sons: *The Sociology of Crime and Delinquency* by M. E. Wolfgang, Leonard Savitz, and Norman Johnston. Professor T. C. N. Gibbens: *Psychiatric Studies of Borstal Lads* by T. C. N. Gibbens, A. Marriage, and A. Walker. George Weidenfeld & Nicolson Limited: *Causes of Crime* by Lord Paken-ham. The Macmillan Company: *Human Society* by Kingsley Davis (Copyright, 1948 and 1949, by The Macmillan Company). The Editor of the *American Journal of Sociology*: 'A Comment on Hartung, F. E., White Collar Offences in the Wholesale Meat Indus-try' by E. W. Burgess; 'White Collar Offences in the Wholesale Meat Industry in Detroit' by F. E. Hartung; 'Institutions of Privacy in the Determination of Police Administrative Practice' by Arthur L. Stinchcombe. Macmillan & Co. Ltd. (for their series of *Cambridge Studies in Criminology* edited by Professor L. Radzinowicz): *Offenders as Employees* by J. P. Martin; *The Habitual Prisoner* by D. J. West. The Institute for the Study & Treatment of Delinquency: *Shoplifting* by T. C. N. Gibbens and J. Prince. The Editor of the *American Sociological Review*: 'White Collar Criminality' by Edwin A. Suther-land. Reprinted by permission of the World Publishing Co.: 'Social Inquiry and the Autonomy of the Individual' by E. Shils in *The Human Meaning of the Social Sciences* (edited by D. Lerner). The Editor of the *Police Review*: 'Suppressing Vice'. Penguin Books Ltd: *The Challenor Case* by Mary Grigg. Victor Gollancz Ltd.: *The Trial of Stephen Ward* by Ludovic Kennedy (Copyright

© Ludovic Kennedy 1965) (published in the United States by Simon & Schuster, Inc.). Dr William Sargant, and William Heinemann Ltd: *Battle for the Mind* by W. Sargant (Copyright © 1957 by William Sargant). The Williams & Wilkins Co.: *Criminal Interrogation and Confessions* by F. E. Inbau and J. E. Reid. Michael Joseph Ltd: *A Calendar of Murder* by T. Morris and L. Blom-Cooper. University of Chicago Press: *The Professional Thief* by Edwin H. Sutherland. Sigmund Freud Copyrights Ltd., the Estate of Mr James Strachey, The Hogarth Press Ltd., and Routledge & Kegan Paul Ltd.: *Totem and Taboo* (1913) in Volume 13 of the Standard Edition of *The Complete Psychological Works of Sigmund Freud* (published in the United States by W. W. Norton & Co., Inc.). The Author, and the Editor of the *British Journal of Sociology*: 'Full-time Miscreants, Delinquent Neighbourhoods and Criminal Networks' by J. Mack. Holt, Rinehart and Winston, Inc.: *The Prison Community* by Donald Clemmer (Copyright 1940, © 1958, by Donald Clemmer). Mrs Pauline Morris, and the Editor of the *Prison Service Journal*: 'Staff Problems in a Maximum Security Prison', by P. Morris; 'It's the Prisoners who run this Prison', by T. Morris, P. Morris, and B. Biely. Mr D. L. Howard, and Methuen & Co. Ltd: *The English Prisons* by D. L. Howard.

The Author is also grateful to the editors of the *Daily Express*, the *Daily Mail*, the *Daily Telegraph and Morning Post*, the *Economist*, *The Field*, the *Financial Times*, the *Guardian*, the *Hoylake News and Advertiser*, the *Liverpool Echo*, the *Liverpool Daily Post*, *The Times*, the *Sunday Times*, and the *Observer*, for permission to quote from their pages and to the Press Association Ltd. to quote copyright material published in several of the above newspapers.

CHAPTER ONE

Introduction

SOCIOLOGY AS A SCIENCE AND THE STUDY OF CRIME

Sociology is a science. It arises from the recognition of order in society. The discipline describes this order and its antecedents, and from these predicts the future course of human behaviour. A definition as austere as this is not readily acceptable to the layman or even to many social scientists because, first, it asserts that human behaviour is predictable and thus conflicts with ideas of free-will, and, second, it implies that all social processes are of interest to the sociologist and that he does not necessarily accept the popular valuations of different social processes that divide them into good, to be encouraged, and bad, to be discouraged.

Functional analysis in sociology describes the imperatives for the survival of a given social system and in particular examines the great variety of functional alternatives that have arisen with the increase of production over the needs of subsistence. This process has accompanied what was the central interest of classical sociology, the transformation of social relationships from status to contract, from *Gemeinschaft* to *Gesellschaft*, or from primary to secondary group relationships. The climax of this development in interest has been the concept of *anomie* and the associated concept of *alienation* in sociology and corresponding concepts in psycho-analytic social psychology. The process has been one in which relationships between one person and another give way to relationships between one person and groups, these groups becoming larger and more remote and nameless. The change is a continuous reduction in the element of identification with the 'other' in the relationship and a corresponding and increasing interest in the material products of the relationship.

1

This formulation derives from the concepts of *mechanical* and *organic solidarity* of Durkheim, the transformation of relationships from persons to positions, the concept of *bureaucracy* in Weber, the *Generalized Other* of G. H. Mead and the concept of *stereotypes* employed in social psychology (Mead, 1934). Relationships become a technique for the manipulation of symbols, the success of which manipulation produces advantage in status, power, or material. The criminal is discussed in his role as scapegoat; what remains to be explored is the relevance of role theory to the criminal's acceptance of and adaptation to the role of scapegoat.

Human society is characterized by rationality, that is, ends can be expressed symbolically and means can be appraised in terms of effort, and economical choices made; from past experience rules can be stated. Thus, over a wide range of behaviours, the best means for ends which command general acceptance are known and inculcated. Likewise, rules have been established that depend not on primary rationality, but simply on the basis that any rule that makes for predictability of behaviour increases the efficiency of society (even though there may be other rules that might be more economical). It is customary to describe such mechanisms as folkways and mores. Complex societies have, however, hierarchical social systems, with differential distributions of status, power, reward, and property, and, in that there is a high correlation between the possession of any one of these attributes and the rest, both customary and statute law tend to control behaviour in the interests of the groups with high scores on these variables. Social control is, however, not simply exercised through administrative and punitive organizations, but is supported by elaborate symbolic systems which are learned and become cues to behaviour. The control of the apparatus for the diffusion of the symbolic system is distributed in much the same way as status, power, reward, and property. In popular language this is described as the 'Establishment'.

The importance of this argument depends on the observation that actions need not be directed to ends but may arise from stimuli which may be symbolic, or may arise from conditioning (may be fetishistic), or may result from the reification or personification of concepts. This corresponds to the concept of the displaced goal in social psychology.

The range of social control is large and complex, from inhibitions acquired in infancy before speech and rational thought – the conscience or superego – through ethics taught as a technique of social adjustment or as a part of divine revelation, to the control of law. Parents are the agents through which many of the mechanisms operate, and those elements of the ideology that can be implanted before rational thought is developed become a permanent addition to a continuously implanted ideology in successive generations.

In a society divided into groups with and without power, the legal system and the ideology function together to maintain the existing social structure. At the same time, the diffusion of the ideology, even among sociologists, makes a scientific appraisal of the situation difficult. Some inkling of this situation has, however, been possible when looking at other societies; thus we find the popular concept of the 'slave mentality' applied to the 'victims' of the ideologies of other social systems. It is therefore not surprising that 'crime' and 'delinquency' greatly preoccupy social scientists and that they generally accept the thesis that crime is bad, that society could function without crime, and that crime is a special category of behaviour with special discoverable causes. It is further believed that if these causes were known, crime would be prevented. There are many other associated theses, such as those concerned with the distinguishing characteristics of criminals or the modifications of the treatment of criminals that would transform them into non-criminals.

THE THESIS

The thesis of this study is broadly to argue the negative of all the foregoing. The thesis is, however, elaborate and must be presented in many parts.

1. That any behaviour that has a disapproved form also has objectively identical forms that are neutral or approved.
2. That if a behaviour is seen as goal-seeking, then the choice of the form of behaviour between objectively identical forms –

approved, neutral, or disapproved – may depend on chance, knowledge, learning, or training.

3. That apart from the factor of conviction there are no differences between criminals and non-criminals.

4. That criminal behaviour is general, but the incidence of conviction is controlled in part by chance and in part by social processes which divide society into the criminal and non-criminal classes, the former corresponding to, roughly, the poor and underprivileged.

5. That a 'crime' is a behaviour, defined in place and time, of a person, in some cases with another person (victim), with police, lawyers, magistrates, and/or judges and juries.[1] All these variables are causal in the scientific sense.

6. That all the foregoing operate to select individuals from a larger universe of individuals with identical behaviours, both objectively and symbolically cued, and that, therefore, no test of the familiar hypotheses about crime is possible unless the scientist selects his subjects independently of the social system.

7. That crime is a functional part of the social system. This part of the thesis has itself several parts. The first is that the designation of certain actions as permitted, tolerated, or condemned in different circumstances is arbitrary; the second is that there is a lack of correspondence between the ideology and behaviour; and the third is that there is differential treatment of different social groups for behaviours which are objectively identical, identical in that they transgress the same traditional mores, but different in their treatment at law. The designation and social isolation of a relatively small group of victims permit the guilt of others to be symbolically discharged; the identification of the criminal class and its social ostracism permit the reduction of social-class hostility by deflecting aggression that could otherwise be directed towards those with status, power, reward, and property. A special part of the ideology functions to prevent the designated criminal from escaping from his sacrificial role, and institutional record-keeping maintains his identity.

8. That, following this, there is a special problem of the immunity of certain members of society and certain groups. This arises mainly from the protective institutional environment in which they pass part, or all, of their lives, or in which

---

[1] 'A criminality which is regulated partly by chronology, partly by longitude, does not easily admit of scientific discussion' (Ellis, 1914, p. 2).

they spend part of their time or engage in some of their activities.

9. That associated with this are covert social processes which extend whole or partial immunity to, or reduce the impact of, the legal system on members of certain social groups.

10. That associated with the general thesis is a separate problem – that of the legal system as a crime-creating institution. That is, once an institution is created it develops a dynamic of its own and becomes involved in the behaviour with which it is concerned as a participant and, in special circumstances, as an instigator. It may do this in response to social pressures, e.g. the demand that 'criminals' shall be caught and punished.

11. Finally, that the general preoccupation with contravention of the mores in symbolic culture – except, perhaps, some of the graphic arts – can be functionally related to the real situation expounded in items one to ten.

The exposition of this set of related theses presents difficulties. To test many of them would require great expenditure of time and treasure, nor can many of them be verified from such data as are available from administrative sources, because the theses question the very basis of the administrative process. Published work in the field of criminology is of some assistance, but most of it accepts as a basis the results of the administrative, legal, and social systems which identify the criminal and again cannot be used to criticize these systems. In consequence, this study will present tentative arguments based on fragmentary and anecdotal data not crucial in themselves but persuasive enough, it is hoped, to compel consideration of the argument.

It is recognized that, while one or more cases chosen fortuitously may suggest hypotheses, they cannot establish theories. On the other hand, it is important to appreciate that a general theory must account for all the instances that are found.

THE FALLACY OF RATIONALITY

Much of the evidence that will be discussed arises from the application of naïve or mechanical concepts of rationality to the problems of social control; the assumptions, for example, that if there are criminals they must differ in discoverable ways from non-criminals or that if punishment fails in its aims then penal reform is justified. Some sociologists do not study the changes in the penal system as a social process that is part of the larger social process, but as an evolutionary tendency towards enlightenment that is to be encouraged. Sociologists are thereby involved in reform movements, often devoting a major part of their texts to propounding preventive or remedial policies, or even in participating in the parliamentary process of law-making and in the administration of justice; in all this the fallacy of rationality is displayed. In this, sociology appears to be less effective than anthropology, which has successfully studied the processes of social control using functional analysis and appears to be able to avoid the 'rational' fallacy. Merton illustrates the issue thus: 'some conception like that of latent function has very often, almost invariably, been employed by social scientists observing a *standardized practice designed to achieve an objective which one knows from accredited physical science cannot be thus achieved*. This would plainly be the case, for example, with Pueblo rituals dealing with rain or fertility' (Merton, 1957, p. 65).

In criminology the existence of latent function is generally ignored.

Difficulties arise at every stage of the analysis, beginning with the identification of the data, behaviours or action, persons or actors.

Only brief reference need be made to the problem of definition: crime is defined in law; a criminal is a person convicted of a crime. Other authors have noted the extraordinary variety of possible crimes and the somewhat arbitrary nature of the division of crime into indictable and non-indictable offences, serious and less serious – or the apparently inconsistent pattern of punishment possible for different offences and the differences in the extent to which powers to punish are employed by judges and magistrates in different situations. Here is a rich field for sociological analysis, as yet only lightly cultivated, and, here again, it has been studied in terms of rationality or 'justice' (Wootton, 1963; Hood, 1962).

Dissatisfaction with the apparently arbitrary nature of legal definition, and the confusion arising from the inclusion of actions of such variety and the exclusion of many behaviours of interest to some sociologists and psychologists, have led to attempts to extend the field to include 'social pathology' on the one hand and the study of psychopaths on the other – the term socio-path has not yet come into use, but the literature on 'problem families' and the like displays the fact that he has been identified if not as yet labelled. This has been the approach of Barbara Wootton, who defines social pathology in terms of action and expenditure by the administrative organs of the state. By so doing, she concentrates on the behavioural problems of the poor, since the agencies with which she is concerned are almost all derived from the Poor Law: in consequence the behaviour of those who can maintain themselves is not considered (Wootton, 1959, p. 14). A valuable attempt to solve the problem appears in the 'Report of the Committee on Homosexual Offences and Prostitution' (1957, pp. 9 and 10) which states:

'There appears to be no unquestioned definition of what constitutes or ought to constitute a crime. To define it as "an act which is punished by the State" does not answer the question. What acts ought to be punished by the State? We have therefore worked with our own formulation of the function of the criminal law so far as it concerns the subjects of this enquiry. In this field, its function as we see it is to preserve public order and decency, to protect the citizen from what is offensive or injurious, and to provide sufficient safeguards against exploitations and corruption of others, particularly those who are especially vulnerable because they are young, weak in body or mind, inexperienced, or in a state of special physical, official or economic dependence.'

Useful though this is, it does not get over the problem that the discernment of offences for scientific purposes must be independent of administrative processes.

AN ANALYTICAL MODEL

To cope with these difficulties what is needed is a set of operational definitions which would make it possible to identify behaviours and to account for the degree of approval or disapproval they invoke and the social consequences of approval or disapproval.

7

Sociology and the Stereotype of the Criminal

In a scientific analysis (outside sociology) any phenomenon that occurs as the result of the interaction of many variables can be studied by reference to the part played by any one of them. If the absence of any variable is accompanied by the absence of the phenomenon, then the variable may be considered as causal. Such a model would lead, if applied to crime, to such a conclusion as that the cause of crime is legislation – a conclusion that might at first sight appear irritating or even absurd. Yet the modification or repeal of laws is frequently advocated to achieve this end, as witness the recent attempt to raise the age of criminal responsibility of children from 8 years to 12 (which has resulted in a typically British decision to fix it at 10).

In spite of the offence to common sense of using the scientific model, it will be persisted in, in the hope that the result will justify the means.

Thus for any behaviour we may isolate the following variables, absence of which, or variations of which, may be crucial in determining crime or non-crime.

1. The actor.
2. The action.
3. The object of the action.
4. The result of the action.
5. The place of the action.
6. The time of the action.
7. The social environment of the action.
8. The observation of the action.
9. The reporting of the action.
10. The reference of the action to the courts.
11. Trial and conviction.
12. Appeal and confirmation.

Two simple illustrations will serve to exemplify these arguments. The crucial importance of the actor is evident when it is considered that no action of the royal Head of State can be criminal, and there is much legislation which designates actions as legal or illegal depending upon the time of day or the day of the week when they take place.

In practice most writers on, and students of, social pathology solve the problems presented here by first treating the statistical evidence of all crime as revealing the problem and then selecting for study a group of specialists, for example, the offenders against the laws of property, the violent or sexual offenders.

The purpose of the analysis set out above is to call attention to the fact that identical actions with identical results can be criminal or non-criminal or even virtuous, dependent upon the age, sex, status, or profession of the actor, the age, sex, status, or other social characteristics of the object, the time or place of the action, and the observation, reporting, and trial of the actor.

THE UNDERLYING PROBLEM

The main thesis of this essay having thus been presented in as economical a fashion as possible, a brief discussion of some of the underlying issues will be attempted before the exposition of particular arguments.

The essential question that has to be answered is: why is it thought necessary to have a special theory or a number of special theories to account for behaviour prohibited by law? The answer offered here is that this happens because workers in this field begin with a definition of the situation, a stereotype, which determines their thinking and their researches.

Why, for example, when we have well-developed theories of learning which are assumed to have general application, are these only rarely employed to account for criminal behaviour, and new theories developed when established theories are found to be inadequate? (Wolfgang and Ferracuti, 1967, p. 148 *et seq.*). Why also is so much attention devoted to the aetiology of the occupational choice of whores and prostitutes rather than to a general consideration of occupational choice, for which material exists scattered throughout the literature? Learning theory can throw light on the choice of both means and ends, and socialization theory has much to contribute to the understanding of aggression, of which illegal aggression is but a small part.

A second area in which difficulties arise is in the assumption that the crime that is settled by the conviction of a criminal represents crime as a whole. There are many problems here. In crimes of property there is a continuous variation between $\frac{1}{2}$d and infinity, and the question of the value threshold and changes in the value threshold must be taken into account; whereas in some crimes of violence the data are discontinuous. Estimates differ both as to the proportion of different crimes which come to light and as to the extent to which the criminality of different groups in the population is known. In general it is believed that about 20 per cent of crimes against property are cleared up, but the majority of murderers are discovered, although this latter success is probably the result of ignoring the practice of ending the lives of those dying in great pain and of allowing grossly defective children to die of systematic neglect at birth.

In that it is a widespread practice to minimize the defective nature of official statistics for scientific purposes, it may be useful to state why it is considered that the under-reporting of crime is systematic.

First, there is much crime within families and organizations, the reporting of which depends on the solidarity of the group and on the status of the participant.

Second, the detection of crime is in part a function of the social range of the police, who are drawn from the lower middle class and from the working class and, in addition, find their social relations restricted by their occupation.[1] In general, the effectiveness of the police may be expected to decline as the social-class area of the problem is raised; this is offset in part by specialization, e.g. the 'fraud squad' (Banton, 1964, p. 176).

Third, on general grounds we should expect the same patterns of occupational choice in relation to approved and disapproved occupations, the poor and ill-educated in unskilled and semi-skilled pursuits and the middle class in the clerical and professional fields. This pattern of occupational choice has two influences: first, that, all other things being equal, the higher the skill and the higher the status, the greater the chances of success; and, second, in that the unskilled is likely to be concerned with property (scrap metal, for example) and the skilled with

[1] Royal Commission on the Police (1962), appendix to the minutes of evidence (1-10), pp. 17-18; also Banton (1964), especially Chapters 8 and 9 and p. 249.

symbols and paper (cheques), the chances of concealment are much greater for the latter. Compare the problems of concealing a quantity of lead with those of hiding from the inland revenue authority entries in accounts of which you are the legitimate custodian.

A fourth source of systematic error, discussed in detail later, arises from the interaction of privacy and police practice. In working-class districts the police observe crime on patrol or are called in to mediate in disputes, some of which may involve crime. In middle-class districts, the police patrol much less frequently and are called in generally only when there is an invasion from outside. Middle-class crimes such as defrauding the inland revenue may be the cause of envy amongst less fortunate members of the same class, but rarely the subject of a report by them to the revenue authorities.

Another part of the thesis deals with punishment and the social role of the prisoner. Imprisonment as a technique of social change did not develop on the basis of any evidence, but as an historical accident. The sentence to death by the method of cortical dislocation by hanging is as accidental in origin as it is technically primitive. These forms of punishment demonstrably fail in their avowed objectives, as does flogging, yet methods of education based on well-established theory and practice are still not employed. Moreover, even where the use of such practices is declining they are still retained for certain classes of persons, e.g. flogging of children in the Isle of Man, convicts in prison,[1] the inhabitants of colonial territories, and the caning of boys under 18 in a Naval training establishment;[2] and, in spite of all that is known about capital punishment, its use was extended in an 'Emergency' in British Guiana (1964).

A clue to the underlying problem is given by parliamentary practice. Where there is an issue in biology, chemistry, physics, engineering, or economics (agriculture, defence, industry, or trade), policy is determined by the government on the advice of experts and enforced by the Whips; where, on the other hand, it is an issue in the field of human relations, like capital punishment or homosexuality, it becomes, to quote the Rt. Hon.

[1] Abolished by Section 65 of the Criminal Justice Act 1967.
[2] Abolished 9 May 1967.

Harold Wilson, member for the Huyton division of Lancashire (now Prime Minister), a 'matter of deep conscience' – that is, not subject to rational thought.

In a society where there is much ambivalence and confusion about morals (including crime), the difficulty of controlling and resolving the resulting tension is acute.

Techniques of conflict resolution are many and not all of them are consciously recognized as such. They include movements of wide religious, social, and political reform, the reform of the law and of the penal system through Parliament (here we find the direct intervention of the social scientist), and organizations devoted to the protection of the individual and the improvement of justice. The responses of the institutions and organizations of social control are ambivalent, and in general we may note a resistance to change and a tendency to offer symbolic changes in place of real ones. The Royal Commission may be relied on both to delay change by up to five years and to present ambiguous and often conflicting recommendations.

Professor Robert Park said, 'We are always passing laws in America. We might as well get up and dance. The laws are largely to relieve emotion, and the legislatures are quite unaware of the fact.'[1]

These 'real' activities are important in the long run, but marginal in the immediate situation. Here forms of symbolic tension-resolution predominate. There is the dramatic form of 'popular' fiction, the drama, radio, television, where the author describes either murder or major crimes against property by persons generally of unattractive appearance and unpleasant social and personal characteristics, crimes which are almost inevitably solved by charming and highly intelligent policemen and detectives who only raise their voices and never their hands in moments of extreme exasperation. Incidentally, identical behaviours form the subject-matter of the next most popular form of drama, the spy story. Here the murders and thefts are undertaken by the charming ones, their victims (from behind the Iron Curtain) the ugly ones. It is interesting to observe the parts played by well-known television actors as they switch roles from night to night.

[1] Quoted in Sutherland & Cressey, *Principles of Criminology* (1955).

The stereotype presented in dramatic form is generally diffused and it permits both the direction of the aggression of the majority towards the under-privileged and the redefinition of the situation of the majority in relation to their own moral conflicts.[1]

There is, however, much literature and drama and some cinema which provide profound insights into the nature of aggression and of social conflict. There is likewise much which illuminates the social processes of institutions. This material is often profoundly disturbing at the time of its first appearance and stimulates hostile responses; nevertheless, it endures and is an agent of social change.

In that this essay appears to argue against the main stream of theoretical explanations of selected human behaviours, the concept of crime and its place in the content of sociological theory will be examined.

Very little sociological theory has been explicitly propounded in the precise form familiar in physics or chemistry. Marx attempted such a presentation in his law of falling profits, Engel, in his law of the relationship between income and expenditure on food, and, more recently, a number of phenomena have been shown to have growth patterns of a form which can be expressed mathematically (Young, 1965). Most theory is a description of general tendencies expressed in literary form or in models; that is, descriptions of patterns or sequences of events found in a variety of social situations. Such primitive theories allow some predictions to be made, permit some persons as individuals or administrators to achieve their aims with a greater economy of effort than without them, or allow the observer to 'understand' a situation. This often means simply to achieve a position of intellectual 'rest'; that is, to stop thinking about the problem. Much of the controversy around sociological theory arises out of failure to agree on definitions, failure to agree upon what variables are to be isolated for the purpose of discussion, and failure to agree on the objects of sociological inquiry. A further complication is that much sociological theory has inevitably been

[1] It is significant that a recent review of the penal system is called 'The *War* Against Crime in England and Wales 1959-1964' (1964) – thus confirming the stereotype of the criminal as the enemy.

anticipated by oral tradition and by literature. Many of the problems of human adjustment have existed in their present form as far back as historical evidence is available – even in the particular forms that are characteristic of large-scale urban settlement – Babylonian litigation may be taken as a guide. What is new is not the problem-solving process, but calling problem-solving Sociology, Social Psychology, and Psychology. This process has, in the past, been recorded as precept, proverb, literature, and drama. It can be readily presented as a series of predictions: if you covet your neighbour's wife, then . . .; if you love your neighbour, then . . .; if you fall in love with your mother, then . . . . Literary tradition may, however, be regarded as having three forms for the purpose of this discussion. The first is the realistic, where a situation of high frequency and generality is described, and the climax or conclusion accords with the probabilities found in nature. The reader or listener is thus equipped to determine his behaviour knowing the odds are in favour of or against his objectives. A second form is the fantasy in which the probabilities are ignored and the desired solution presented. This may be a tension-relieving device, as in the religious concept of eternal life. It may, on the other hand, be an alternative to problem-solving behaviour – this was the point of view taken by Marx about the concept of eternal life. Between these two extremes is a group of forms, in which fantasy and reality are presented together, and these may function in a variety of ways to relieve individual tensions variously described as increasing self-awareness, relieving guilt, increasing understanding, and the like. They may also serve to increase consensus and to replace individual goals by communal ones.

It is to be expected, therefore, that where sociology has a literary form, and deals with situations of conflict, or where psychology deals with conflict within the person, these disciplines will possess the characteristics of literary forms of problem-solving. This will take the third form in many cases because of the socialization to which the scientist has unwittingly been exposed, or the social, political, or economic pressures to which he will respond. The very rationalizations with which he accompanies his behaviour are part of the process with which this essay is concerned.

14

The form in which the reality and fantasy are often presented
is as follows. Data are collected with a greater or lesser degree of
scientific procedure (or ritual). They are then presented with an
unexpressed assumption in which the criminal is presented with
the attributes of the devil in a medieval mystery play. Finally,
a fantasy solution is presented in the form, if only boys' mothers
would breast-feed them for nine months, then, etc., etc. To this
the reasonable man might object, if this is so, why does the process persist? The answer is, because, in societies where the moral
order and the social practice are in large-scale conflict, the
criminal and the criminologist are functionally necessary to control tension, and the form of criminology is determined by this
need. In the same manner the scapegoat-creating process of the
criminal law makes the fantasy true.

It is ironical to observe that the essayist, poet, and play-
wright Oscar Wilde anticipated much of this thesis when he
wrote of the attitude of 'Humanity' towards 'people whom, in a
very arbitrary manner, it chooses to call criminals'. In the same
essay, 'The Soul of Man Under Socialism', he wrote:

'As one reads history, not in the expurgated editions written for
schoolboys and passmen, but in the original authorities of each
time, one is absolutely sickened, not by the crimes that the wicked
have committed, but by the punishments the good have inflicted; and a community is infinitely more brutalized by the
habitual employment of punishment, than it is by the occurrence
of crime' (Wilde, 1891).

His relevance does not end here; this statement was prophetic
for Wilde was to suffer the extremes of punishment in Wandsworth and Reading gaols, and from this experience he wrote 'The
Ballad of Reading Gaol'. This poem has more of relevance to
say about the desocialization of the prisoner and the destruction
of his personality than much of the 'scientific' literature of
crime. It provides also deep insight (if colleagues will permit
such an unscientific concept) into the moral order and social
system of the prison (Wilde, 1898).

So much for the form of the argument. The general place in
sociology of the thesis is that it attempts to explore the theme
of W. I. Thomas, who wrote that, when people define situations

15

as real, they are real. This is a tantalizing theme which awaits the immense task of systematic exploration. Much has been achieved in existential psycho-analytic psychology, since this is the systematic study of the symbolic systems by which persons represent themselves to themselves. The processes are comprehensible when the behaviours of schizophrenic patients are described (Laing and Esterson, 1964), but where whole societies are involved the difficulties are much greater.

The hypothesis has a double relevance. It argues that the behaviour is a learned, culturally patterned response to a situation which fails to provide for the needs of the patient and that it is accompanied by a symbolic representation of the world – delusion, hallucination, or fantasy – which allows the patient to accommodate the behaviour.

The problem exists at two levels. The first is that of comprehending the symbolic system, the second that of tracing the social processes which have been selected out of the infinite range of alternatives, which occur by chance and are maintained because they 'fit' the belief system. Prison is one such process.

It is easier to become aware of the scope of Thomas's thesis if consideration is given to the range of symbolic systems with which modern society functions. Only seeing, touching, smelling, hearing, and tasting provide experience not mediated by symbols. Even thinking – if this is regarded as talking with oneself – is subject to the inadequacies of words to represent things and relationships. It is only in mathematics, where the results of symbolic manipulations are checked against reality, that the influence of the process of representation can be minimized (Braithwaite, 1953). In social life, unlike mathematics, if the results of the manipulation of symbols do not conform to reality, it rarely happens that the calculus is discarded.

The nature of the problem was demonstrated when Myrdal initiated the series of studies of the Negro/white conflict in the U.S.A., of which *An American Dilemma* is the main work. As a Swede, he conceived the possibility of viewing the American situation through the 'prism' of an 'alien *milieu*'. He wrote, 'There are some ideas concerning the larger society, in which our special problem has its play, which are so general that they are hard to grasp and give definite form, and in any case, almost impossible to prove. Everyone has such ideas, and of necessity they determine the scientific treatment of a specific social problem' (Myrdal, 1944, p. xlix). He goes on, 'No doubt most social scientists honestly believe that they have no such preoccupations. Their prevalence becomes obvious, however, when time has passed and the milieu changed' (Myrdal, ibid, p. 1).

Following Myrdal, it is possible to show a parallelism between beliefs about the Negro amongst American sociologists, and beliefs about criminals held by sociologists elsewhere. His fourth chapter, 'Racial Beliefs and the Role of Science', has affinities to Chapter 2 of this work. The parallelism becomes more striking when the situation in some parts of the South is considered; here Negro and criminal are synonymous. It is easier to see the self-fulfilling prophecy at work in America, when the inferior education of the Negro is justified by his inferior performance in occupations requiring higher education, than it is to appreciate the consequences of long prison sentences to the recidivist in Britain.

The parallelism with the Negro/white problem displays an important fact. In the case of the criminal and the non-criminal population, the relationship is between a few thousands and some fifty millions; the sacrifice of the few may be a small cost to achieve the social solidarity of the many. Where, however, the numbers are more nearly equal, political difficulties of a major order arise, although there is little evidence that the increase in real experience over symbolic is enough to change the nature of the relationship between Negroes and whites.

Much more exciting prospects appear when it is realized that the same processes as determine these relationships apply also in relationships between major states with different religions or ideologies. In these, behaviours are controlled almost entirely by the stereotype of the enemy presented by selective reporting – or even deliberate invention. While this analysis may make no contribution towards preventing the progress of humanity to self-destruction, it will make possible a reliable prediction of the manner, time, and certainty of it.

The implication of this analysis is that there is an indivisibility of morals; this has an interesting consequence as behaviour is examined, and that of the individual is contrasted with that of society. When the individual wishes to perform a forbidden act, he may redefine it to escape the symbols which evoke the emotionally disturbing conditional response – he rationalizes – and his friends will tell him so. If he redefines the world, he may be considered to be mad and have to receive treatment – or he may become a great political leader and achieve the power to modify the world to match his delusion. If, however, an ideology has grown over historical time and is universally accepted, then it will not change unless it ceases to be functional. This point is reached with defeat in an international war. It is approaching in Britain in relation to the crime of theft, with the realization of the predatory nature of much business and the business-like nature of much theft. The rapid growth in the number and size of crimes of theft, unaccompanied by any change in the variables assumed to be associated with crime, may be a turning-point (Wilkins, 1965). The scientific problem is then how to acquire the capacity to see the processes concealed in the symbolic system. In psycho-analysis, the patient is made to redefine this world by a long and painful process requiring the continuous support of the analyst. Myrdal has suggested the 'prism' of the 'alien *milieu*' and Tom Harrisson, returning to England from Malekula, the employment of black anthropologists to enlighten us about the nature of our culture. What is attempted here is to employ the method of operational definition developed in the physical sciences to solve a simpler problem of objectivity. By this means the behaviour, and those symbols which both identify it and give it moral reference, are separated. By this means the reality, the myth, and the reality created by the myth can be separated and studied.

The thesis of Thomas represents the first approximation to a model of the situation. In this work it is modified in two ways; one to take account of the role of the power elite, and the other to take account of the class divisions in society. If it is objected that the class divisions do not exist, it can equally be argued that the fact that many persons believe them to exist creates a real division which requires explanation. In detail, the work explores the real consequences in police behaviour, the courts, and the prisons, of the beliefs which exist as stereotypes in society. What cannot be demonstrated here is the nature of the accommodation that these beliefs make possible within the person in conflict with the behaviours appropriate to a competitive society and the traditional or natural moral order with which he has been socialized.

An attempt will now be made to set out in concise general terms the main provisional theoretical assumptions referred to above, in the form of a model. This will assume a number of conflict situations in which the beliefs about crime and the criminal, and the behaviours that arise from these beliefs, function to control the conflicts and maintain the stability of the system.

I. *The Conflict within the Moral Order*

(*a*) The fundamental moral order consists of rules appropriate to a small population, most of whose social experience is in primary groups.

(*b*) A large part of modern urban social life is conducted in secondary groups and is mediated by symbols.

(*c*) Much social action, including many 'compulsory' forms, is contrary to the moral order.

(*d*) Many socially approved goals are contrary to the moral order.

(*e*) There are contradictions between the *nature* of actions and their moral referents.

(*f*) In many actions that are contrary to the moral order the 'criminal' and the 'victim' are symbiotically involved.

(*g*) The increase in wealth and the wider distribution of wealth are accompanied by insecurity and fear of loss among a large part of the population.

II. *The Conflict within the Social Order*

(*a*) Political, social, religious, and administrative power is concentrated in the hands of a relatively homogeneous elite who control the sources of information and means of communication.

(*b*) The values and outlook of the 'power elite' are accepted by a large prosperous stratum, the middle and upper classes. (These include the executives, the professions, the priesthood, the educators, and the magistracy).

(c) There is a substantial minority in the population deprived of material satisfactions, education, and vocational opportunity.

The responses to these conflicts are in social processes which contribute to both individual and social stability.

III. *Generalized Patterns of Conflict Resolution*

(a) By redefinition, which takes the form of changing the symbols representing the behaviour, thus changing the conditional response. This is called 'rationalization' in the individual, and may take many forms in society, from a change in legislation to a Papal Encyclical. (This process of revaluation is of special interest in the adjustment pattern of minority groups, as Wilkins argues below).

(b) By the transfer of the guilt to an identifiable minority and their designation as an 'outgroup'.

(c) By the direction of aggression on to the 'outgroup' minority.

(d) This requires the arbitrary absolution of the victims and the others symbiotically involved in the behaviour.

(e) It may involve means of exemption of some persons or groups from the rules in the moral order either overtly or covertly through the operation of secrecy (see below).

IV. *The Criminal as Scapegoat*

(a) The criminal of the stereotype is a lawbreaker who has been sent to prison. All other lawbreakers do not become identified with the scapegoat.

(b) The scapegoat is chosen largely from the lower-working-class group, who are vulnerable because of poverty, lack of privacy, lack of education, social disconnection, weakness of kinship ties, visibility through colour, foreign name or origin, etc.

(c) The process of selection is operated by employers, property-owners, the police, magistrates, and judges—all, except the lower ranks of the police, members of the middle and upper classes.

(*d*) Once he is identified by imprisonment, incorporation of the criminal in normal social life is difficult, sometimes impossible.

(*e*) The pathways to normal social life are controlled by employers, administrators, and property-owners. Most of these are members of the middle class.

(*f*) Once the victim has been chosen, his vulnerability increases with each successive offence and his desocialization is progressive.

(*g*) He may accept the role and become adapted to prison.

(*h*) Professional, successful criminals exist and contribute to the conflict situation. This relative invulnerability increases the aggression directed against the scapegoat.

(Wilkins has developed a theoretical system to describe this group, which is given below).

(*i*) Professional criminals enter this occupation in the same way as other occupations, but tend to be drawn from groups in society for whom the normal paths to approved goals are blocked.

(*j*) The penal system is justified by the 'recidivist', who corresponds to the stereotype. He is the product of the penal system. The process is self-maintaining.

(*k*) The process of stereotype-creation contains its dialectical opposite: the highly successful criminal may become a 'folk-hero'.

(*l*) Many criminals whose aggressive behaviour contributes to the stereotype could, with vocational guidance, be accommodated in socially approved occupations.

There is a third subsidiary conflict created by the fact that much of the penal system is contrary to the traditional moral order.

V. *The Conflict between the Moral Order and the Penal System*

(*a*) Problems arise because not all victims have the characteristics of the stereotype (discussion of the Oscar Wilde case has gone on for over fifty years).

(*b*) The behaviour of the police, generally concealed by the *corps d'élite* pattern, is on occasion contrary to the moral order.

C

(c) The penal system, with its arbitrary punishments and deprivations, is contrary to the moral order.

(d) The penal system compels its victims to participate in behaviour contrary to the moral order.

VI. *The Resolution of the Conflict between the Moral Order and the Penal System*

(a) As in other conflicts, redefinition plays a part, but more generalized symbolic systems are more important. These take the form of continuous discussions, writing, research, and inquiry, of which the Royal Commission is the archetype. The characteristic of this process is that the situation remains unchanged, while for the duration of the symbolic process the conflict is resolved. The symbolic process is continuous.

(b) The level of toleration of penal practices varies with the quantity and quality of 'crime'; particular incidents raise or lower the thresholds of toleration.

(c) The penal system is highly resistant to change, in a society with a steadily rising standard of life and amenity.

(d) Such changes as take place through penal reform are relative to changes in society and may have the effect of keeping constant the degree of relative deprivation of the criminal.

(e) Since, if there was no change in conditions, the penal system would fall below the threshold of tolerance, the function of penal reform is to preserve the system by adapting it to social change.

The fifth area of conflict concerns the place of the social sciences in society.

VII. *The Role of the Social Sciences in the Conflict Situation*

(a) The social sciences are a part of the symbolic system by which societies adapt and are controlled.

(b) The social sciences and social scientists compete for power, esteem, and reward with administrators, priests, and doctors, and among themselves.

(*c*) The social sciences accept the stereotype of the criminal as given, for to challenge it would involve heavy penalties. The penalties are, to be isolated from the main stream of professional activity, to be denied resources for research, and to be denied official patronage with its rewards in material and status.

(*d*) The social sciences attempt to provide rational-scientific explanations in competition with the magical and quasi-magical explanation of the priesthood and of some parts of the medical profession.

(*e*) Social scientists are heavily involved in penal-reform movements which are adaptive to the system.

(*f*) The growth in the quantity and change in the scale of crime is producing new types of social science in conflict with the old. This is not committed or wholly committed to the prevailing value system (Wilkins, 1965).

This highly abstract theoretical system requires the support of many theoretical subsystems to deal with problems of differential immunity, privacy, the role of the victim, the nature of symbiosis, changes in symbolic systems, the *corps d'élite*, and other matters described in later chapters. This cannot be attempted here. Mention must be made, however, of an extremely relevant general theory developed by Wilkins, which deals with the 'deviant group' of which the professional criminal organization is one example, and the police may be another. This theory also throws light on the social consequences of the existence of successful deviant groups. It also accounts for the role of secrecy in deviant groups or institutions and is relevant to the concept of the *corps d'élite* in the power structure.

Wilkins's model is given here.

'Summarizing the general theory, in so far as it is possible, the following statements are set forth:

(*a*) certain types of information in relation to certain systems lead to more acts being defined as deviant to the extent that the individuals whose behaviour is so defined are "cut off" from the values of the parent system;

(b) the defining act leads to more action being taken against those perceived as deviant, and the individuals defined begin to see themselves as deviant (as unacceptable within the general system or culture). Perhaps it is mainly through information received from other persons that we get to know what sort of persons we "are";

(c) the self-definition and the action taken by society at large leads to the isolation and alienation of the persons defined as deviant;

(d) the deviant groups tend to develop their own values which may run counter to the values of the parent system which has defined them as "out-laws" (or in terms of the probability calculus "outliers");

(e) the deviation-amplifying (centrifugal) forces are thus generated and develop within the deviant group, and lead to more deviant behaviour by the alienated groups;

(f) the increased deviance demonstrated by the deviant groups (resulting from a deviation amplification or feed-back system) results in more forceful action by the conforming groups against the non-conformists;

(g) thus information about the behaviour of the non-conformists (f) received by the conforming groups, leads to more acts being defined as deviant and back to (a) and round, and round again' (Wilkins, 1965).

The theory expounded by Wilkins, taken with those advanced here, suggests, that the creation of the scapegoat is a part of the hostility displayed by the macro-society to deviants in general, and makes an important contribution to the maintenance of deviant groups as an ongoing part of the system. The thesis advanced here is that deviant groups are a functionally necessary part of the system, as is the sociology of deviance. This analysis becomes more cogent as deviance is traced from the extreme of actions generally condemned and punished at law, through to actions such as gambling and drug-taking (including alcohol), which, although contrary to the mores, are widely undertaken, but not in most instances contrary to law.

Taken together, the theories suggest that social change, that is processes which take account of the theoretical analysis of society, is very different from social reform, which is a part of the adaptive mechanism by which a society maintains stability.

24

CHAPTER TWO

The Stereotype of the Criminal and the Strategy of Social Investigation

THE STEREOTYPE OF THE CRIMINAL

The creation of stereotypes is an important functional necessity in all societies and the stereotype of the 'villain' is of especial interest. Originally the lowest and most deprived group in feudal society (except for the slave), villains have in their stereotyped symbolic form continued to represent the evil concentrated in the lowest social groups. As Nigel Balchin expresses it:

'I submit, therefore, that the monumental villain is a projection of two of man's most important subconscious characteristics . . . the sense of frustration and the sense of guilt' (Balchin, 1950, p. 255).

Associated with the stereotype are elaborations, mainly discarded by the criminologist but still affecting popular thinking and social action, that criminals and other socially pathological persons are physically, psychologically, or racially inferior, or – a recent variation – members of a cultural sub-group: the racial theory reborn in modern anthropological language. Historically the Saxon villain in Norman society lost status, and the revolt of 1381 created the identification of the villain as the enemy in class conflict. Later, the nineteenth-century European migrant with his German argot fitted the stereotype.

The pattern is consistent with that which represented women as inferior through their spiritual uncleanness and smaller brains, and with the stereotype of all aboriginal peoples as morally and intellectually inferior and appropriately subject to salvation, exploitation, and extermination. The attempts to establish criminal types, to show their physical and intellectual distinguishing characteristics, are now less frequent but the

25

attempts to demonstrate the socially inferior qualities of the criminal persist.

Two separate theoretical problems are involved: the first is that of the social function of hostility to the criminal, and the second the way in which class conflict, with the resultant hostility of the middle and upper classes to the working classes, concentrates hostility onto the working-class criminal.

G. H. Mead, in a brilliant essay published over forty years ago, describes the hostility of society to the law breaker and the dilemma of the helplessness of the reformer, exemplified in the work of Barbara Wootton to be described later:

'Thus we see society almost helpless in the grip of the hostile attitude it has taken toward those who break its laws and contravene its institutions. Hostility towards the lawbreaker inevitably brings with it the attitudes of retribution, and exclusion. These provide no principles for the eradication of crime, for returning the delinquent to normal social relations, nor for stating the transgressed rights and institutions of their positive social functions' (Mead, 1918, p. 590).

He then goes on to expound a functional analysis of crime in society:

'On the other side of the ledger stands the fact that the attitude of hostility toward the lawbreaker has the unique advantage of uniting all members of the community in the emotional solidarity of aggression. While the most admirable of humanitarian efforts are sure to run counter to the individual interests of very many in the community, or fail to touch the interest and imagination of the multitude and to leave the community divided or indifferent, the cry of thief or murder is attuned to profound complexes, lying below the surface of competing individual effort, and citizens who have separated by divergent interests stand together against the common enemy' (ibid, p. 591).

Mead argues that hostility to the criminal reinforces the common values that unite society and that are challenged by crime. He pointed out that – at the time when he was writing – the activities of criminals were economically insignificant and did not seriously endanger the working of society. The criminal courts in spite of their many defects continuously bring the value system to the notice of society and create the essential consensus needed for its survival. He did not, however, argue that the different treatments of crimes of different types but of the same economic magnitude also function to preserve the particular class relationships within a society.

This becomes more obvious when the statements made by judges when sentencing or when summing up in a divorce case are studied. In these situations the judge speaks on behalf of 'society'. What happens then is that newspaper, radio, and television report the judgement and its accompanying gloss, and society learns what is expected of it. It is curious that while sentences, which affect the individual primarily, have been studied, sentencing, the whole process which affects society, has been taken for granted.

However, Mead was over-optimistic when he continued:

'I am willing to admit that this statement is distorted, not however in its analysis of the efficacy of the procedure against the criminal, but in its failure to recognize the growing consciousness of the many common interests which is slowly changing our institutional conception of society, and its consequent exaggerated estimate upon the import of the criminal' (ibid, p. 591).

In fact, it would not be too much to say that, far from following the brilliant insight of G. H. Mead, sociology has simply added its voice to the cry of 'stop thief'.

The second issue, that of social class, is demonstrated in the pattern of criminological research. This is shown in the popular hypotheses about the nature of criminal behaviour, and the methods employed to test them.

POPULAR HYPOTHESES ABOUT THE CAUSES OF CRIME

Barbara Wootton has devoted the central argument of her work to an examination of the 'popular current hypotheses about the causes of characteristic features of crime and delinquency'. In this she examined some twenty-one researches chosen from the whole field of criminological literature which had first to be

27

scrutinized to eliminate the irrelevant, the inadequate, and the unreliable (Wootton, 1959).

Her study then dealt with the following:

'The twelve factors on whose possible association with criminality or delinquency light is sought from these studies are as follows:

(1) the size of the delinquent's family,
(2) the presence of other criminals in the family,
(3) club membership,
(4) church attendance,
(5) employment record,
(6) social status,
(7) poverty,
(8) mother's employment outside the home,
(9) school truancy,
(10) broken home,
(11) health,
(12) educational attainment.'

She commented:

'It must be admitted that this selection looks about as arbitrary as the list of investigations just given. Here again, however, choice is limited by what there is to choose from. This miscellaneous list is the result of trying to cover, on the one hand, those hypotheses which underlie currently popular explanations and, on the other hand, those which happen actually to have attracted the interest of investigators: it necessarily, therefore, reflects the influence of fashion in social research' (Wootton, 1959, p. 84).

It is not necessary to follow Barbara Wootton's careful analysis in detail – it is readily available – only to quote her conclusion:

'All in all, therefore, this collection of studies, although chosen for its comparative methodological merit, produces only the most meagre, and dubiously supported, generalizations. On the whole it seems that offenders come from relatively large families. Not infrequently (according to some investigators very frequently) other members of the delinquents' (variously defined) families have also been in trouble with the law. Offenders are unlikely to be regular churchgoers, but the evidence as to whether club membership discourages delinquency is "widely contradictory". If they are of age to be employed, they are likely to be classified as "poor" rather than as "good" workers. Most of them come from the lower social classes, but again the evidence as to the extent to which they can be described as exceptionally poor is conflicting; nor is there any clear indication that their delinquency is associated with the employment of their mothers outside the home. Their health is probably no worse than that of other people, but many of them have earned poor reputations at school, though these may well be prejudiced by their teachers' knowledge of their delinquencies. In their schooldays they are quite likely to have truanted from school, and perhaps an unusually large proportion of them come from homes in which at some (frequently unspecified) time both parents were not, for whatever reason, living together; yet even on these points, the findings of some enquiries are negative. And beyond this we cannot go' (ibid, p. 134).

It will be observed that even these tentative conclusions do not demonstrate differences between offenders and non-offenders, for example, the statement that 'offenders are unlikely to be regular churchgoers' would not appear to differentiate them from any distinctive social group except ministers of religion and church organists.

The next stage of the discussion is an examination of theories of the 'effects of Maternal Separation or Deprivation'. Here it is possible to be even briefer and to record Barbara Wootton's conclusion:

'That the damage is lifelong or irreversible, that maternal deprivation is a major factor in criminal behaviour, or that the younger the child the greater the risk, all these must be regarded as quite unproven hypotheses' (ibid, p. 156).

This is not to deny the value of research into the relationship between socialization and learning in childhood and later behaviour, especially those regular and patterned responses to social situations comprehended by the term personality, but only of the researches which attempt to relate certain childhood experiences to later conviction in the courts for specific offences.

The examination of the significance of an early start in criminal behaviour was no more conclusive:

'. . . we are thus left with a mass of confused and contradictory evidence. On the one hand the theory that criminality is a

29

symptom of "immaturity" seems to amount to little more than a repetition in somewhat grandiose terms of well-known facts about the age-distribution of offenders; while, on the other hand, the hypothesis that those who begin early are likely to go on is certainly not proven, and cannot even claim to be supported by a preponderance of the available evidence' (ibid, p. 172).

The studies of the psychologist appear to offer no solution either, although they raise many interesting problems:

Wootton quotes the work of Schuessler and Cressey, who in 1950 evaluated all the research published in the previous 25 years which considered the differences in the personalities of criminals and non-criminals. They established that the components of personality believed to be associated with criminality have about the same distribution in the criminal and non-criminal population. This is what would be expected; while personality factors, skills, and intelligence play a part in vocational choice and success, the identification of a person as a criminal from amongst all those who act in a particular form, approved or disapproved, would only be affected at the margin by such factors. That is, all other things being equal, the more intelligent and more athletic will escape and the dull and slow will be caught. Wootton refers also to the study by Metfessel and Lovell who reviewed the mainly American literature on the subject of the individual factors in crime for the decade 1930 to 1940 and she reports their finding that age and sex are the only constants. These, it will be shown, are equally likely to be determined by legislation and by the practice of the police and the courts. The American authors came to the important conclusion that those factors which deal in relatively vague categories such as bad parents survive longest, while those which deal with measurable variables and can be tested have failed to survive when tested rigorously. Wootton reports the same fate for theories which explain criminality in terms of differences in intelligence (Wootton, 1959, pp. 301 and 302).

Of especial interest is the discussion of the so-called motiveless crime, as when a rich person steals, for example. When this happens, special explanations are provided: these are designed to evoke sympathy for the accused as the victim of ill health or emotional disturbance. The term kleptomania is commonly

applied in such cases. A curious point about such discussions is the
lack of interest in the parallel situation of the rich person who
devotes endless time and energy to becoming richer – the end-
product of which can only be additional zeros on the credit side
of his bank statement. In this regard it is interesting to observe
from reports the extent to which the psychological explanation
is advanced in the defence of the rich offender, a matter which
will be dealt with at length later.

This discussion by Barbara Wootton is important because it
raises the question of how far the psychologist and psychiatrist
have undermined the notion of free will and responsibility by
orienting criminological studies in the direction of prediction
rather than explanation. As Wilkins has expressed it: 'In prediction methods we do not necessarily seek a "meaningful result" (a subjectively satisfying explanation?) but a "powerful"
result' (Wilkins, 1962, p. 97).

In spite of the lack of established theory, the production of
literature which repeats or elaborates all the unsubstantiated
hypotheses listed above continues; it comes from social workers,
magistrates, judges, prison commissioners, priests, and criminologists, all of whom are trapped in the cultural stereotype.
Barbara Wootton comes near to escaping the pattern when she
writes:

'This faith in the overwhelming importance of criminality as a
thing-in-itself has certainly had a stultifying effect upon the trend
of research in this field. Ultimately it seems to have its roots in the
implicit self-righteousness of those who range themselves, as it
were, instinctively, on the side of authority. It expresses the
characteristic, if unspoken, premises of what Marx would have
called the ruling class, and what today has become known as the
Establishment' (Wootton, 1959, p. 306).

Wootton then goes on to consider two related issues which are
central to this study, the different attitudes of the members of
the Establishment to their own contraventions of the moral
order and the social consequences of the emergence of an influential academic discipline with its own techniques and tradi-
tions based on concepts of crime and the criminal which determine the form and conclusions of their studies.

Having advanced the argument thus far, she proceeds to ask for studies of specific types of offender and improvements in the methods of social inquiry.

At this point she appears to accept the concept of criminality, perhaps influenced by the other role, that of police court magistrate, that she has played for many years, and goes on to argue against psychiatric studies of individuals and in favour of ecological studies. These are studies which are based on the assumption that there are distinctive sub-cultural areas in cities with different systems of morals. Two criticisms of this point of view may be offered here: the hostility displayed to psychiatry neglects the very considerable development of learning theory and its application in social work and psychological medicine, and the fact that ecological studies display the same Establishment influences as other studies (Wootton, 1959, p. 329; Jehu, 1967).

SUBCULTURAL THEORIES

Research that seeks to establish that the environment causes the poor to be criminal is suspect. The commonest form selects an area in which poor people live, or a group of poor children, and either asks questions of them or records published information about them. In the former case the information obtained is not compared with information obtained in the same way from other groups in the population, but is compared with an *assumed* standard. In the latter case, little account is taken of the arbitrary nature of the selective process of both legal action and reporting, or of the symbiotic nature of delinquent and non-delinquent areas.

Terence Morris states the argument thus:

'The problem is posed quite simply because, however reluctant we may be to feel that the poor are less honest or the rich more law-abiding, the facts of the matter are that crime and delinquency are almost exclusively a proletarian phenomenon. Such is the experience of every Probation Officer, Approved School Teacher and Prison Governor' (Morris, 1958, p. 116).

He dismisses the suggestion that differential selection by the police is important:

'It has often been argued, of course, that differential arrest or charge rate merely reflects partiality on the part of the police or those responsible for prosecution. Such a charge cannot really be sustained for several reasons. In Britain, certainly, partiality would make headline news, and in any case the average policeman on the beat has a good deal of kindly sympathy towards the socially under-privileged child if not always perhaps towards the adult' (ibid, p. 166).

But he explains the relative immunity of the middle classes in a somewhat different way:

'The assumption that there is a valid class differential suggests that delinquency may be studied within a class frame of reference. This is not saying that morality varies inversely with social status, but merely that legally defined delinquency is a social characteristic, of the working classes in general and the family of the unskilled worker in particular. The behaviour of individuals in other social classes is so organised that departure from established norms is far less likely to bring the non-conformist into collision with the criminal law' (ibid, p. 167).

This assumption needs further qualification: the intensity of police surveillance is highest in the poorest areas and there is a tendency to regard the poor with suspicion both in their own areas and in areas where higher-income groups live, unless they have an obvious functional role like gardener. As will be discussed later, there is a tendency for the police to assume a legitimate explanation for middle-class behaviours such as carrying a suitcase at night and an illegitimate one for members of the working class.

F. C. McClintock, fellow of Churchill College, Cambridge, however, in a paper to the British Association for the Advancement of Science at Aberdeen in 1963, reported that police failures had an important influence in creating the stereotype of the criminal; they had a failure rate of seven in ten in discovering robberies where the victims were persons in charge of money or goods. He describes the effect thus:

'Statements about the characteristics of robbers relate to an extremely biased group, those convicted, in particular. The emphasis is on those who committed the most serious and unplanned robberies, upon the less efficient offenders, upon juveniles and those whose past records, or certainly easily identifiable personal peculiarities such as race or foreign nationality, make them more easily traceable' (*Guardian*, 30-8-63, p. 3).

It is likely that both processes are at work in making for the relative immunity of the middle and upper classes. (A discussion of the differential immunity of the middle and upper classes is attempted in Chapter 3.)

A widely quoted statement of the 'subculture' point of view is J. B. Mays's *Growing up in the City* (1954). His main thesis is:

'When we talk of a criminal area or of a delinquent subculture we are not saying that every individual living spatially close to the offenders is so powerfully conditioned by their attitude and behaviour that he is obliged to break the law himself. What we are saying is that within a broad zone which can be drawn on a map a very substantial number of people commit offences and there is a general social tolerance extended towards this behaviour' (Mays, 1963, p. 219).

In this thesis, culture and subculture are by implication narrowly defined to include only behaviours prohibited by law; no evidence is provided, except by implication, of the nature of the culture, nor is any allowance made for the possibility described by Morris above that class differences may be due to the form rather than the nature of the behaviour. The key study was based on interviews with eighty boys. It is apparent from the account of the method that the subjects were not chosen on any basis which made generalization possible, that the data were obtained by interview and not observation, that the interviews were not standardized, and that the subjects were not isolated from each other during the study. Moreover, although the norm is evoked for comparative purposes, no evidence is adduced from groups outside the alleged subcultural area to validate this comparison.

'In order to follow up Mannheim's points and discover what is the cultural background to the extensive, yet milder sort of delinquency in a typical under-privileged neighbourhood it was necessary to obtain a cross-sectional group to study. Such a group needed to consist of ordinary young people, and, since delinquency is largely confined to boys, average boys, inhabiting one of the older city areas. Such a group was fortunately available and willing to co-operate. Eighty boys, all of them members of a city youth club, were interviewed individually over a period of months by the same investigator. As he started with the initial advantage of being known personally to many of them some of the usual difficulties confronting the research worker were, therefore, avoided. But with the boys who were strangers more time had to be spent in establishing mutual confidence. With well over half the interviews it was not necessary to spend any time building up good relationships since a feeling of trust and confidence already existed.

Certain routine questions were asked and certain broad themes were pursued in each interview, *but the rigid questionnaire method was not employed and each session was permitted to follow its natural course.* The conversation though guided was sometimes permitted to wander into side-tracks whenever it was felt that such digressions would assist the establishment of rapport between investigator and boy. The length of interviews varied between one and two hours. Reports of the discussions were noted down immediately after the interviews and fuller accounts compiled as soon as possible after that. Usually the longer accounts were written at no more than twenty-four hours' remove from the original session. In some cases a second interview was undertaken or a home visit was made or material was checked up with school teachers or other knowledgeable social workers.'

He continues:

'Because of the small number of boys interviewed, *it is not possible to provide findings which are statistically valid for the youth of the neighbourhood as a whole.* It can only be claimed that the findings hold good for the total membership of the youth club from which the eighty boys were drawn. *Nevertheless, the remainder of the book is based on the assumption that the findings that are valid for the limited group can in fact be taken as being sufficiently accurate for the area as a whole for all practical purposes'* [My italics, D.C.] (Mays, 1954, pp. 29 and 31).

His conclusion from this study is:

'In such circumstances, therefore, it was argued that delinquency
is not so much a symptom of maladjustment, as of adjustment to
a sub-culture in conflict with the culture of the city as a whole'
(ibid, p. 147).

It may be worth while here to mention, in view of the influence of this and other works of the same kind, some of the
prerequisites of scientific research. The subjects chosen must be
all of those concerned in the inquiry, or, if they are less than all,
they must be selected in numbers adequate to give significant
results and chosen so that they are representative of the population from which they are drawn – there is, of course, a large body
of accepted practice here. Where comparisons are made with
another population, the two populations must be discrete in
relation to at least one variable (the problems are usually those
in which many variables are concerned), and the second population must be treated in all respects as the first.[1]

The interview method is essentially a technique of stimulus
and response so that in order to appraise response it is necessary
that the stimulus be known and constant. In physics, particularly in the measurement of electricity, a variable stimulus may
be applied in order to obtain a constant response; in such case
the stimulus must be recorded.

The implications of this analogy for social research are interesting, for the analogy implies that the desired response is known
and the stimuli are varied in quantity and quality until it is
obtained. There can, of course, be no objection to this if a full
account of both stimuli and response is published, but in the
absence of these data it is possible neither to repeat the experiment nor to evaluate those responses, selected from the total,
which are reported in studies of this kind. Moreover it is necessary that the subjects should not undergo change during the
period of study (the process of 'cross-infection', even through a
city, during the course of a study can be very rapid indeed).

[1] Mays recognizes these difficulties; in the *British Journal of Criminology*,
Jan. 1963, he writes 'My own researches, of course, have also been based on
selective samples but this does not invalidate their significance *as this bias
was taken into account in formulating the conclusions*'. To do this it would be
necessary to repeat the investigation using random samples, the bias, if any,
could then be ascertained.

Interviewing children presents special difficulties. Children are very suggestible and may respond to cues of which the interviewer may be unaware, even such responses in the interviewer as 'hum' and 'good', designed to maintain interaction and assure continuation, can influence responses (Krasner, 1958, p. 160; Richardson *et al.*, 1965, p. 198). It is also possible that the relationship between the interviewer and the respondent, in this case the warden of a boys' club and a member, could influence the outcome of the interview.

An American study of the relationship between reported delinquent behaviour and social status throws considerable doubt on the subcultural theory. This study did not deal with areas in which the poor live, but took a sample of high-school boys from three contiguous Midwestern cities, ranging in population from 10,000 to 25,000, and compared the behaviour reported by boys of different socio-economic status. In that in all cities there tends to be residential segregation by socio-economic status, the study is directly relevant.

The method employed was to use a large questionnaire, the responses to which were in the form of a checklist of items. The authors described their methods thus:

'Information on delinquency involvement in this study was obtained from a delinquency check list which was "buried" in a larger questionnaire. The introduction to these items explained: "Recent research has found that everyone breaks some laws, rules, and regulations during his lifetime. Some break them regularly, others less often. Below are some frequently broken. Check those that you have broken since beginning grade school." The list of delinquencies ranged from "Driving a car without a driver's licence or permit", "Skipped school without a legitimate excuse", and other less serious forms of delinquency, through very serious items such as "Taken things of large value (over $50) that did not belong to you" and "Used or sold narcotic drugs" ' (Short and Nye, 1962, pp. 44-49).

These subjects were divided into two groups for purposes of analysis; those reporting the 'most' and those reporting the 'least' delinquent behaviour. The evidence gives no support to the traditional thesis of an association of delinquency with low socio-economic status.

D

A second analysis in the same study threw light on the inter-action between administrative practice and the popular stereo-type. The criteria chosen were institutionalization, the placing of boys in a training school for delinquents, and the influence of the 'broken home'.

DELINQUENCY BY SOCIO-ECONOMIC STATUS:
REPORTED BEHAVIOUR AS THE CRITERION OF
DELINQUENCY

Socio-economic Status	Most Delinquent (Scales types 8-15)		Least Delinquent (Scales types 1-7)	
	No.	%	No.	%
I (Lowest)	42	16·0	69	12·0
II	101	38·4	233	40·4
III	91	34·6	191	33·1
IV (Highest)	29	11·0	84	14·5
Total	263	100·0	577	100·0

$\chi^2 = 4\cdot2$ $P < 0\cdot30$ $C = 0\cdot10$

DELINQUENCY BY SOCIO-ECONOMIC STATUS:
INSTITUTIONALIZATION AS THE CRITERION OF DELINQUENCY

Socio-economic Status	Training School Boys		High School Boys	
	No.	%	No.	%
I (Lowest)	73	50·0	112	13·3
II	48	32·9	333	39·6
III	19	13·0	282	33·5
IV (Highest)	6	4·1	114	13·6
Total	146	100·0	841	100·0

$\chi^2 = 117\cdot0$ $P < 0\cdot001$ $C = 0\cdot45$

Comparing the evidence presented in the two tables, the authors conclude that, while reported behaviour shows very little difference in the delinquent behaviour of different socio-economic groups, 50 per cent of all institutional boys came from 13 per cent of the high-school population – the lowest group.

The broken home, like poverty, is a common element in the popular stereotype, and the authors' examination of this is equally illuminating.

DELINQUENCY BY FAMILY STATE:
INSTITUTIONALIZATION AS THE CRITERION OF DELINQUENCY

State of Family	Training School Boys		High School Boys	
	No.	%	No.	%
Unbroken	81	51·9	934	80·5
Broken	75	48·1	226	19·5
Total	156	100·0	1160	100·0

$\chi^2 = 63\cdot7$ $\quad P < 0\cdot001$ $\quad C = 0\cdot34$

DELINQUENCY BY FAMILY STATE:
REPORTED BEHAVIOUR AS THE CRITERION OF DELINQUENCY

State of Family	Most Delinquent (Scale types 8-15)		Least Delinquent (Scale types 1-7)	
	No.	%	No.	%
Unbroken	281	76·4	653	82·4
Broken	87	23·6	139	17·6
Total	368	100·0	792	100·0

$\chi^2 = 5\cdot9$ $\quad P < 0\cdot02$ $\quad C = 0\cdot11$

The authors conclude: 'The inference must be made that children from broken homes as well as from the lower socio-economic strata are more likely, as the result of the same delinquent behaviour, to be committed to institutions.'

The results of an interview programme even most rigorously conducted only report the verbal responses to a verbal stimulus: in the case of a sample inquiry it states that another sample drawn in the same way would respond in a similar way within predictable limits.

What remains to establish is the relationship between past actions of the subjects or future actions of the subjects and their responses to questions. Here the information will relate to the group, not to the individual. Once this is done, then the verbal stimulus and response method has its use. There is, of course, a considerable literature on this subject but an example will illustrate the problem. In York, in 1936, a count of all churchgoers was made and immediately following an interviewing inquiry was made. The results showed that to discover the number of Anglican attendances the verbal responses must be divided by 41, the Scottish Presbyterians were correct (they keep a register), and the Elim Foursquare Gospel Church must be multiplied by 2 (the use of correction factors is of course commonplace in the 'natural' sciences).

The subcultural theory is, of course, maintained not only by the studies already discussed, but also by administrative statistics, and it must be regarded as not proven rather than disproven. Barbara Wootton does, however, point out that areas of social pathology are dependent on the arbitrary selection of criteria, ignoring, for example, motoring offences, and she discusses the possibility that even the subsequent processes of law may be arbitrary here too. This will be discussed at length in later chapters.

A THEORY OF SYMBIOSIS

From the sociological point of view, it is possible, accepting the thesis that there are areas of delinquent subculture, to argue that these are essential to and symbiotic with non-delinquent areas. That is, these areas are not in conflict with the larger culture, but are an essential component of it, without which the culture could not continue.

Arthur Sherwell, writing over sixty years ago, described Soho in London as an area on the borders of the wealthy West End of London and the impoverished East End where the depraved poor catered for the depravities of the rich (Sherwell, 1898). In the course of time this area has become a specialized functional tract, to use the language of the Chicago ecologists, in which brothels, strip shows, clubs, public houses, hotels, cinemas, theatres, picture galleries, restaurants, pornographic galleries, and pornographic bookshops are found, drawing its clientele from the whole country and abroad, and its personnel from the poor of the United Kingdom, Malta, Cyprus, Italy, Spain, and the West Indies. Sherwell's descriptions and his analysis of the situation are penetrating and relevant:

> 'Another, by no means inconsiderable, factor which confronts us in an analysis of the industrial life of Soho and the immediately adjacent districts, is the strangely heterogeneous army of "touts", "loafers", and "casuals", who are attracted by the wealth of the West-End, and who succeed, by almost infinite resource, in eking out a sort of parasitic existence, feeding upon the follies and vices and pleasures of wealthy West London. Included in this innumerable army are hotel, theatrical, and music-hall employees (e.g. waiters, kitchen-porters, theatrical "supers", ballet-girls, chorus singers, wig-makers, etc.), cab "touts", and "runners" (who literally swarm in the squares and other wealthy thoroughfares of the West); sandwichmen (for whom the numerous theatres, music-halls, art-galleries, exhibitions, etc., of the West-End provide ready but miserable employment); and "dossers" of every description – a pitiable and parasitic host who seriously affect the moral as well as the industrial life of the district' (Sherwell, 1898, p. 75).

He continues:

> '. . . the roots of the problem lie deep down in spiritual facts, and that the problem itself represents what is at the bottom a mad and irresistible craving for excitement, stimulated by the excitement and vicious luxury of the West-End life – a serious and wilful revolt against the monotony of commonplace ideals, and the uninspired drudgery of every-day life. It at least should be

remembered that it is in no sense an accident that prostitution has its recognised centre in the West-End. It is rather the inevitable consequence of the conditions of life that prevail there. Prostitution is a symptom: an outward and visible sign of a hidden moral disease induced by false habits and corrupt ideas of life. It is the pathetic but hideous "supply" of a corrupt "demand" coming for the most part – in West London at least – from men whose every ideal is impoverished, whose every habit is anti-social, and whose lives are vicious in their very uselessness. It cannot too often be insisted upon, that the effect – the logical, inevitable effect – of the idleness and extravagance of the West is entirely demoralising, and those who are concerned to discover the ultimate cause of the miserable but pathetic infamy of Piccadilly should begin to look for it in the idle luxury and vicious irresponsibility of West-End life (ibid, p. 147).

The revelations of the Profumo-Ward-Keeler affair in 1963 confirm Sherwell's diagnosis.

The complexity of the social process of symbiosis and its independence of the wills of persons involved in it is well displayed in this affair. The situation revealed was one in which working-class girls of relatively poor education and high physical attractions were brought to the capital as entertainers, dancers, night-club hostesses, and models; the agents in this process ranged from the pimps of foreign extraction deliberately pursuing their trade to salesmen and advertising executives who were accidentally involved. A leading witness in the case had been brought to London by a manufacturer to adorn a stand at the motor show (Rice-Davies, 1964, p. 2).

These girls from the age of 15 and 16 found employment in a well-known night club patronized by the very rich, where the principal requirement of the artistic staff is a willingness to appear in the minimum of dress with the breasts exposed. From this employment and sometimes concurrently with it, the girls were introduced (not by the night club) into prostitution, including the more bizarre forms demanded – according to one witness – by the wealthy, the cultured, and the well-connected.

The central figure in the case, Stephen Ward, was a middle-class osteopath, son of a canon of the established church, whose activities were perhaps more of a hobby than a profession; his clients or the friends for whom he provided introductions included a minister of the crown, a diplomat, a peer, and various wealthy business men.

One wealthy property speculator, Peter Rachman, who was involved illustrated in himself the symbiotic process. He drew his wealth from the gross and often illegal exploitation of a 'delinquency area', drawing revenue at one remove from prostitution and directly from slum housing. He lived, however, in a neo-Georgian mansion valued at £70,000 in Hampstead, impeccably furnished in Louis XV style, owned two Rolls Royce cars, and was a respected member of London's Polish community (*Sunday Times*, 7-7-63, p. 3).

The scandal, from being concerned with sexual morals, extended to include the underworld of clubs and drugs.

The revelations about the London property market made public what had long been known to social workers and such urban sociologists as Dr Ruth Glass, that 'delinquency areas' were consciously and systematically created for profit by wealthy middle-class property-owners with the assistance of building societies and insurance companies during the process of which the law was broken with impunity. The police ignored what was happening since it was mainly in the 'private sphere', and the local authority made only inadequate efforts to take action.

In passing, it is interesting to note that where an offence is committed against property, action by the police is automatic. Where the offence is by a property-owner against his tenant, and even where the offence may seriously affect the tenant's health, the initiative must come from the tenant, who is often in a very weak position because after an interval he may sacrifice his tenancy; or it must come from the local authority.

Writers about the City of Liverpool have called attention to a particular area as having a high concentration of social defect, including 'immorality' as judged by illegitimacy. Happily the advent of the motor-car makes it possible to apply the observation techniques of ornithology – bird-watching – to one aspect of this problem. Observation of parked cars outside brothels in the area of social defect show that these cars are the same as may be found parked in the commercial centre of the city by day and in the middle-class residential area by night – the number plate performing the same function as the numbered ring. Likewise, disorderly houses, staffed by personnel whose homes are in poor working-class districts, have been observed in the area devoted to specialist medical practice, adjacent to an expensive private dining club, and in a commercial office block.

During the period of food-rationing some expensive eating-places did in fact contravene the law in respect of both prices and foodstuffs; here the restaurateur was the intermediary between the middle-class customer and his supplier, an 'illegal' butcher or a dock thief (to quote cases known to the author). In that much of the social, administrative, and judicial life of a great city revolves around ceremonial eating, the involvement of the local establishment was considerable.

In these cases the symbiosis is obvious. In eighteenth-century London the ideology had not been developed to conceal this, as the engravings of Hogarth, the plays of Sheridan, the operas of John Gay, and the memoirs of William Hickey show (Quennell, 1960).

Also, it must not be forgotten that the mutual dependence of the middle-class social and economic groups and the areas of social defect have other forms. Thus the physical fabric of the homes of the poor is to a considerable extent owned by wealthy members of the middle class or investors in property companies.

The following is an account of a case where exorbitant rents were charged for defective dwellings. In such cases the property-owner has a simple choice, a higher standard of amenity in the area of social defect, or a higher standard of personal wealth.

' "The Minister of Housing, Sir Keith Joseph, has confirmed a compulsory purchase order covering 20 blocks of tenement flats at Bethnal Green. In a letter to the owners (Greencoat Properties Ltd.) published yesterday, the Minister states that he is unable to resist the conclusion that they have failed to look after the property with proper consideration for the tenants."

The letter added: "The Minister adds that he agrees with his inspector that the new rents are exorbitant for what the tenants are getting or seem likely to get." The flats are in Waterlow Buildings. The order involves 198 of them and two shops with attached living accommodation. The buildings, which are 90 years old, consist of 102 terrace blocks, of which Bethnal Green council originally proposed compulsorily to purchase 21.

In his letter to Greencoat Properties, Sir Keith Joseph said it was clear that there was a threat of homelessness which the Bethnal Green council was in no position to meet. Of the new rents, he said there was a conflict of evidence about whether these could be said to be in excess of market value.

The flats in the estate have one to four rooms, plus scullery, with electricity, gas, and cold water and their own lavatory, but no bath. The gross values vary between £14 and £28. In the estate as a whole, the rents are from 4·4 to 6·5 times the gross value and the new rents in the flats covered by the order are from 4·4 to 6·2 times the gross value. The 30 tenants who refused to pay had been asked for between £1 and £2 a month more.

At the public inquiry, Dr S. A. Boyd, the borough medical officer, said he had examined 81 flats. The kitchens were all less than 100 square feet, "dark, ill lit, and inadequately ventilated". There was no proper food storage provision.

The Minister's letter of yesterday states: "The inspector has drawn attention to the poor condition of the property, to serious defects in maintenance and management, and the absence of any serious attempt to improve the property notwithstanding the progressive rent increases in recent years".

The Ministry of Housing statement said that the inspector in his report had concluded that there were 29 families under threat of eviction. Greencoat Properties Ltd. is a £3 million concern. Its chairman is Lord Broughshane and Mr Ronald Armstrong-Jones, Q.C., is the deputy chairman. The company, which changed its name in 1958 from the Improved Industrial Dwellings Company, was formed in 1863 "to provide homes for the working classes" ' (*Guardian*, 2-8-62).

Greencoat Properties Ltd paid dividends of 26 per cent in 1958-59, 20 per cent in 1959-60, 1960-61, 1961-62, and in 1962 paid 20 per cent plus a centenary distribution of $2\frac{1}{2}$ per cent free of tax.

The recent legislation offering grants for the provision of baths, hot-water systems, and inside water closets shows the situation quite clearly:

'The contractor told me that 95 per cent of his orders are coming from one category of residents – the owner-occupiers. Tenants in identical houses in the same streets, who would dearly like to have their houses improved and would gladly pay the few shillings a week extra, find that their landlords just cannot be bothered with having the work done.

This is in line with national experience. Of the 125,807 improvement grants made in 1960, only 21,807 were for privately owned tenanted houses. In spite of even more generous grants made available in 1961, the number of landlords using the grants has actually declined" (*Guardian*, 20-8-62).

Many property owners are inhibited from improving poor dwellings by a belief or knowledge that they are breaking the law by allowing a dwelling to be inhabited in a dangerous or insanitary condition and will, if the dwelling is inspected, be compelled to spend money to have it brought up to the minimum standard.

An extract from a letter by the Chairman of the National Federation of Property Owners, Mr S. C. Hand, illustrates this point:

'... there is undoubtedly a fear among many applicants for grants that public health inspectors will insist on other work being done which will not rank for grant, as a condition of the grant being obtained. This might even extend to service of a sanitary notice, and hence compulsion on the owner to do this work. Owners are therefore often deterred from even inquiring about a grant' (*Guardian*, 19-2-63).

To add to the landlords the other middle-class interests, the following must be listed: the brewery companies, publicans, bookmakers, retail traders, pawnbrokers, doctors, and social workers, some of whom are parasitic on the slum-dwellers, others of whom are functionally and economically dependent.

The overwhelming difficulty of the subcultural theory is that its proponents have not first of all identified the society and sub-society with which they are concerned and have not identified and described the major culture and shown how it differs from the subculture. To do this they would need to show that the behaviour differences with which they are concerned are functional in each society. Even if all the assumptions, such as that of the impartiality of the police, made by the subcultural theorists are accepted and if the differential exposure to risk is discounted, the most that can be claimed is that, for certain behaviours classified on a scale ranging from virtue to vice, the distribution of the behaviour on the 'negative side' is skewed for the poor compared with the rest. No subcultural theorist has considered virtue and its distribution, and it is possible that this quality also might show a difference in the distribution by socio-economic class.

What has been argued so far is that none of the popular arguments about the causes of criminality, will, as Barbara Wootton has shown, bear critical examination and that the evidence for the subcultural theory will likewise not stand up to critical examination. It is, moreover, argued that the rich and the poor do not represent different cultures (the poor, of course, being identified as the *sub*cultural group) but that the rich and poor are a functional unity and that their culture is inextricably interwoven.

In spite of the cogency of Barbara Wootton's argument, new and ingenious attempts are continuously made by experts in the field of psychological medicine and the administration of justice to identify the stigmata of criminality.

The school of 'physical' psychiatry have attempted to show that certain 'psychopaths' have particular types of electro-encephalograms and from this it is assumed that criminals may have a cerebral abnormality. At the other extreme, Mr C. L. S. Cornwall-Lech, Deputy-Lieutenant of Cheshire, Chairman of the Juvenile Court at Lymn, Cheshire, stated that:

'I look forward to the time when it will be standard practice to have available for magistrates an interpreted horoscope of every child charged with a serious offence'[1] (*Sunday Times*, 3-2-63).

The fundamental difficulty of theories of this kind is the assumption implicit in them that when the number of criminals changes through legislation, or through changes in retail distribution, like the opening of a supermarket, such changes will be accompanied by changes in the E.E.G. patterns or the horoscopes of certain persons.

---

[1] De Quirós, writing in 1911, was perhaps premature in noting, 'the physical or cosmic factors did not produce a third school which might have been called Criminal Meteorology or Judiciary Astrology' (p.34).

The determination of social scientists to pursue the belief of the special nature of the criminal is well illustrated in *Psychiatric Studies of Borstal Lads* by Gibbens, Marriage, and Walker. At once the reader is struck by the employment of the pejorative form 'lads', who are in the text contrasted on occasion with 'middle-class youths' (Gibbens *et al.*, 1963).

This is a study of unselected offenders, not specialists, but, in spite of the authors' own caution, when they describe the sample: 'The vast experience of the London courts in dealing with hundreds of offenders a year has produced a *remarkable uniformity* in those selected as in need of this kind of training' (Gibbens *et al.*, 1963, p. 7), they assume that the characteristics that they establish, and incidentally some that they fail to establish, are typical of the young criminal.

The methods employed included the uncontrolled interview, certain tests, and photographs to establish physical types.

It is of interest that, whereas an interview in other disciplines must be replicable, the psychiatrist has a special dispensation which relieves him of this handicap.

The authors are convinced of the lower-class nature of delinquency and give one of the most complete and concise statements of the stereotype available in the literature.

They write, 'Delinquency is strongly class-linked', and go on to list the familiar qualities which are assumed to be operative: overcrowding, large families, ill health, poor intelligence, inability to keep up with the 'respectable' working class, belief in the importance of money and possessions rather than the approbation of the community, 'community status' and being influenced by mass media rather than 'local community feeling'. What is meant by 'community status' or 'community feeling' and how these variables are measured is not explained nor is the evidence given which would enable the reader to estimate the relative importance of these variables in the lives, say, of residents in Stepney and Golders Green.

The authors go on to give a general picture of the family life of their subjects, drawing their evidence from limited studies, some made with quite other functions. They mention Bernstein's work on language and social class, for example, which described the differences in vocabulary and syntax of boys in different schools and make assumptions about the emotional consequences for which there is no evidence.

Other factors which are listed include anxiety about puberty, emphasis on the different social roles of the sexes, aggressiveness as an expression of masculinity, not however that displayed on the rugby football field or in the gymnasium, restricted parental roles severely administered, and many others.

They conclude:

> 'Very briefly, these are some social theories put forward to account for the personality characteristics of mentally normal delinquents; inability to postpone immediate gratification (through fear that the opportunity may be lost altogether) or to plan for the future, cheerful lack of concern for property offences which the rest of society regards as serious, physical restlessness and tendency to react to anxiety by increased exploratory activity, stoic resistance to punishment, strong emotional bond to a home which appears incapable of exercising control, association in gangs or groups. Some of these features are among those which in an extreme form have been regarded as characteristic of the psychopath' (Gibbens *et al.*, 1963, pp. 96-98).

What is of importance here is the great variety of characteristics that are listed, the fact that for most of them their distribution in different social groups is unknown, and the fact that their relationship either to behaviour or to conviction is not established. Indeed, the quotation is the commonplace stereotype in its academic form.

Further, what does not appear to have occurred to the authors is that the working-class culture that they purport to describe could be adaptive to the social and economic conditions in which the working class live, and the middle-class norm which they assume as an ideal might be dysfunctional.

From a consideration of all this the author will argue that there are no differences of any kind between criminals and noncriminals, apart from the accident of conviction and disapprobation (both variables are required), except those which operate in vocational choice generally. This leads inevitably to two kinds of further inquiry, the first into 'faith in the overwhelming importance of criminality as a thing in itself' and the second into categories of behaviour of a general kind, like aggression, not specific examples of behaviours which arise arbitrarily from the belief stated above. The situation is exactly that discussed by Zetterberg, which he illustrates thus:

> 'In our childhood many of us enjoyed reading some popular book in physics containing chapters called "Automobiles", "Aeroplanes", "Radios", "Guns", etc. In high school, however, our texts did not have these titles. Now the chapter headers were "Mechanics", "Optics", "Thermodynamics", etc., and the cars, planes, radios, and guns occurred only as illustrations of the principles valid in these various branches of physics. The remarkable accomplishment of physical scientists made it possible to explain all the phenomena of the physical world in terms of a limited number of definitions and laws. We learned these definitions and laws, that is, the theories of physics, and we understood the operation of planes, radios, guns and many other things' (Zetterberg, 1927, p. 9).

What is suggested under the second heading is that the social scientist should himself define and observe specific behaviours *independently* of the ideology and administration and seek to establish general theories about behaviours determinable by criteria independent of the value system. Already, of course, much has been done, the study of 'aggression' as a social-psychological variable is highly developed in the work of Berkowitz and of Sears, Maccoby, and Levin, to cite two examples (Sears *et al.*, 1957; Berkowitz, 1962).

THE NATURE OF THE INTELLECTUAL CONFLICT

The dangers to the sociologist of the scientific approach are foreseen by Barbara Wootton and by the American sociologist, Kingsley Davis; these are that the sociologist may be adversely critical of some social institutions and that he will call in doubt the most sacred beliefs of society and compel a reappraisal of its structure. Barbara Wootton argues:

> 'Inevitably, the first result of a demand for evidence which will stand up to rigorous scientific examination is the destruction

of myths, and such destructive activity is likely for sometime to come to be the main preoccupation of the social sciences' (Wootton, 1959, p. 328).

Among the myths that are threatened is the belief in sin. The terror of the believer when faced with the possibility of a scientific study of behaviour is displayed by Lord Pakenham:

'How far can we ever hope to progress beyond our present stage? How far can we ever expect that the researches and generalizations of the social scientists including the criminologists will ever remedy the shortcomings and supplement the experience and intuitions of the statesmen and social reformers? A greatly gifted sociologist like Mrs Wootton in a well-known book (*Testament for Social Science*, 1950) has conjured up a picture of the social assimilated to natural sciences in methods and results. In her view, "the raw material of the social and the natural sciences is identical over a large area . . . each of these two branches of science uses the same methods, formulating hypotheses which, after empirical verification, become laws of association between phenomena". But there is no disguising the Christian apprehensions aroused by any dream of interpreting and guiding and ultimately controlling human conduct according to the same kind of rules as govern inanimate matter.

A Christian inevitably suspects that the freedom of the will is thereby threatened; that so too is the uniqueness of each human being and of each human action, criminal or crimogenic, law-abiding or law-promoting, that a perfectable view of human nature is entertained; that the concept of sin is discarded in favour of an explanation of crime entirely in terms of disease or deviation from a norm. He fears that revelation and natural theology have been discarded, not to mention traditional wisdom, and that all understanding of human nature is being sought in partial and contemporary experiments, conducted it may be with little tenderness for religious values. These apprehensions in my opinion should not be lightly set aside' (Pakenham, 1958, pp. 110 and 111; see Wilkins, 1962, p. 96, for the opposite point of view).

Kingsley Davis is more explicit and describes both the dangers to the sociologist of independent thinking and the hazards of the alternative of social conformity:

51

'A social system is always normative. Its integration rests upon the fact that its members carry in their heads, as part of the cultural heritage, the notion that they ought or ought not to do certain things, that some actions are right or good and others wrong or bad. Each person judges himself and his fellows according to these subtle and ubiquitous rules; and the violation is punished by some negative reaction, be it slight or great. An evaluative attitude, an attitude of praise and blame, or accusation and justification, thus pervades every human society. To question the rules, or worse yet, to question the sentiments lying behind them, is to incur certain penalties, the least of which is controversy. The person who tries in his own thinking to escape entirely the moralistic system in order to study behaviour objectively, who tries to analyse social norms and values as if they were amoebae or atoms, is quickly branded as an agnostic, cynic, traitor, or worse. Instead of public support for his work, he must count on public hostility.

To protect himself the social scientist usually accepts certain social values (the ones generally agreed upon in his society) and merely studies the means of attaining them. He thus eliminates from his inquiry the very phenomena that from a sociological point of view are the most fundamental bases of a social existence. But his failure to adopt a scientific attitude may go still further. He may willingly or unwillingly get involved in controversies – i.e. disputes in which the public has taken sides – and espouse one set of values as against another. In this case he frequently winds up by becoming a special pleader, a propagandist or wishful thinker, the very opposite of a scientist. No one thinks ill of him for this, except those on the other side, because partisanship on public issues is the expected thing' (Davis, 1959, pp. 10 and 11).

The argument of this chapter is that many sociologists have, perhaps unwittingly, perhaps consciously adopted the position thus described by Kingsley Davis.

On all this, a final comment must be passed. Almost all the familiar hypotheses about crime are at least a century old. They have been employed in inquiry after inquiry, few, if any, of which have been conducted with the rigour necessary for a reliable prediction to be made from them. They function to sustain the popular stereotype of the criminal, to provide the basis for the employment of the social worker, and to maintain the professional criminologist and sociologist as valued members of society. Almost none of the studies is based on observation, most are based on question and answer – a technique vulnerable to unconscious social influences – and even where observation is employed the categories into which observations are grouped frequently reflect the current stereotype.[1]

Thus encouraged, we may now examine some other problems.

[1] The persistence of the stereotype is interestingly shown if the biographical ledger of Ottolenghi (1905) is compared with the Bristol Social Adjustment Guides of D. H. Stott. (De Quirós, 1911, p. 218 and Stott, 1950, Appendix III, p. 422 *et seq.*)

CHAPTER THREE

Social Class and the Differential
Distribution of Immunity

The actions of the legal system are normally governed by the concept of equality before the law. This concept is, however, subject to many modifications in statute and in application. The most obvious example of the first is the immunity given to young children, and, of the second, the differential treatment of men and women. The concept of diminished responsibility and the application of the M'Naughten rules and arguments advanced in court in mitigation of offences likewise show the tendency to treat different groups, including social classes, of the population differently.

This discussion is concerned with a special problem, that of the relative immunity and, in some cases, the absolute immunity of the professional and higher middle- and upper-class groups from the processes of law.

In the absence of observations made independently of the police, there can be no reliable way of knowing the class distribution of any or all of the behaviours proscribed or punished by society. The prosecution, treatment, and reporting of these behaviours gives the impression that generally crime is an attribute of the lower-status groups in society. This is the point of view accepted by many sociologists and taken as a datum in their studies.

Many factors contribute to this situation, but they all derive from the division of society into social classes and the dominance of the middle and upper classes in the control of ideology. This is not to suggest that the ideology is wholly consciously created as part of a process of domination, or exploitation, but that the middle and upper classes propagate what is to them a system of beliefs which enables them to adjust without emotional strain to reality. Nor is it correct to regard the middle and upper classes as a single unified ingroup; there are many grades, and the degree of immunity conferred by institutional pattern and made acceptable by the ideology differs from grade to grade. Immunity is only complete for the royal Head of State (Phillips, 1967, p. 244).

There is, moreover, extreme difficulty in discovering the nature and distribution of immunities. The sociologist, as a member of the middle class, enjoys many of them, often without being aware of it, and much that he knows about the function of immunity systems is learned as a privileged member of institutions and organizations.

In passing, it should be noted that some professional bodies have their own organs of social control which may subject their members to deprivation from which non-members may be immune.

The origins of immunity are many; they include the differential policing of working-class and middle-class areas, the differential distribution of privacy, the availability to the middle class of institutional immunity, and the fact that middle-class crime is treated differently by the police and the courts from working-class crime. The result of all these processes is to reduce the likelihood of a middle-class person's being prosecuted, found guilty, and sent to prison, which is the crucial distinguishing feature in the stereotype of the criminal.

Any crime is a behaviour that involves the actor and the police, so any distribution of police to persons that is differentiated may, all other things being equal, favour one group rather than another. The intensity of policing of different areas of cities is explained by the police as a policy which reflects the incidence of crime. On the other hand it could be argued that as there is a direct relation between the presence of a policeman and the detection of crime, persons in areas rarely visited by the police have a high degree of immunity. There is an element of the self-fulfilling prophecy here.

An accidental circumstance made observation possible in such an area for a period of six months. This circumstance was that one house had been completed in a developing upper-middle-class suburb, and for a period of six months other houses were being built around it.

Each evening and every weekend, after the workmen had departed, the site was visited by between five and fifteen men with motor-cars or wheelbarrows. They removed bricks, tiles, paving slabs, timber, mortar, and other building materials systematically, and often in large quantities. (The builder estimated his losses as between 5 and 10 per cent of the total.) It was possible to identify them and to classify them by occupation; they were all in the Registrar General's occupational Groups I and II.

On one occasion when a patrolling policeman was present, the observer asked him why he did not intervene. The policeman's reply was that he assumed that they all had had permission. Even though the site was visited on many occasions by the police, no one was questioned at any time.

Another example occurred in an upper-middle-class suburb (Registrar General's occupational Groups I and II). Here the local authority planted the roadside grass verges with floribunda roses, and within three weeks some 20 per cent of them had found their way into adjoining gardens. The local authority gardeners claimed that they could identify the missing bushes, but stated that the policy of the local authority was not to take action on 'public relations grounds'.

When some of the 'thieves' were interviewed they argued that, with an ill-educated gardener opposed to a good lawyer, not only would the prosecution fail, but the local authority would suffer a considerable loss of face. In effect, they were consciously exploiting the immunity conferred by their class position.

THE DIFFERENTIAL DISTRIBUTION OF PRIVACY

The institutions of privacy have been little studied by sociologists, yet the degree to which a person's life is spent in public rather than private places will have a quantitative effect on his liability to break the law and to be detected in breaking the law; moreover, evidence has to be adduced to show that conviction is more certain in offences committed in public than in private.

It would be possible to measure social status in terms of the ratio of time spent in public places (places to which the police have continuous unfettered access) to time spent in private places (places to which the police have access only in special circumstances and after due safeguards). The range would be from one hundred to none in the case of the person 'of no fixed abode', automatically suspect, to something of the order of five to ninety-five in the case of the very wealthy who has access to private transport on all occasions, conducts all his business in privacy, or through intermediaries, and can purchase private space in hotels, restaurants, and theatres.[1]

The issue is excellently described by Arthur L. Stinchcombe thus:

'Most of our daily life is lived in a number of small, bounded social systems, such as families, schools, factories, clubs, etc., that have their own norms, goals, and facilities. The maintenance of the boundaries of these systems is necessary to their free and autonomous development. If agents of the state or strange private citizens could enter these systems arbitrarily and interfere with interaction within them, they cannot develop freely.

The central practical boundaries are such mundane things as walls, doors, window shades, and locks. But in modern society few of these are made to withstand a concerted effort by a group of men to breach them (in contrast to feudal societies, for example). Yet these fragile doors and windows effectively prevent police or private citizens from interfering with our sleep, our classrooms, our

---

[1] There is an important exception to this where middle-class persons are believed to hold certain beliefs. These include pacifists, anarchists, communists, syndicalists, supporters of Irish, Welsh, Scottish, and other nationalist movements, and, it is believed, members of societies concerned with the reform of the law relating to homosexuality and abortion. Such persons are subject to surveillance, to photography, and to having their correspondence opened and read and their telephones tapped. Such information has been passed to foreign governments and, in one instance, to the British Medical Association, where information about unprofessional conduct was incidentally obtained. It may be assumed that information obtained in this way about breaches of the law would be acted upon.

This suggests an important issue of principle. The relative immunity of the middle classes is reduced for those who hold a variety of disapproved political, ethical and social beliefs. (On all this, see Street (1964), and Anon., 'Mail Interception and Telephone Tapping in Britain' (1965)).

toolbenches, or our bars, at least most of the time. This is because a door is a legal entity of great importance: legitimate concerted social efforts to break down a door may only take place on legally defined occasions. These occasions are defined in the law of arrest[1] and the law of search and seizure,[2] and therefore, derivatively, in the criminal law.

The legal defense of doors and walls and windows means that small social systems which have legal possession of a place can maintain continuous, discretionary control over who crosses their boundaries. And this discretion may be enforced against agents of the state unless they have legal cause to penetrate the system or are invited in. Whenever such continuous discretionary control is maintained, the law speaks of "private places". The legal existence of "private places", then, is the main source of the capacity of small social systems to maintain their boundaries and determine their own interaction without interference from the outside.

The distinctive feature of a modern liberal state is that it uses the monopoly of violence (which all modern industrial states have) to guarantee the boundaries of small, autonomous social systems' (Stinchcombe, 1963, p. 150).

This discussion is primarily concerned with the effects of privacy in reducing the liability of those who possess it to the processes of law. Stinchcombe, however, makes an important sociological point. He argues, especially in relation to crimes of coercion, that those crimes that occur in public concern persons with few or weak social ties, and that those that take place in private concern those with more permanent and intense social relationships. He states the results, confirmed by statistical evidence, thus:

'Because the people who participate in small social systems are highly visible once the system is penetrated, and because often the complainant knows perfectly well who coerced whom, arrests are fairly easy to make. Crimes against persons generally have a high proportion of " 'crimes' known to the police" that are "cleared by arrest".

[1] A good summary of the law of arrest is R. M. Perkins, 'The Law of Arrest', *Iowa Law Review*, XXV (1940), 201-89.
[2] See E. W. Machen, Jr., *The Law of Search and Seizure* (Chapel Hill: University of North Carolina Press, 1950).

But the same conditions that produce easy arrests create another characteristic of enforcement against these crimes, namely, that arrests quite often do not result in conviction. Legal responsibility of the assailant must be established. His intentions are not immediately obvious from the nature of the act (as they are, for example, in burglary). The kind of passionate conflicts that lead to murders rarely make the motives of the crime absolutely clear. In the highly intensive interaction between the presumed offender and the victim the crime may have been provoked, for example, by requiring self-defence, or by consent before the presumed rape of a woman.

In addition, conviction before a jury generally requires that the defendant be judged not only legally, but also morally responsible for the crime. In spite of the legal tradition, rape of a prostitute, or murder of a really oppressive husband, seems to be a lesser crime. Evidence of moral responsibility is much harder to produce in crimes of passion. Finally, complaint to the police is something of a betrayal of those to whom we have close personal ties. Once the complaint is made, and the immediate danger and anger past, the personal ties or embarrassment of the complainant quite often reassert themselves, and the main source of evidence refuses to testify further' (ibid, p. 154).

The factors of concealment have a wide range, from the simple privacy conferred by a dwelling to the immunity of the large landed estate, which may be a state within a state.

The ownership of house property at once gives privilege, since many proscribed behaviours are only proscribed if seen, or if they take place in public. The report of the Wolfenden Committee states the issue in this categorical form:

'It is not, in our view, the function of the law to intervene in the *private lives* of citizens, or to seek to enforce any particular pattern of behaviour, further than is necessary to carry out the purposes we have outlined. It follows that we do not believe it to be a function of the law to cover all the fields of sexual behaviour. Certain forms of sexual behaviour are regarded by many as sinful, morally wrong, or objectionable, for reasons of conscience, or of religious or cultural tradition; and such actions may be reprobated on these grounds. But the criminal law does not cover all such actions at the present time; for instance, adultery and fornication are not offences for which a person can be punished by the

59

criminal law. Nor indeed is prostitution as such' (Committee on Homosexual Offences and Prostitution, 1957, p, 10).

The ownership of a dwelling confers on an individual advantages over the person who can command no privacy at all, and, with greater resources, buildings can be adapted which make a variety of behaviours possible with a high degree of immunity. The use of mirrors which act as one-way vision screens in walls or in ceilings permit the occupants of one room to view the actions of those in another without their knowledge. This has been used in factories to prevent women workers idling in the lavatories and was a feature of Stephen Ward's flat and of the house in which Miss Diana Dors and her husband Dennis Hamilton lived (Irving, Hall, and Wallington 1963, p. 32; Dors, 1960, pp. 72, 73).

Ownership of land likewise increases immunity through simple physical effects, the large house surrounded by many acres is closed to police observation in all normal circumstances. Where the great estate includes dwellings, even villages, the police may become, through the ordinary pressures of the status system, agents of the estate. The problems of the rural police force are twofold; the acceptance of the role of feudal dependant by the junior officer and the identification with the higher social group of the senior officer, who may, in the past, have come to the office from an upper-class family *via* service in the armed forces. The influence of feudal tradition on the landed estate modifies the processes of law thus (Banton, 1964, p. 268).

'A holiday party from St Mary's Church, Newark-on-Trent, was fired on six times with a shotgun by a gamekeeper of Lord N. at Cynwyd, Merioneth, Corwen magistrates were told yesterday.

Pellets fell among the party of 30, mostly children, said Mr M. W. prosecuting. The gamekeeper, J. W. (48), had told police: "They were making a terrible noise and upsetting the grouse."

He was fined £2 and ordered to pay £6. 3s. 6d. costs for damaging a camera case belonging to the party's leader during a brief scuffle. W. said the party was trespassing' (*Guardian*, 25-2-67).

This situation is critically displayed in cases where persons from outside the rural community endeavour to instigate actions for cruelty in hunting. It is noteworthy that such actions are rarely initiated by the police. The Cruelty to Animals Act of 1911 explicitly excludes *wild* animals from its provisions and was designed to grant immunity to the rural feudal middle classes in their sports (*The Times* Law Report, 14-11-63). The practice of hunting carted deer is of interest. While the deer is in the control of the huntsman and being carried to the field it is a tame animal and as such is protected; on release, however, it reverts to its wild status and loses its protection!

That the rural middle and upper classes consider themselves above the law is revealed in the following editorial from *The Field*:

> 'Considering that the Wild Birds Protection Act is now nearly 10 years old, precedents for its enforcement have been slow to emerge. In particular much uncertainty remains in Law of *those who find themselves obliged to kill a protected bird in order to safeguard their property, or interests*' (*The Field*, 13-6-63, p. 1095).

Even for the farmer, the privacy of the farm allows the practice of many procedures with animals, the dehorning of cattle; the castration of bulls, rams, and boars without anaesthetic, using a primitive instrument resembling a joiner's pincers[1]; the docking of lambs' tails and the like, all of which can inflict pain, if the noise the animals make can be assumed to be evidence of suffering. It is only when the drover leaves the farm and reaches the highway, or market, that the beating of an animal becomes an offence.

INDUSTRY AS A PROTECTIVE ENVIRONMENT

In the industrial situation the plant is likewise a private area, and immunities may extend over wide social domains. There are often traditional perquisites, the extent of which is status-graded, which, if publicly acknowledged, would rank as thefts

[1] Now no longer permitted except for castration of bulls and sheep under three months, and goats and pigs under two months: Protection of Animals (Anaesthetics) Act, 1964.

(Martin, 1962, p. 108 *et seq.*). More important, however, are the policies of large companies with respect to offenders; these are very hard to discover from the outside, but, in the author's experience, in some large public companies internal private justice is operated for monthly staff and public justice for the hourly paid.

The internal private justice takes the form, in offences concerned with property, of permitting restitution, often by regular deductions from pay; in serious cases resignation is permitted. In some situations the offence is regarded as symptomatic of domestic problems and the occasion is taken to give sympathetic assistance in the solution of the problem. This is especially so in firms with personnel managers and welfare officers.

The only major study of the problem made in Britain, *Offenders as Employees* by J. P. Martin (1962), did not classify its subjects by social class, so the extent of status differentiation remains unknown. In cases where it was possible to compare those with responsibility for others with the rest there was no difference in treatment. The study did, nevertheless, reveal the very considerable extent of private justice in industry, the considerations upon which it is based, and the social consequences, one of the most remarkable of which is that the employer more than any other civil person has the power to decide whether a man is to be prosecuted or not.

The facts are:

'In the larger firms, only 41% of the 61 offences connected with employment were brought to court, and in only 31% did the firm call the police. Similarly, in the smaller firms, out of 29 offences only 7 (24%) resulted in prosecution, and in only 6 (21%) did the firm call the police.

It seems an indisputable conclusion from these figures that where possible firms neither prosecute nor call the police but deal with the matter themselves. In our sample this was particularly true in cases involving personal violence against a fellow-employee, and stealing from a customer' (Martin, 1962, pp. 106, 107).

The consequences of this policy are described by Martin thus:

'This revelation of the extent to which employers prefer to take the law into their own hands has a number of implications which should be discussed. As we have said, it is clear, from the high dismissal rate of men not prosecuted, that employers do not treat these offences lightly. Their policy may be described as a mixture of humanity and expediency.

It is human because the man concerned does not appear in court, and therefore does not get his name in the papers. Indeed he may even be able to hide the matter from his family by using a "cover story" such as that he had "had a row with the foreman". Furthermore, he does not become a man with "a record". This may be of importance on subsequent occasions as a man known to have been convicted is perhaps more likely to be regarded as a potential suspect if there should be any unsolved crimes in his neighbourhood. This is not to say that he would be unfairly accused, merely that, other things being equal, a man with a record is more likely to be suspected than one with an apparently unblemished past.

These social consequences of conviction may reasonably be feared, and to some they will be of overwhelming importance; quite apart from them the man who is prosecuted has most likely to pay a fine, and may even risk imprisonment (about one in four in our sample). It is not surprising, therefore, that the employer faced by an offence committed by a man possibly well-known to him, should when possible take the lenient course.

Finally, this evidence emphasises one fact of fundamental legal and sociological importance. It is that an employer, more perhaps than any other civil person (policemen excepted), is in a position where he has to decide whether or not to put a man in the hands of the law. The extent of this power and responsibility has tended to go unrecognised. It seems clear that all but the smallest employers are likely to face this problem at some time, and that in the larger firms they will have to do so regularly. This report is not the place for a full discussion of the legal implications, but now that the facts are known it is to be hoped that their significance will be noted.

To the layman, one question stands out. How far is it a good thing for standards of the law enforcement to vary as widely as they do between different sections of the community, and between different social situations?' (ibid, pp. 104-106).

This study is one of the few which do not start with the convicted criminal as the basis for generalization, but deal with the whole of a category of behaviour in a given social situation.

It reveals in a most impressive way the gross difference between the quantity of 'crime' that occurs in industry and the amount that results in police action.

The study, however, since it was based on information from management, did not examine in any detail those behaviours of management which, operationally defined, would be identical with crime, some of which have been noted elsewhere in this chapter.

THE PROTECTION OF THE INSTITUTION

A special situation occurs in institutions like the church, universities, and professional and commercial undertakings, where the ratio of middle-class to working-class employees is very high. In some there is a sharp differentiation in the treatment of the different social groups, the working classes being subject to public justice, the middle classes to private justice. In some cases, however, immunity is extended to the whole population. The problem here is that these institutions are heavily involved in the moral order, the church must appear virtuous, the university wise, the profession competent, and commerce honest, so that, in addition to ingroup sentiment, public relations and financial interest all contribute to the tendency to deal internally with the delinquent. This may be illustrated by an example, one of several known to the author, of an employee of a university. As treasurer of a club whose funds he used for his own purposes, he was permitted to make restitution by bankers order, and, when found to have a large deficiency in his accounts in the university, was invited to resign; but when later, in business on his own account, and no longer in the area of institutional immunity, he defrauded his customers, he was found guilty and sent to prison.

The permitting of restitution favours the middle classes as does the differential distribution of the capacity to make restitution before or after the discovery. The middle classes have as a rule, through family and friends, much greater resources with which to make restitution in a wide range of situations that, if brought to the courts, would rank as criminal. In the value system of the middle classes, a gift, or loan, to save a friend from prison and his family from disgrace is 'good'. Membership of exclusive societies and clubs, such as the Freemasons, is important here not only for settling problems out of court, but also for the accommodation of mutual assistance afforded to members.

In the church, sexual offences, if detected by the ecclesiastical authorities before they attract the attention of the police, may be dealt with by special bodies of the institution as problems of sin, or of mental health, and in some cases even where the police and the courts have become involved, the offender may be bound over into the care of his superior priest for treatment in the internal and private sphere of the church.

The position of schoolmasters is, in contrast, much less favourable; dismissal is inevitable and prosecution and punishment frequent.

The police have under their disciplinary regulations an internal system of justice which, in cases not brought to court, imposes penalties differing from those that the court would have imposed; additional penalties may also be added to those imposed by the courts. The situation is illustrated from the Sheffield case.

'Details of conversation between a Solicitor and the Chief Constable of Sheffield were given at a tribunal in Sheffield yesterday.

The tribunal, in its seventh day, is hearing appeals by Derek Edward Millicheap and Derek Leslie Streets against their dismissal from Sheffield City Police Force after being convicted of assaulting suspects.

Mr Arthur Hewitt, a solicitor whose firm acted for the assaulted men, said in reply to Mr Baker (counsel for Sheffield watch committee) that he telephoned for an appointment with the chief constable after not receiving a reply to a letter.

"I was anxious to see the chief constable and put the position before him and see what he had to say. He indicated that he did not know a great deal about it. I told him that from our point of view it was an extremely serious matter and handed him an album of photographs."

The chief constable appeared to be obviously shocked by the photographs and when asked if he would prosecute said that if the matter was handed over to him steps would be taken under the police disciplinary regulations.

Mr Hewitt said he told the chief constable that it was far too serious a matter to be dealt with in that way, and should go to the criminal courts.

When the chief constable asked him what charges he had in mind he told him it was one of grievous bodily harm. The chief constable said: "Well, I can tell you this, you have no chance – no chance at all."

Mr Hewitt said it had appeared to him that if proceedings were not brought on behalf of the men they would not be brought by the police. The chief constable had told him he would receive every assistance in the preparation of the case and the matter was left in that way' (*Guardian*, 18-9-63).

THE ARMED FORCES AS A PROTECTIVE ENVIRONMENT

The armed forces are of special interest in that they are closed communities with a total internal system of social control. Although the regulations are public, the practices are largely secret, and from what little is known it would appear that the basis of the practice is an assumption that 'other ranks' are mainly inferior members of the working class whose training must be to create a number of conditional responses. This training is reinforced by graded deprivations and punishments, most of which become oppressive, not by their inherent nature but by the speed, frequency, and duration of their performance. Thus when described in words their significance is lost. It is worth noting that the 'glass-house' has not, so far, been studied by the social scientist, although the general issues involved in the life of total institutions are brilliantly described by Goffman (Goffman, 1961).

For the officers, except in battle or in matters of money, largely informal procedures are employed to maintain behaviour appropriate to 'an officer and a gentleman': the persistence of the phrase is an important clue to the status differential. The ultimate sanction is disgrace and expulsion. The following extract from *The Times* is valuable not only in that it describes the system of justice in a closed community, but also in its use of stereotypes designed to absolve a member of the middle class from the stigma of criminality:

'A Royal Navy commander who fraudulently misapplied £1,289 from the Rosyth Fleet Club Fund was ordered to be dismissed from the Service at a court martial at H.M.S. Cochrane, the Royal Navy shore establishment, near Inverkeithing, Fife, today.

The accused was Commander X, aged 42, former base supply officer, Rosyth. He admitted having on September 22, 1961, when acting as honorary treasurer of the Rosyth Fleet Club Fund, fraudulently misapplied £700; and between June 30th, 1961 and June 18, 1962, fraudulently misapplied £589 belonging to the Fund.

The circumstantial letter read to the Court stated that on June 12 this year X was relieved as base supply officer by Y. On June 14, X went to say farewell to his commanding officer, Captain Z. He told the captain that he had embezzled the money from the Club Funds and was placed under arrest.

An audit was taken and there was an overall deficiency of £1,289. A cheque for £700 which had been drawn on the Club Funds by X had not been entered and a transfer from bank to cash, and from the accounts produced by X the audit board was unable to find what had happened to the money.

Giving evidence as to X's character, Rear Admiral George A. F. Norfolk said that for eight years X had been his secretary in two appointments – as chief of staff to the Commander-in-Chief Far East Station, and as Deputy Chief of Navy Personnel. During that time X's conduct had been quite exceptional in every way. He showed intense loyalty to the Crown, the Service and to his superiors. "He was always extremely honest and forthright with me," he said. "The misapplication of funds is completely inconsistent with his character."

In a plea in mitigation the defending officer, Commander John Arthur Hassard-Short, said that X had served in the Navy for over 23 years and during that time had rendered excellent service.

Commander Hassard-Short pointed out that *all the money had been repaid* and that X had come forward of his own accord and told his captain what he had done. It had been his intention from the start to disclose the offence at what he considered to be a proper time.

"Why did he do it"?, asked the defending officer. "Over a period of years he brooded over his wife's unreasonableness and aggressiveness about money and finally, rather than endure this any longer, he decided to take the cash from the fund, give himself up in due

67

course, risk being flung out of the Navy, break up the marriage but at least achieve peace of mind. This, he said to himself, would sort out his family troubles and make his wife sorry for her behaviour."

The defence then submitted a report from a leading Scottish psychiatrist who had examined X and said that X had gone to him because he feared he was going mad, not to try to concoct some fairy story.

Commander Hassard-Short said of Mrs X: "She was anxious to come here today, but he wished to spare her that. As a family with their two young daughters they are back where they were many years ago – united and at peace with themselves. This ordeal will, I am sure, keep them in that state," he concluded' (*The Times*, 26-7-62).

It should be noted that whereas the Army Act, 1955, and the Air Force Act, 1955, provide two possible punishments for officers, 'cashiering', (that is, dismissal with disgrace), and 'dismissal from Her Majesty's Service', for other ranks a simple punishment is prescribed, 'discharge with *ignominy*'. For other ranks disgrace is inevitable, as is implied in the different terms applied, 'dismissal' and 'discharge'. The Naval Discipline Act, 1957, in contrast provides the same punishment for officers and ratings, 'dismissal with disgrace from Her Majesty's Service', and 'dismissal from her Majesty's Service'.[1]

THE RELATIVE IMMUNITY OF THE MIDDLE AND UPPER CLASSES

The generalized pattern of immunity of the middle classes is based on the education system – the preparatory school, the private boarding-school (including the public school), and the residential university college. The child spends most of his life, often up to early manhood, in a series of closed and frequently physically isolated communities. In all these he is almost entirely immune from the system of public justice. At school, minor offences are dealt with informally by his peers, more

[1] Army Act 1955 (3 and 4 Eliz. 2, c. 18), Sections 71 and 72; Air Force Act 1955 (3 and 4 Eliz. 2, c. 19), Sections 71 and 72; and Naval Discipline Act 1957 (5 and 6 Eliz. 2, c. 53), Section 43.

serious offences by the housemaster, and major offences by the head; the ultimate sanction, 'sending down' or 'rustication', is deprivation of immunity. Where the offences concern non-members of the closed community, the general public, the immunity though not absolute is still considerable, and it is often the policy of the police to refer the offender to the headmaster for punishment, and in other situations the head acts as an arbitrator between the aggrieved party, the boy, and his parents.[1] In one case reported to the author, the boy fired a hay-rick, the parents made restitution, and the school punished the boy. This partial immunity extends to the student at university, but is greater in Oxford and Cambridge where the universities dominate the local community.

Thus British Railways complained to the headmaster of a school about vandalism by children from the school on a special train taking them to Christchurch (Hampshire) for the holidays. A Southern Region spokesman said:

'When the train reached Christchurch it was found that twenty-three electric light bulbs, and a number of shades were missing, a safety rail across one of the long corridor windows was broken, window blinds were pulled down, and toilet rolls and towels were scattered throughout the train.

During the journey the communication cord was pulled twice; five fire extinguishers were thrown out of windows and two were discharged in corridors.

We have not received a reply to our letter, but we don't expect to hear until after the holidays, as the school is closed.

In the past when we have complained to the school authorities of minor incidents we have always received the utmost co-operation and have recovered a certain amount of cash for the

---

[1] Long after this was written, the following account appeared under the heading 'Eton Boy Expelled for Shop Lifting'. 'A 15-year-old Eton College boy has been expelled following his admission to shoplifting in shops in Windsor and at the school shop.

'The boy was reported to his housemaster by his house captain following his boasting about his activities as a shop-lifter.

'The headmaster, Mr Anthony Chevenix-Trench, got in touch with the boy's father and said the boy must leave school.

'It is understood that the boy made a complete admission and his father has paid for all the goods he took' (*Daily Mail*, 5-2-65).
The pattern is *exactly* that described above.

damage, and we have no doubt this matter will be settled in the same way.

We are concerned in this case not only over the cost, but also over the inconvenience caused, the railwaymen's time in putting things right, and the element of danger in safety devices being removed' (*Liverpool Daily Post*, 17-7-62).

This may be compared with the attitude of the railway police when the vandals are travellers to and from a football match. Again the report below shows a quite different situation from those that describe the 'friendly scuffles' and 'knifings' that occur in the working-class areas of Liverpool.

'R. N., 16, a pupil of Blundell's School, Tiverton, Devon, was operated on in hospital yesterday for a stomach injury. The Rev. J. M. S., the headmaster, said N., whose home is at Liphook, Hants., had been injured in a "friendly scuffle" with another boy for possession of a knife on the wall of N.'s study' (*Daily Telegraph and Morning Post*, 1-10-62).

In leisure the middle-class child, and in due course the middle-class adult, is more frequently in a private social area, and the member of the working class in a public area. Members of golf clubs, tennis clubs, and sailing clubs, or of gentlemen's clubs, are almost exclusively middle class and the delinquencies which take place within them are rarely investigated and almost never brought to the notice of the police. A demand that the member resign is the ultimate sanction and because of its social consequences it is employed only rarely, and often only when other undesirable characteristics are present in him. However, observation and inquiries show that most sailing and golf clubs find it necessary to post notices in their cloakrooms reminding members that it is unwise to leave valuables in garments, or to leave lockers unfastened.

Amongst the many areas of criminal behaviour where the higher social groups enjoy substantial immunity is that of abortion. This functions in two ways, legally and illegally. For the educated private patient with a high income, a therapeutic abortion on psychological grounds is much more possible than for a member of the working class who is on the National Health

Service list of a general practitioner. For some groups in society
an unwanted pregnancy can be dealt with illegally in ideal conditions without inconvenience, though at great expense.

Discussions with general practitioners with a large working-
class practice disclose a number of factors. Some state that they
receive many requests for abortions, often several a week. These
are refused for a variety of reasons: that the operation is illegal,
or, in certain cases where it might be legal, that there is the
possibility of being challenged in the courts; that if an abortion
were performed, news of it would spread rapidly and the doctor
would be overwhelmed with demands (and threats); that his
patients would not be able to guarantee the skilled aftercare
and rest that would make the operation safe; that the presence
of police informers would make detection likely; and that the
police would exercise pressure on patients as accessories to give
evidence against them in courts. This latter is a real threat as
was shown in the case of a Cornish doctor sentenced to three
years' imprisonment in 1964. The case was commented upon in
a letter to the *Guardian* thus:

'The one thing the five anonymous ladies who gave evidence
against Dr William Tellam had in common was, according to their
own confession, that they had all been desperate to have their
pregnancies terminated, and had all begged him to undertake this
for them.

One can only speculate, therefore, as to what could have persuaded them to turn against him all of a sudden, and to agree to
appear in court to testify against him.

Do not the methods by which "evidence" of this kind is obtained
raise important issues of civil liberties?

Only the most naive will believe that these five ladies were all
suddenly and simultaneously overcome by remorse and repentance' *(Guardian,* 15-8-64).

Legal abortions are possible for the National Health Service
patient, but she is at a disadvantage compared with the private
patient.

'Although 1,500 legal abortions are performed each year in
N.H.S. Hospitals, a considerably greater number of legal abortions
are performed in private nursing homes. This is hardly surprising

71

when one considers the difficulties of arranging two consultant opinions and admission to hospital before the patient's pregnancy is more than twelve weeks' duration' (Darby, 1964).

Immunity operates also for the middle class during the process of offending, thus it is found that the policy of retail stores towards shoplifters differs along class lines. Once again, the problem of evidence arises. A study of press reports suggests that stores patronized mainly by the working class and the lower middle class have a regular pattern of prosecution, whereas stores with a high-class clientele rarely appear in the courts as complainants. This could, of course, be simply that the middle-class customer is more honest. Likewise most of the customers who are prosecuted are of working-class origin, judged by address, occupation, or husband's occupation, even by stores with a wide class range of customer.

It has been possible to interview the senior executives of a number of stores and groups of stores on policy in relation to detected shoplifters, from which it emerges that the more exclusively working class the trade of the store, the more automatic the practice of prosecution. In stores with a mixed clientele the fact that the middle-class offender is interviewed by a middle-class executive often changes the social situation. It has been argued that the middle-class offender does not *need* to steal and is, therefore, in a different category from the working-class offender who is assumed to *need* to steal and who must, therefore, be prevented by the threat of prosecution. The executives interviewed approach the middle-class offender assuming that she is emotionally disturbed, or ill, and conduct their interviews in accordance with this stereotype. The responses they receive, as might be anticipated, confirm their expectations, so that they are frequently able to accept restitution and leave the matter at that.

In some stores of the highest class, interesting variants have been discovered. In one even to appear to consider the possibility of theft is unthinkable. The customer who seems likely to leave without paying is reminded of the omission; if she lacks cash, she is invited to pay by cheque, or even to open an account. Such procedures are claimed to be good both for public relations and to attach the new customer loyally to the shop. A variant in the case of customers, known to the firm, who are observed taking goods without paying is to send an account for the items the same day.

Gibbens and Prince in their study of shoplifting confirm that there is a wide difference in the policy of different stores and that there is a wide variation in the treatment of individuals. They consider that there is little evidence to suggest that discrimination is on a class basis, but as they do not analyse their stores by the class of customers and did not make independent social classification of the apprehended shoplifter, their conclusions cannot be regarded as proved.

'The policy of stores with regard to detection, arrest and prosecution varies widely. At one extreme are the few stores that never make a charge, some of which make little or no attempt at detection. The blatant thieves who cannot be ignored are dealt with "in the manager's office". At the other extreme the policy is to "catch" as many thieves as possible and charge everyone without making any enquiries into their circumstances. Most stores adopt a scheme somewhere about the "golden mean". Two quite different reasons were given for adopting the no-charge policy. Some say they simply cannot afford the time involved in sending an assistant to court to give evidence. The cost of court proceedings is out of all proportion to the value of the goods involved, and there was a feeling among some that the cost of bringing aberrant shoplifters to book should be borne by society and not by the store itself. On the other hand, one managing director suggested that he could not bring himself to prefer a charge as the store is equally culpable – "Who's to blame, the tempter or the tempted?" He deplored the open counter system, many features of which encourage lax moral standards, but had adopted it as a necessary evil. The second reason given by the more expensive shops was that they were reluctant to charge offenders because of adverse publicity. One, in fact, found the idea of a police court quite unthinkable. In practice, such stores have much more trouble with cheque frauds and impersonations of account customers than with shoplifting. [This suggests a high-status clientele. D.C.] . . . Some of the no-charge stores seem to have their own methods of private jurisdiction, with the offender being asked to pay for the goods and to sign an undertaking not to enter the store again.

Then there are the stores which arrest as many thieves as possible and charge them automatically, no matter what their health, age, circumstances or explanation. [No classification of these stores was attempted D.C.]. It is maintained that it is the business of the court to discover extenuating circumstances. If there are genuine social or psychological problems motivating the shoplifter, the quicker he or she is brought to the notice of the relevant social agency, the better. If the person is really innocent, then this will be revealed by the evidence produced in court. Between these two extremes, those who never charge even if they detect and arrest and those who prefer a charge in all cases, are many variations. One store, for instance, never prosecutes except for some outstanding reason. An example was that a woman of 35 was very abusive when arrested and appeared to be drunk. Another store refrains from prosecuting only for some outstanding reason – examples were given of the very old, the obviously confused and women in late pregnancy. Unfortunately, these are probably the people who could benefit most from social or medical help deriving from a court appearance. Some stores ignore thieves who steal goods of little value. The manager of a book-shop and bookstall on the other hand was adamant that the value was no criterion, that he would prosecute for the theft of a 2½d newspaper as readily as for a ten-guinea book. Some of the chain stores leave the local manager to deal with the pilferage problems as he sees fit. There is no consistent policy between the branches, or, indeed in one branch from one time to another as the local manager may manipulate the system according to the season and rate of sales. One large concern with an ex-police officer as security manager has an almost case-work attitude to offenders, and seems unusually adaptable in approach. They have detailed records of the number of offenders caught and those charged, their age, sex, marital status and social circumstances. Two or three young people who have seemed in difficulties have been offered jobs with the firm.

Apart from the variation in policy between stores, there was little evidence, as indeed there is little in the court records, to suggest that any discrimination is made on a personal basis. The professional man or woman is as likely to be charged as the teddy boy or girl; the rich, foreign visitor as the housewife doing her local shopping. Of course, at the time of arrest no one knows anything about the offender, and the personalities – national or international – who are sometimes arrested will be familiar to all' (Gibbens and Prince, 1962, pp. 147, 148).

This last statement surely does less than justice to the store detective who could probably judge age, sex, social class, and even nationality from the many indicators in dress and toilette. Indeed it could be argued that certain people are much more visible than others and if these are more carefully watched than the rest they are likely, assuming a constant rate of stealing over the whole population, to be found out; thus creating the familiar phenomenon of the self-fulfilling prophecy. This quotation from the same study supports this hypothesis:

'Two detectives claimed their experience had taught them to be specially watchful of someone with a physical deformity, such as a wooden leg, strabismus or a withered limb' (ibid, p. 150).

It is fascinating to find the stereotype which originated with Lombroso in 1869 incorporated in the thinking of a store detective in the 1960s.

Not only are the middle class more often immune from prosecution than the working class, but if apprehended the consequences are likely to be less severe.

Underlying the attitudes expressed by the police, the prosecution, and the magistrates and judges is the belief that the wealthy do not need to commit crimes, especially crimes of theft, so that if they do it is because of physical ill health, mental illness, or evil influence.

The daily press reports offer many examples, and the pattern of reporting assists in the creation of the stereotypes expounded above. A few examples will suffice:

'The ex-public schoolboy who became a motor mechanic was jilted because he did not have a white-collar job.

So he started his own business and stole to get quick success, a court was told yesterday.

Thus the heartbreak of 25-year-old X of Sale, Cheshire, was revealed at Knutsford Quarter Sessions yesterday.

"His four-year engagement was broken off because the girl's family objected to the fact that their daughter was to marry a mechanic," said Mr David Morgan Hughes, defending.

The phrase was used "Why should she have a white wedding when she is marrying a man with a dirty job?"

So X branched out on his own account, setting up a one-man repair business at rented workshops in Rusholme.

Then he stole equipment from other garages to speed the build-up.

After his engagement was broken off, X did not like to ask his father for money to buy the equipment he needed, "so he did this most rash and wrong thing".

Then the court was told of the other heartbreaks in X's life.

How he failed his examinations to become an accountant like his father and his elder brother.

How polio had ended his hopes of shining at athletics.

X stole an engine-tuner and equipment worth £160 after breaking into one garage.

From another he took two spray guns worth 14 guineas. He asked for the theft of a battery tester to be taken into consideration.

Fining him a total of £20, the chairman, Judge Lind-Smith, said: "If you want equipment, pay to hire it in future, don't just take it. Go away and see what the doctor can do for you."

Afterwards X said: "I hope to carry on my own business, and I shall go to the doctor for his help" ' (*Daily Mail*, 10-1-62).

In this case social status anxiety, ill health, and emotional disturbance are all regarded as providing substantial extenuating circumstances for a series of systematic thefts.

'A West Kirby doctor's son was bound over in his own recognisance for two years in the sum of £5 at London Sessions on Wednesday, on condition that he did not return to London alone. X, 18, trainee manager, was allowed to return home with his father, X Senior of West Kirby.

He pleaded guilty to breaking out of the flats of Miss Y, a television actress, and Z an actor, at Bywater Street, Chelsea, after stealing a record player and other articles, and to possessing Indian Hemp.

Mr Henry Pownall, prosecuting, said that Miss Y was an acquaintance of X, who came from her home town of West Kirby. On Good Friday it was found that the self-contained flats on the ground and first floor had been ransacked.

At 4.00 a.m. on May 9th, X kept his finger on Miss Y's bell until she answered the door. He told her that he had been evicted from his flat and she allowed him to stay the night in her lounge.

Later she rang the police because he fitted the description of a man who had been loitering near the flats.

He was seen by the Police and admitted that he had stolen the articles.

In his possession was a match-box which contained a hand-rolled cigarette which had Indian Hemp in it.

On the way to the police station X had an epileptic fit and, after he had recovered, he made a written statement. He said he paid £1 for the Indian Hemp and rolled the cigarette himself. He said he was sorry for stealing the articles, which he did on impulse.

Det. Constable Dennis Burke said that X had no previous convictions and went to a public school until he was 17 and-a-half. He then had various jobs as a trainee manager and came to London in April. His parents were allowing him £5 a week.

He was satisfied the flat-breaking was the work of two men.

Mr J. H. Peppitt, defending, said that it was tragic that a youth of X's background should be in the dock, as it seemed he had every prospect of a successful career. He contracted epilepsy at the age of 13, and ever since had to take anti-convulsive drugs which had had an unusual effect upon his personality. It had more or less produced in him a grudge against society.

He came to London to find other work as his jobs had not been exciting and he lived in a flat in Chelsea with others who had the practice of smoking Indian Hemp. His prospects of getting a job did not materialise and his money ran out.

On the spur of the moment he robbed a flat in company with another man, and his share of the proceeds was about £10.

"His father intends to pay the losers and recoup himself from his son as soon as he can afford to pay," added Counsel.

"This has been a severe shock to this boy, and he assures me that he will never come before a court again. If allowed his freedom he intends to emigrate to South Africa, or South America and work on farms with cattle, which he is fit to do."

X Senior gave evidence and said he had noticed a change in his son since taking the drugs, which he would have to take for the rest of his life. His behaviour was most variable and he only had epileptic fits when he forgot to take the drugs.

Binding X over, the chairman, Mr R. E. Seaton, told him: "The prodigal son is going to return to West Kirby. You came to a city which is full of evil and got mixed up and tarnished with it. I hope this will be a lesson to you."

"I dare say it will be better for you to go abroad and associate with cattle which will get you into less trouble than people in London.

A condition of the order is that for two years you must not come to London alone. You have had a lucky escape." ' (*Hoylake News and Advertiser*, 8-6-62).

Here is an example of the classic form of expiation, namely, emigration.

The persistence of the stereotype that the delinquent public school boy goes to an undeveloped country to make good is well illustrated in this quotation from a book of short stories called *The Last Chukka*, a valuable source of material on the ideology of the middle classes. It describes two public-schoolboys at the moment of being discovered drinking brandy:

" 'What'll happen?" he whispered. "Will it mean the sack?" "How can I tell?"
"If it does, I don't know what my father'll say. He's the sort of chap who'd give me fifty pounds and a ticket to the colonies' "
(Waugh, 1928, p. 7).

In the third case a 'businessman of some standing' and 'a well-known and impeccable character' had been found guilty of shoplifting. After his parish priest had attested to his many virtues the stipendiary magistrate said he was *reluctantly* driven to the conclusion that the case had been proved beyond any doubt (*Hull Daily Mail*, 21-6-62).

It is illuminating to compare the sentence of seven years' imprisonment imposed on an unemployed Garston, Liverpool, labourer for living on the immoral earnings of one woman with the fine imposed on a London millionaire property owner of £25,000 for exploiting a number of women systematically by letting flats to them at very high rents (*Liverpool Echo*, 17-10-63).

The following reports are interesting in that they present the familiar stereotype designed to exculpate the middle-class offender.

'An accountant at the Atomic Energy Centre, Risley, near Warrington, has forfeited his pension rights of £825 a year and a lump sum of £1,600 as a result of stealing a wallet containing £1. 10s. 0d. from a colleague, Mr Alastair Bell, defending, said at Newton-le-Willows yesterday.

Mr X (51) of Davyhulme, who pleaded guilty to stealing the money, was put on probation for two years on condition that he had voluntary medical treatment.

Chief Inspector Norman Lindsay said that after reports of property being missing a security officer left his jacket over a chair in an office and kept watch. Mr X entered and later the wallet was found to be missing. It was afterwards found in a litter basket.

Mr X was alleged to have told police: "I don't know why I did it. The money is of little value to me." Later he said: "It took me two hours to convince my wife." Mr X asked for five similar offences to be taken into consideration. The Court was told that all the money had been repaid.

Chief Inspector Lindsay said Mr X's salary was £2,200 a year, and he resigned his post on the day the offence was discovered.

Mr Bell said there was no reason for Mr X to commit such an offence. He had been examined by psychiatrists who had stated that the offence was due to his state of health' (*Guardian*, 13-9-63).

'Y, aged 19, secretary, of South Kensington, said to have once worked as assistant to dress designer Norman Hartnell, was fined £100 at Marylebone to-day.

She pleaded guilty to stealing a cheque book from a house in Onslow Gardens, South Kensington, where she was then living, and to three offences of obtaining clothing and other items by false pretences.

She asked the court to consider 18 similar offences concerning cheques involving property worth £105.

Mr C. Frere Smith, defending, said Y was privately educated and has been in good employment, but she had missed a happy home background, and since the age of eight, when her parents separated, had been virtually alone.

Her mother later remarried, disastrously, and divorced again.

"There was constant friction on every side and she (Miss Y) was the butt", said Mr Frere Smith.

Mr Frere Smith said she came to London alone. She "got in with a thoroughly bad set of layabouts."

She started gambling and, after a spell of beginner's luck, got into financial difficulties. She then started taking "purple heart" tablets and finally, persuaded by her friends, who commended that kind of behaviour, committed the offences.

Arrangements had now been made for her to live with a vicar and his wife in the West Country' (*Liverpool Echo*, 15-10-63).

The treatment of the rural middle class is in the same pattern.

'Two east Kent farmers, A. aged 53, of Hothe Court Farm, Blean, a former Canterbury Justice of the Peace, and his brother, B, aged 54, of North Court Farm, Stourmouth, were each fined £40 with 50 guineas costs yesterday at Kent Quarter Sessions, Maidstone.

Both pleaded Guilty to making false P.A.Y.E. tax deduction returns with intent to defraud over a period of eight years by omitting overtime payments made to regular employees.

Mr Kenneth Jupp, for the *prosecution* said *both men were hitherto of impeccable character*. The total amount of the omissions from the returns was £8,596 and the tax involved was £1,078, which had since been paid.

The matter came to light in a random check by the audit department of the Inland Revenue authorities. When the defendants were interviewed in the presence of their accountant, both explained that the discrepancies were due to overtime not being shown on the tax deduction cards.

Both had made similar statements in which they said that employees would not have worked the required overtime hours if the overtime payments were taxed. They said that they had paid the overtime untaxed for the benefit of their employees.

But Mr Jupp said, this gave the defendants an unfair advantage over their competitors. If they had wanted to pay the overtime free of tax they could have done so provided they paid the tax themselves.

Mr John Gower, for the defence, said that not one penny piece had been lost to the Revenue. It all started when the employees made it clear they would not work overtime unless it was paid in full without deduction.

It was said that other farmers were paying the full amount and that the defendants foolishly adopted the practice of paying full overtime without disclosing the fact to the authorities. *Unfortunately they did not seek advice about how it could be done legally, but in effect they had done it legally now in retrospect.*

In his submission, the defendants had already suffered grave punishment. They received great publicity. Both men had done much public work and were well respected in the community. As a result of the case, A had tendered his resignation as a Justice of the Peace' (*The Times*, 8-10-63).

The remarks of both the prosecuting and defending counsel tending to excuse the defendants are of great interest. The defendants themselves sought to excuse themselves as *victims* of their *employees*, who would 'not have worked the required over-time hours if the overtime payments had been taxed'.

The following is of interest, not only for the treatment of the criminal by the court, but also as showing the protective en-vironment of his institutional employment and the belief that, for the middle-class criminal, psychiatry is the appropriate treatment.

'A civil servant, said by the police to be earning £2,500 at the Foreign Office, was given a conditional discharge for 12 months when he pleaded Guilty at Bow Street Magistrates' Court yester-day to stealing a book from a Mayfair bookshop. The Court was told that the book, entitled *Wodenotes* and printed in 1649, was valued at £30.

Mr X, aged 51, of Cromwell Place, Kensington, S.W., asked for the theft of a book in Persian, valued at £35, from another book store to be considered also.

Detective-Inspector R. Taylor said that later X readily ad-mitted taking the books, but could in no way account for his actions.

It was stated that the Foreign Office was arranging for X to have psychiatric treatment' (*The Times*, 1-11-63).

Two cases are now presented to show the mechanism which works to prevent members of the middle class from going to prison, the crucial factor in creating the 'criminal' of the stereo-type, and to select a member of the working class for prison.

'Between 1950 and 1960, Jay Richard Attenborough & Co. Ltd. Jewellers, of Oxford Street, W., defrauded the Inland Revenue of £31,920 in purchase tax by describing new jewelery as second-hand, Mr Kenneth Jones, Q.C., for the prosecution, said yesterday at the Central Criminal Court.

Before the court were the company, and two of the firm's directors, A, aged 36, of Radlett, Hertfordshire, and B, aged 75, of Cheam, also P. A. Sinclair & Co. Ltd., of Poland Street, Soho, C, aged 71, of Worcester Park, D, aged 69, processing jeweller, of Potters Bar, and E, aged 45, processing jeweller, of St John's Wood, N.W.

All pleaded Guilty to conspiring with F, and other persons un-known to cheat and defraud the Inland Revenue of purchase tax by falsely describing certain jewelry as second-hand. They further pleaded Guilty to other substantive charges alleging the fraudulent evasion of purchase tax on certain items of jewelry.

Attenborough & Co. were fined £5,000 and ordered to pay a sum not exceeding £500 towards the costs of the prosecution.

A was fined £1,500 (or, in default, 12 months' imprisonment), B was fined £1,000 (or nine months). C and D and E were each fined £500 (or nine months). No separate penalty was imposed on Sinclair & Co.

Mr Kenneth Jones, Q.C., said the Court was concerned with three conspiracies to defraud the Commissioners of Purchase Tax. In each conspiracy the Company, Attenborough & Co., A and B were involved together with a man named F who died in the early part of 1961.

Jay Richard Attenborough & Co. were a very well known firm of jewellers carrying on business in Oxford Street, but they were in no way connected with another company bearing a similar name. A and B were directors of Jay Richard Attenborough & Co., F was head of the jewelry department for 30 years until he died, which was about a month after this investigation started.

C, D and E were processing jewellers.

The allegation in this case was Attenborough & Co. bought from the public secondhand gem jewelry. They then agreed with the processers, C, D, and E to make the stones into quite new pieces of jewelry and these of course attracted purchase tax.

The prosecution claimed that throughout there was the false pretence to describe the jewelry as secondhand so that no purchase tax was ever paid.

It was further alleged that this was done with deliberation as a regular trading practice over many years.

The result of this fraud meant that Attenborough & Co. were able to obtain new jewelry at a lower price than other honest jewellers who had met their purchase tax obligations.

The benefit to the processing jewellers may well have been that they were able to charge black market prices for the work they did for Attenborough & Co. They gained at the expense of honest processers who charged purchase tax.

As far as Sinclair and Attenborough & Co. were concerned the purchase tax evaded was £29,093 over 11 years. In the case of D and E, who were in business together, the figure was £1,058 over six years. The grand total of tax evaded was £31,920.

Mr Jones said it was quite clear that as far as the day to day working of this conspiracy was concerned, F was in charge until he died. Whether he organized the fraud in the first place one simply did not know, but he carried it out assiduously.

A's attitude to this investigation was disingenuous and dishonest. Had he adopted a different attitude many hundreds of hours might have been saved.

B had been with Attenborough's for 30 years. He and F valued the jewelry.

Mr G. R. F. Morris, Q.C. (for Attenborough & Co.), said arrangements had been made for the unpaid purchase tax to be remitted to the Revenue. F was the man solely in charge of the jewelry department and no one had the right or the inclination to challenge what he was doing. The situation now confronting the company sprang entirely from the conduct of F, although as far as one could see he derived no financial benefit to himself at all. Whether he had a distorted sense of zeal it was impossible to say.

Mr Dingle Foot, Q.C. (for A and B), said it was always distasteful to put the blame on someone who was dead, but there could be no doubt that F was the prime mover in these operations.

The Recorder, Sir Anthony Hawke, said he refrained from passing a sentence of imprisonment on A and B only because of B's great age. In that respect A could regard himself as being fortunate' (*The Times*, 24-9-63).

The logic of this statement is curious to say the least!

In the next case the defendant, being a time clerk on a building site, was suitable as a candidate for the stereotype role of the criminal, quite unlike the 36-year-old company director with a Home Counties address, whose offence was a fraud of £31,920 compared with the clerk's balance of £5.

'The Court dismissed an appeal against conviction on a charge of larceny as a servant of £5 and refused leave to appeal against the sentence of 12 months' imprisonment imposed at London Sessions by Deputy Chairman, Mr Edward Clarke, Q.C., on May 3rd, 1963.

The appeal was heard one day later than scheduled. The prosecution was brought by the employer. The money in question had been entrusted to the appellant by way of a float for petty cash 10 days after his employment had started. He had been employed on a building site as a time clerk from January 14th, 1963 until February 14th, 1963, when he disappeared with the £5.

Counsel for the appellant had submitted that the Deputy Chairman of London Sessions had failed in his summing-up to put part of the defence to the jury, and, after being reminded of the omission, had failed to rectify it properly. The part of the defence not mentioned in the summing-up was whether an IOU given by the appellant for the sum of money entrusted to him by his employers was an acknowledgement of a debt or a mere receipt for the money.

Mr Justice Hinchcliffe, delivering judgement of the Court, said that the main defence put forward by the appellant at his trial concerned the amount of money due from him to his employers. The issue of the nature of the IOU hardly arose. Counsel for the appellant had, at the trial, used the expression "receipt" and "IOU" as synonymous. Whatever the document was called, the case concerned the stealing of £5 belonging to the employers, who, at all material times, had retained ownership and control of that sum of money.

The Deputy Chairman had presented the defence adequately in his summing-up to the jury by telling them that it was the defendant's case that he never took £5, and that he honestly thought he owed his employers a small balance of the £5 which remained after items of expenditure for which he had not been reimbursed' (*Guardian*, 18-9-63).

An example of the different treatment of white-collar crime compared with, for example, train-robbing is the case of Messrs. E. S. and S. K., who pleaded guilty to four charges of fraudulent conversion involving the sums of £81,249, £67,568, £366,686, and £43,449. E. S. and S. K. were each fined £60,000 and given 6 months to pay. E. S. in an interview with the *Sunday Times* commented that his fine could not be charged as an expense in his income-tax return. It would not be unreasonable to observe that the fault of the train robbers was a failure to be educated (*Daily Mail*, 23-2-66; *Financial Times*, 23-2-66).

Less dramatic, but still impressively different, was the case of A. G. P. who pleaded guilty to defrauding three finance companies of a total of £577,960, and was sentenced to five years' imprisonment (*Guardian*, 1-3-67).

It must be borne in mind that a few selected cases *prove nothing*. They do, however, suggest a hypothesis, which could be tested either by a field investigation or by the criminal statistics if they were compiled so as to reveal the treatment by the police and the courts of offenders classified by social status.

The hypothesis is a simple one. It is that the middle class are rarely sent to prison and that the working class are frequently sent to prison for offences of the same gravity.

BANKRUPTCY

If the legal definition of such crimes as theft, larceny, and fraud is translated into an operational definition that would cover them all – 'the transfer of goods or rights from one person to another without the former's full knowledge and consent' – it is evident that the legal framework within which business is conducted makes possible the exploitation of credit and bankruptcy in a way that falls within the definition but does not incur a liability to prosecution. Such possibilities are open to individuals with education and a knowledge of the law or with access to the services of those who have knowledge of the law.

In that many businesses involve risk, and this is known, the taking of risks is normal, and the law allows that men should not be punished for disasters arising from unforeseen circumstances or even for lack of foresight or for incompetence. Nevertheless, there are some bankrupts, who, without breaking the law, succeed in obtaining and disposing of large sums of money at the expense of their creditors.

The pages of the local, national, and financial press contain many reports of the proceedings of bankruptcy courts and frequently include the comments of the Registrars. These comments are often extreme in their condemnation of the bankrupt and describe in detail the deliberate way in which money has been transferred from the creditors to be used for the private purposes of the bankrupt. Attendance at such a court is instructive, since many of the more striking comments of the Registrar do not reach the press.

It had been the intention at this point to quote reports of a small selection of cases exactly as they appeared in the press, omitting only the names. However, the author has been advised that he might be liable to proceedings for libel, involving himself and his publisher in the payment of heavy damages, if he were to reprint a report of a bankruptcy, even after taking the precaution of rendering the litigants anonymous, in a book with 'Criminal' in its title in which a similarity is suggested between the behaviour leading to bankruptcy and behaviours that are criminal.

This is a remarkable illustration of the extent of the immunity of members of the middle classes; not only may they on occasion deprive their creditors of tens of thousands, and in some cases over hundreds of thousands, of pounds (there may be peril in quoting the exact sums), but their behaviour may not be discussed in a serious text.

The commonest kinds of case are those of relatively small businesses in which the director or directors are responsible for day-to-day management. Typical are house agents, stock-brokers, insurance brokers, retail traders, wholesalers, and small manufacturers. A common pattern here is that the director or directors draw from the firm sums of money to meet day-to-day expenses with a reckoning at the year-end, when it is decided whether or not drawings have exceeded the salary and share of the profits; appropriate adjustments are then made. There are cases where companies have enjoyed long periods of prosperity during which the directors have become accustomed to a high rate of drawings and have then been caught out when trading prospects have changed.

In some recent cases the deficiencies have arisen where the money drawn from the business has been used to finance the education of children – some tens of thousands of pounds; to house and provide an income for a mistress of extravagant habits; to indulge in a passion for gambling on the race-tracks; or even to cover the cost of a few hundred pounds' worth of shirts.

The appointment of a managing director's mistress to the board of directors, with the provision of a motor-car and a flat as a part of her remuneration – a situation revealed in a recent divorce suit – does not constitute an offence.

In a case where the directors had falsified their books, a case with liabilities of tens of thousands of pounds, they were fined some hundreds and given six months to pay. The directors claimed they had spent the money on bribing the buyers of their products. The treatment of the offence of conspiracy to defraud

– to which they pleaded guilty – a white-collar offence, is in marked contrast to that of theft.

In another case where the deficiency was over two hundred thousand pounds, made up largely of 'excess' drawings from the company, the author spent some time looking into the circumstances of the director concerned. He found that he was still living in a large detached house in the Home Counties with many acres of parkland, that he still drove his Rolls Royce motor-car, and that his children were still at expensive boarding-schools. The situation that makes it impossible to quote the original report has the advantage on this occasion of permitting the supplementary data to be mentioned.

It may be argued that some of these activities are unplanned and should, therefore, be disregarded. There are, however, techniques of trading by obtaining credit and going into liquidation that must be carefully planned and are profitable.

Such techniques fit into the general description of white-collar crime. This classification includes a wide range of activities that are common among the middle class, are often highly profitable, and are rarely the subject of police action. If they are the subject of successful prosecution they are likely to be punished by a fine, rather than imprisonment; if imprisonment is the penalty, then the convicted person is likely to serve his sentence in an open prison. Many of the offences are referred to even by sociologists as 'administrative', thus removing them from the source of disapproval.

Among the many offences concerned are: defrauding the revenue by making false tax returns, customs offences, purchase-tax offences, offences relating to agricultural subsidies, bribery practised by manufacturers and wholesalers to gain favours from large buyers, offences against the Factories Acts, offences against the Food and Drugs Acts, breaches of the laws concerned with health and safety (such as those relating to heavy vehicles and to housing), and conspiracies by antique dealers at auction sales to eliminate competition ('knock-outs'). Such conspiracies are so common at auction sales of antiques and government surplus equipment as to be 'normal', yet they are almost never subject to interference by the police, even though they are illegal under the Auctions (Bidding Agreements) Act 1927. The

87

author has attended furniture sales where such conspiracies have taken place, and confirmed his observation by discussion with the auctioneer and with a leading antique dealer who was a participant. On occasion, he has been present in the private room of an inn where, after the sale, the valuable antique items have been resold at considerably higher prices in the 'knock-out'. He has also received precise accounts of such conspiracies at the sales of government surplus stocks from a dealer who participates regularly in them. This dealer has told the author that, in addition to agreeing over bidding, dealers also operate a form of retail price maintenance on some of the 'standard' items. It had been the intention of the author to reproduce an account from a daily newspaper of the operation of the knock-out at a sale of antique furniture which resulted in an eighteenth-century piece valued at about ten thousand pounds realizing about one-twelfth of its value; he is, however, advised that, since it might be possible to identify three antique dealers who were involved, it would be dangerous to do so.

In some instances the law is deliberately broken, but insurance is taken out against possible financial penalties. This may be illustrated in relation to window-cleaning. Many local authorities, including the Greater London Council and the City of Liverpool, have by-laws designed to make window-cleaning safe for window-cleaners and for the general public in the street. Such by-laws prescribe the use of ladders, cradles, safety belts, or other devices designed to prevent falling. In spite of this, many new buildings are erected without safety provision. Some owners of buildings have insurances to indemnify them against claims for damages by window-cleaners; others attempt to transfer the liability by the form of contract they negotiate with cleaning firms. The author is informed that such insurances and contracts are probably unenforceable, as being contrary to the public interest.

ANOTHER FINANCIAL STRATAGEM

The directors of public companies are in a special position; they are often in possession of information about the performance and prospects of their companies which, if known, would affect the value of the shares of their company. This value is determined largely by the performance of the company as expressed in the annual balance sheet, by the announcements of interim dividends, and by statements put out from time to time about policy changes, the take-over of other businesses, dramatic success in obtaining orders, and the like. If the managing director of a public company published information he knew to be untrue, and thus changed the value of the shares, and if he then bought or sold shares to his advantage, it is possible that such an action would be a conspiracy to defraud and he would, if prosecuted, and found guilty, be liable to a fine or imprisonment. If, however, the director – or any other person with special knowledge – is aware that if his knowledge was made public the value of the shares would change, and he then buys or sells to his advantage, providing he maintains silence his behaviour would not be actionable as a crime.

Members of elites are often in the position to benefit from 'inside' information of the kind described above, and the obtaining and passing on of such knowledge is an important medium of social intercourse. In some cases the process takes another form. Thus it would be unprofessional, to say the least, for an architect to receive a consideration for specifying the products of a particular manufacturer; on the other hand, a manufacturer whose products had been recommended by an architect would be churlish if, towards the end of a good year, he did not acquaint his friends of the fact that his shares were undervalued in the market. This practice, examples of which are known to the author, would fall under the operational definition given above.

At this point it had been intended to reprint without alteration an account from the *Financial Times* of a Stock Exchange inquiry into share dealings in a well-known Midland company. The author has, however, been advised that this would be the subject of an action for libel. Such inquiries are held from time to time, and a description of the general features of such cases will enable them to be recognized.

The pattern is simple: shortly before the accounts are to be presented, the managing director of a company sells some tens of thousands of shares; upon publication of the accounts, the value of the shares falls, leaving the London jobbers with a heavy loss. There are well-known cases where the sums have been much larger, but in these cases the loss more often falls on the general public, who are not skilled in recognizing the signs of changes of fortune in the affairs of companies.

It has been argued that the operational definition given here is wide, in that a crime such as theft depends on a transfer of goods against the will of the owner and that the seriousness of the crime depends to some extent on the degree to which the will of the owner is acted against. Thus robbery with violence is more serious than the picking of a pocket, where the owner may be unconscious of the loss at the time. The problem is a subtle one. In the case of the confidence trick, the subject may 'will' the action by which he loses; indeed he often displays enthusiasm. At the other extreme, a theft is no less a crime when the owner of the property is unaware of his loss. In reply to the argument, it could be said that the will of the owner can operate only where there is full knowledge and consent; the law, on the other hand, assumes that the subject must actively guard his interest, both in the literal sense and by seeking information – *caveat emptor!*

Thus far it has been argued that members of the middle class are substantially immune from prosecution if they commit offences and, if prosecuted, receive treatment that is sympathetic rather than hostile and punishments that do not identify them permanently as criminal.

WHITE-COLLAR CRIME

The crimes for which the middle class are prosecuted differ from those of the working class in that they frequently involve large sums of money and are achieved by the manipulation of symbols rather than artifacts, fraud compared with burglary. The exception to this generalization is the offence with the motor-car.

Dr Terence Morris referred to this matter in his List Lecture to the British Association for the Advancement of Science in August 1963.

'Society tolerates the homicidal motorist because many people are drivers and can easily imagine themselves in the same position as the man in the dock, a sociologist told the British Association at Aberdeen yesterday.

Dr Terence Morris, lecturer in sociology, London School of Economics, said in giving the List Lecture to the association's sociology section, that in spite of the law there were some crimes many people were prepared to accept with equanimity.

For example, of 88 people tried for murder in 1961, 16 were executed, 40 sentenced to life imprisonment and four otherwise disposed of.

In the same year, 429 people were tried for causing death by dangerous driving, of whom 130 were acquitted. Of the 299 found guilty, 234 were fined, the penalty in some cases being less than £10, fifty-four were sent to prison and three to Borstal, and eight otherwise disposed of.

"How can one account for an acquittal rate of 18 per cent in respect of murder and causing death by dangerous driving?" Only 21 per cent of homicidal motorists were deprived of their liberty, while nearly 80 per cent were merely fined.

The lawyers would say murderers intend to kill their victims, while the hapless motorist never intended to kill anybody.

This may well be true, but how do we manage to regard a man as merely unfortunate who drives with reckless abandon not infrequently in a drunken state and sometimes uninsured against third party risks, and regards his victims as in much the same category as livestock' (*Liverpool Daily Post*, 30-8-63).

Dr Morris's statement would have been more exact if it had read 'Middle- and upper-class judges and magistrates (instead of society) tolerate the homicidal motorist because they are drivers and identify themselves with the man in the dock'. These facts raise the issue of how far white-collar criminality is 'real criminality'. This issue is important, for once sociologists admit the identity of all forms of criminality they must cease to concentrate their attention on the 'criminal' of the popular stereotype and look at society as a whole. The kinds of offences described above are not popularly regarded as 'crime' and, as they are not often punished by imprisonment, the persons involved are rarely considered as criminals. In view of this, it will be useful to quote from the American discussion of white-collar crime and examine a few examples of such behaviour, which is accepted as normal in a middle-class area.

Edwin Sutherland presents the following concise statement of the view that white-collar crime is 'real crime':

'That argument, stripped of the description, may be stated in the following propositions:

1. White collar criminality is real criminality, being in all cases in violation of the criminal law.
2. White collar criminality differs from lower class criminality principally in an implementation of the criminal law which segregates white collar criminals administratively from other criminals.
3. The theories of the criminologists that crime is due to poverty or to psychopathic and sociopathic conditions statistically associated with poverty are invalid, because, first, they are derived from samples which are grossly biased with respect to socioeconomic status; second, they do not apply to the white collar criminals; and third, they do not even explain the criminality of the lower class, since the factors are not related to a general process characteristic of all criminality.
4. A theory of criminal behaviour which will explain both white collar criminality and lower class criminality is needed.
5. An hypothesis of this nature is suggested in terms of differential association and social disorganisation.

   The criterion of white collar crime, as here proposed, supplements convictions in the criminal courts in four respects, in each of which the extension is justified because the criminologists who present the conventional theories of criminal behaviour make the same extension in principle.

   First, other agencies than the criminal court must be included, for the criminal court is not the only agency which makes official decisions regarding violations of the criminal law.

   Second, for both classes, behaviour which would have a reasonable expectancy of conviction if tried in a criminal court or substitute agency should be defined as criminal. In this respect, convictability rather than actual conviction should be the criterion of criminality.

   Third, behaviour should be defined as criminal if conviction is avoided merely because of pressure which is brought to bear on the court or substitute agency.

   Fourth, persons who are accessory to a crime should be included among white collar criminals as they are among other criminals' (Sutherland, 1940).

The following are a few examples of white-collar criminality obtained by observation and questioning in an area which could hardly be described either as proletarian or part of a delinquent subculture – an upper-middle-class suburb:

(*a*) A garage built at the home of the subject of material belonging to a company, by craftsmen of the maintenance department, the costs of which were 'absorbed' in general maintenance.

(*b*) The supply of petrol and oil and the servicing of the subject's private motor-car at the works garage.

(*c*) The construction of an Italian garden, with materials and labour of works maintenance depot costs 'absorbed'.

(*d*) A half-acre vegetable garden cultivated by the works gardener (employed to mow lawn in front of the company offices) and the produce sold and the proceeds retained by the subject.

(*e*) Two 'machinists' taken from the plant by works car each day after clocking in to work as domestics in a director's home and returned to the works at the end of each day for clocking out.

(*f*) The distribution at Christmas-time, by a manufacturer, of goods to the value of 10 per cent of the orders placed in the preceding year to buyers of departmental stores and other large users.

(*g*) The provision of a private motor-car taxed, insured, serviced, and provided with oil and petrol to a university student by his father, the car being 'officially' provided by the company for staff use.

The list could be longer and its content more exciting, but the author does not wish to lose all his friends! This dilemma faces all sociologists writing about social pathology: either they must admit Sutherland's thesis, which is to admit their own involvement in activities of this kind, or they must find arguments to sustain the thesis of proletarian criminality.

The dilemma of the sociologist is displayed in a classic form by Ernest W. Burgess, the pioneer urban sociologist, in comments he made on an essay by F. E. Hartung, a disciple of Sutherland,

'White Collar Offences in the Wholesale Meat Industry in Detroit'.

Hartung's thesis may be stated briefly thus:

'The agencies charged with the enforcement and administration of this type of regulatory law need not, of course, be concerned primarily with the application of allowable criminal sanctions. Indeed, with hardly any exception save that of the pre-Taft, Hartley National Labor Relations Board, federal agencies appear to have been more concerned with obtaining compliance with the law than with punishing violations. For whatever reasons, these agencies have not defined themselves as being white-collar police departments charged with law enforcement. The various OPA administrators, charged with the responsibility of discharging the provisions of the laws creating OPA, perhaps fortunately did not have a criminological viewpoint in their work. It was also evident to the writer, from extended discussion with OPA enforcement attorneys over more than a year, that most of these attorneys defined their positions as administrative, law enforcement in any police sense of the term being secondary in their eyes. Nevertheless, violations of the two laws named above and of the regulations to which they gave rise, since they had the full force and effect of law, can legally, logically, and technically be classified as criminal acts' (Hartung, 1950, p. 26).

'OPA violations, in their chain effect, are similar to the bribing of policemen and the operation of organised vice, in that neither of these types of activities can be carried through by the initiator of the illegal deeds, but must necessarily involve other persons' (ibid, p. 32).

Professor Burgess makes the following comments in a discussion of the article:

'The theory of white collar crime implicit in this paper is that little or no distinction should be made between different violations or violators of all laws or regulations which have the sanction of a penalty. It is a legalistic and not a sociological position to regard these as one and the same.

The following are outstanding differences between these violations and offenses generally recognised as criminal by the community.

1. There is no evidence presented that OPA violators conceived themselves as criminal or were so considered by the public. In fact, for only 2 out of 122 is a previous criminal record reported.
2. The Emergency Price Control Act and the Second War Powers Act were suddenly imposed upon business men, defining many business transactions as offences which had previously been legal.
3. No concerted organised effective attempt was made by civic leaders, churches, schools, the press and governmental agencies to apply social condemnation to violations by businessmen and to purchase by consumers. Consequently, these acts were not stigmatised by the public as falling in the same category as murder, burglary, robbery, forgery and rape.
4. Large sections of the populations, comprising perhaps over half the adults, participated in black-market purchases during the war.
5. Few cases of violation (only 6·4 per cent.) drew prison sentences, and these were very light as compared with non-white collar "crimes", averaging only from three months to one year.

The attempt to make little or no distinction between white collar crime and other offences promises confusion rather than clarification in criminology. It is important to distinguish between offences which carry with them strong public disapproval and those violations of regulations (or recently enacted statutes) in which large sections of the public are willing accomplices' (Burgess, 1950, pp. 32 and 33).

These comments are of crucial interest to the arguments of this essay. The first comment states that an activity is assumed to be criminal only if the actor conceives himself as criminal. This is a remarkable doctrine, since it would exclude persons ignorant of the law, members of cultural groups with different norms, certain castes in India, Jehovah's Witnesses, Closed Brethren, Quakers and others, and persons indoctrinated for specific purposes such as the Waffen S.S., paratroopers in the British and French armed forces, marines in the U.S. armed forces, and members of 'security' organizations. It further asserts that criminality derives from the ideology, so that the control of ideology is the crucial causal factor in crime.

His second point is that businessmen cannot be expected to adjust to a 'sudden' change in the law. The idea that businessmen should be treated differently in matters of morals is, of course, not new, but it is unusual to find it advocated by a sociologist.

His third point reinforces his first and states specifically that the 'establishment' did not attempt to change the ideology.

The fourth is in effect that morality is a statistical concept and there is a threshold over which the proportion of offenders to the total population determines crime or non-crime. This is undoubtedly an underlying tendency in the moral order, but such an analysis needs qualification and should be considered in the dynamic rather than the static situation.

The fifth comment simply confirms the Sutherland thesis that the perpetrators of white-collar crimes are substantially immune from punishment.

Professor Burgess makes the following final comment, which is an excellent statement of the underlying assumptions of the traditional approach to the sociology of crime:

'A criminal is a person who regards himself as a criminal and is so regarded by society. He is the product of the criminal-making process. Professor Hartung gives no evidence that the so-called "white collar" criminal that he studied could be included under this definition. Under his definition of criminals the great majority of adults are criminals. But that is only because he employs a legalistic and not a sociological definition of the criminal (Burgess, 1950, p. 34).

Professor Burgess's paragraph contains an interesting circular argument, that is that 'a criminal – is the product of criminal-making process'. This is the assumption usually made, but generally it is accompanied by an attempt to establish what the criminal-making process is. He recognizes the implication of the Sutherland approach 'that the great majority of adults are criminals', but does not see that if this is accepted the problem then becomes to explain why some are designated and others immune.

Professor Burgess does, however, take the point that there is a problem here, although he does not accept the basic argument of the Sutherland School that 'the study of white collar crime will not so much reform the criminal as the criminologist'. To this end the present work is dedicated.

96

CHAPTER FOUR

The Actions of the Police and the Courts as Causal in Relation to Crime

It is not uncommon for discussion of the workings of the police and the courts to take place around the issue of whether guilty persons escape punishment because of the requirement that guilt must be proved beyond reasonable doubt; or whether the guilty who succeed in appeals against sentences on technical grounds should escape; or whether the court of criminal appeal should have the power to order a retrial; or whether the police or some other body should have greater powers of interrogation. In this, the actions of the courts or the limitations of the police are clearly seen as causal in reducing crime and the number of criminals. The tenor of the discussion is that this is a 'bad' thing.

Although, in these discussions the influences of the court and the police are recognized, and the imperfection of the system examined, it is still generally assumed, and assumed by many sociologists and criminologists, that the actions of the courts and the police reliably discriminate between criminals and non-criminals for scientific purposes. In this they believe first that the actions of the police discriminate and that the courts further refine the analytic process.

Unlike the judicial process of primitive societies, the British courts are almost unstudied by *sociologists*, although they have been described by lawyers and political scientists. This is because they have a majesty and a sacred quality that places them beyond the scope of inquiry. Shils has argued that there are important reasons touching the survival of civilized society (not to mention academic sociologists) which make it essential that this should be recognized.

'The nominally secular modern state has no avowedly "sacred" sphere, and the churches no longer have the power to prevent anyone outside their jurisdiction from turning an empirically analytical eye onto their sacred objects and actions. Nonetheless, there is a sacred area even of secular societies. The detached and realistic observation of the actual working of certain institutions arouses feelings approaching horror and terror in some persons, just as it exercises the fascination of sacrilege on others. For the secular state, what goes on in these institutions is sacred, and no social scientist would be unqualifiedly free to disclose, even if he were to know as a participant, what goes on in spheres designated as "secret". Those who possess secret information are not privileged to disclose it in interviews, and the attempts to learn of it without permission are strictly prohibited under severe penalties, even if the intention is politically innocent and scientifically reasonable' (Shils, 1959, p. 136).

This acceptance of such a point of view is consistent with the approach of most sociologists, who broadly accept the present system for the identification of the criminal, who devote their studies exclusively to him and aim at the 'perfecting' of existing institutions of detection, sentencing, and punishment or reform.

Within the compass of this short essay, it will not be possible to do more than to suggest that the processes of the courts and the police have a considerable influence on the selection of the criminal from the general population and on the numbers and social origin of those so selected.

The first issue is to observe the wide range of discretion that the court has in sentencing. Reference has already been made to this in Chapter 3. The crucial issue is that the popular stereotype of the criminal is of someone found guilty and sent to prison or borstal. This is important for a further reason, namely that much criminological research is done on criminals in prison, a captive audience, for whom the interviews and tests of the investigator are a welcome break in routine. The much greater difficulty of dealing with persons fined or bound over allows them to escape the net. In consequence the researchers tend to confirm the stereotype.

At the present time, much attention has been given to the differential treatment of motorists and non-motorists: reference has already been made to the views of Terence Morris on this in

Chapter 3. Barbara Wootton, in her Nottingham lecture 'Crime and the Criminal Law', argues the same point, stating that, in an investigation of 635 serious motoring offences, three-quarters of the offenders were found to believe there was nothing wrong in breaking the law, a point of view widely held by the police and reflected in the sentencing policy of the courts. In the same lecture, Barbara Wootton did, however, deal with the more general problem, describing 'the enormous element of luck that enters into the decision as to who is and who is not to be deprived of his liberty' (*Daily Telegraph*, 9-11-63, p. 23).

The author is not a believer in luck and would agree that differences in sentences are systematic, but that the records of the court do not make it possible, without independent empirical study, to establish what the non-random elements are.

The few facts quoted by Barbara Wootton are impressive:

'Indeed I need only remind you that the proportion of adult men imprisoned for indictable offences in any one of the four years 1951-54 by English courts varied between 3 per cent and 55 per cent.

In a sample of 12 urban courts sentencing adult men for comparable offences of dishonesty in the same period, the imprisonment rate as between one group of courts and another, ranged from about 50 per cent to under 15 per cent' (*Daily Telegraph*, 9-11-63, p. 23).

The nature of the systematic influences inherent in the practices of the British courts is complex and the social-class factors, although pervasive, are not the only ones.

At the root of the matter is the requirement that the magistrate, judge, or jury is charged with the task of establishing beyond reasonable doubt guilt or non-guilt. That is, whether behaviours described or represented by words correspond to words written in Acts of Parliament or to words recorded in previous judgements. There is no requirement to establish all the facts.

The most obvious method of ensuring a conviction is to have the accused plead guilty. The extent to which convictions as a whole are the result of pleas of guilt or of conviction after trial cannot be ascertained from the published records. A partial answer can, however, be given from an investigation made by the Chief Constable of Leicester. He asked the chief constables of forces in the Midlands to complete information about the outcome of cases taken to the higher courts in their districts for the period 1 January 1960 to April 1964. This shows that in 20,940 cases there were 16,647 pleas of guilty. Of the 3,293 people who elected trial, 1,576 were acquitted or discharged. The Chief Constable of Leicester argues that this is clear evidence of the ineffectiveness of the jury system and contrasts the English system of unanimous jury decision with that of the Scottish system of majority verdicts. He argues that 'Accused persons who fight the prosecution to the end are likely to include the kinds of criminal whom the police understandably are most anxious to see convicted'. His evidence shows, first, wide variations in the performance of different courts that could not arise from chance, and, second, the heavy dependence of the police on pleas of guilty to obtain convictions. Nothing is known about the characteristics of those who plead guilty and those who 'fight the prosecution to the end'. The Chief Constable of Leicester believes that these include many of the worst criminals and 'a tiny proportion of persons who believe in their own innocence'. It would appear likely, however, if the nature of the offence and the culpability of the offender are disregarded, that those with higher intelligence, with a knowledge of the law and the working of the courts, and with financial resources, are more likely to defend themselves rather than plead guilty, and, when tried, are more likely to be acquitted (Mark, 1965).

Two further questions arise. The first is the contrast between the continuous variability of human behaviour and the arbitrary thresholds which distinguish crime and non-crime: these thresholds come at 10.30 p.m.; at nine years, eleven months, and twenty-nine days; at fifteen years, eleven months, and twenty-nine days; at twenty-nine and ninety-nine hundredths of a mile an hour; at a penny, where this is taken at the time of a murder, or a few words, if spoken before another kills a policeman. At all these points and many thousands more, the translation of the observations of the police and their records of the words of suspects may be crucial.

From this, it follows that the interest of the police and the

Police District	Accused Persons	Committed[1] for Sentence	Guilty Pleas	Not Guilty Pleas		% of Persons who elected Trial who were Acquitted or Discharged	Standard Deviation
				Found Guilty	Acquitted or Discharged		
Counties							
Leics. and Rutland	1,099	109	756	132	102	44	3·24
Northamptonshire	874	150	373	277	74	21	2·16
Shropshire	742	166	495	50	31	38	5·39
Staffordshire	4,378	411	3,139	520	308	37	1·67
Warwickshire	2,116	355	1,431	173	157	48	2·75
Worcestershire	1,388	274	856	114	144	56	3·10
Cities and Boroughs							
Birmingham	6,611	764	4,813	697	337	33	1·45
Coventry	1,309	284	870	70	85	55	4·00
Dudley	309	65	192	38	14	27	6·16
Leicester	1,445	291	882	177	95	35	2·89
Northampton	465	70	300	63	32	34	4·86
Nottingham	1,808	258	1,190	239	121	34	2·49
Stoke	1,203	344	756	73	30	29	4·47
Walsall	580	71	460	28	21	43	7·07
Worcester	313	88	134	66	25	28	4·70
Totals	24,640	3,700	16,647	2,717	1,576	37	

[1] Persons found guilty in a lower court but sent forward to a higher court for sentencing.

H

prosecuting counsel will be to present words or to extract words from the defendant which correspond to the symbols of guilt, and of the defending counsel to prevent this. For the police the most valuable statement is the admission of guilt.

The situation of the police and that of the magistrates, judge, or jury is very different. The police are under heavy pressure to find criminals, that is to obtain convictions and to clear up crimes, that is, to find persons who can be shown to be responsible or are willing to accept responsibility. Magistrates and judges are not punished or rewarded for different kinds of decision, except perhaps in that appeals are often successful and tend to reflect adversely on the judge in the lower court. Judges have no vested interest in conviction and appear in general to carry out the function of establishing guilt, modified by a tendency to confuse this function with one of deciding whether or not this person should be punished. This is reflected in recommendation for mercy, and in the long and irrelevant evidence of character given by defence witnesses – wives, clergymen, employers, and the like – and elaborated by defence counsel. The effects of this process are discussed elsewhere.

The influence of the police in creating crime in the narrowest sense depends simply on their actions in detecting, apprehending, and successfully prosecuting persons with particular behaviours. This action is widely approved and is measured against popular belief about the extent of 'crime' and records of actions believed to be crimes reported to the police. In passing, it should be noted that the process of reporting is not uniform, either as to actions or as to persons. The other function of the police and that which is claimed to be primary in the legislation and precept concerning police forces is that of crime prevention. This function is not measurable and tends to escape public notice. In consequence, problems arise when the aims of preventing crime and catching suspects conflict, indeed the successful capture of a suspect *in flagrante delicto* necessitates connivance in the crime.

It has been argued with some evidence that attitudes, including the stereotypes of the criminal, may determine whether or not the policeman, when faced with certain behaviour, will decide to inquire into it. It is argued that this is less likely where the person displays middle-class characteristics than where he displays working-class characteristics – a situation frequently exploited by professional criminals.

Having inquired into the behaviour, the policeman may himself issue a caution, or report it to his superiors, who will decide whether or not to prosecute. If, however, the decision is to issue an oral or written caution, then this is recorded.

The likelihood of a caution is widely believed to be affected by a contrite communication from the accused or his solicitor. If this is so, then an advantage is conferred on the literate and the higher-income groups. The Criminal Statistics do not differentiate those cautioned by social class, so there is no means of testing this hypothesis.

The evidence does, however, show that the proportion cautioned is higher amongst the young than the adult, and higher among females than males. Nothing is known systematically about the practice of cautioning, so no firm conclusions can be drawn from this evidence. It does suggest, however, the possibility that the differences in practice arise from, and help to confirm, the belief that crime is a masculine rather than a feminine behaviour.[1]

The statistical evidence is, of course, very imperfect; it shows only those cautioned by a senior officer as a proportion of those found guilty and omits those apprehended, but not found guilty. There is some reason to believe that a caution is sometimes used when the police are convinced of guilt, but doubtful of a successful prosecution. As an example, the data for 1957 are given below. In this table the assumption is made that all who are cautioned are guilty, as are those prosecuted and found guilty; the action of the police in cautioning reduces the extent of crime. It does this for a higher proportion of women than men and for more of the young than the old.

The actions of the police create crime in a secondary way. If any actions increase the likelihood of successful prosecutions, then this in itself can increase crime; moreover, actions may also increase the likelihood that single criminals may admit to

---

[1] If it could be shown that professional crime is mainly a masculine prerogative, it would fit appropriately into the pattern in which all other professions are largely reserved to men.

numbers of crimes. Where the number of offences known to the police is high relative to the numbers of successful prosecutions, pressure to such actions will increase. The range of possible responses is considerable; there are actions that are criminal that are continually practised, for instance, cleaning windows in Liverpool without safety belts. From this available stock, of which there is an almost infinite supply, the police may pick at will (Rolph, 1962, p. 183). There are actions like 'loitering with intent' for which there is no defence, and there are actions that can be prosecuted under many rubrics, some of which give the possibility of a plea of guilt with a small penalty and little publicity, others which, if defended unsuccessfully, bring heavy penalties and much disgrace. The possibility of negotiation here is of interest (Newman, 1962). There are likewise other actions which increase the likelihood of admissions of guilt.

INDICTABLE OFFENCES

Persons Cautioned as a Proportion of all Persons Cautioned and all Persons Prosecuted and Found Guilty in 1957
(*Criminal Statistics* 1957, *p. xxx*)

Age Group	Males %	Females %
8 to 14	28·3	40·2
14 to 17	14·2	21·3
17 to 21	5·1	9·5
21 and over	3·3	9·1
All ages	11·6	15·3

The effects of police behaviour on crime, apart from the foregoing, which will be discussed in detail later, will also be displayed in differences between police forces and differences of police behaviour in relation to different classes of offence.

As there is no independent measure of 'crime', the evidence of criminal statistics shows that the success of police action differs in relation to different types of offence. Information is given below for three offences which show both net efficiency and

RELATION BETWEEN THE NUMBER OF OFFENCES KNOWN TO THE POLICE, THE NUMBER OF OFFENCES CLEARED UP, AND THE NUMBER OF PERSONS PROCEEDED AGAINST, 1937-38 COMPARED WITH 1949-50[1]

Offences	(1) Mean 1937 and 1938	Ratios	(2) Mean 1949 and 1950	Ratios	Ratio of Means (2) to (1)
Indecent assaults on females					
i Offences known to police	2,488		6,435		2·6
ii Offences cleared up	2,016	ii to i 0·8	4,457	ii to i 0·7	2·2
iii Persons proceeded against	1,358	iii to i 0·5	2,414	iii to i 0·4	1·8
Larceny by a servant					
i Offences known to police	5,887		11,963		2·0
ii Offences cleared up	5,447	ii to i 0·9	11,840	ii to i 1·0	2·2
iii Persons proceeded against	3,989	iii to i 0·6	9,409	iii to i 0·8	2·4
Larceny from unattended vehicle					
i Offences known to police	23,543		31,727		1·0
ii Offences cleared up	6,955	ii to i 0·3	7,278	ii to i 0·2	1·0
iii Persons proceeded against	4,154	iii to i 0·2	3,438	iii to i 0·1	0·8

[1] Table adapted from Lodge (1953).

changes in efficiency over time. This shows that police action as a variable is effective both between offences and over time. It could be argued that if police activity is to be 'neutral' then the intensity of policing would be aimed at maintaining constant ratios between offences and over time. In practice, however, the attitudes of Home Secretaries, opinions expressed by Members of Parliament, and even the enthusiasms of chief constables can introduce variability.

Another very simple example of the variability of police action is given by Lodge, who notes that the numbers of persons found guilty of offences against the Wireless Telegraphy Acts for the years 1948, 1949, and 1950 were 5,382, 12,459, and 3,149 (Lodge, 1953, p. 292).

The Wolfenden Committee drew attention to the variability in the rates of prosecution of homosexuals in different areas, thus:

'To some extent the laws relating to homosexual offences, and for that matter, to other sexual offences, are bound to operate un-evenly. Obviously many homosexual acts, especially those committed by consenting parties in private, never come to light, so that the number of those prosecuted in respect of homosexual acts constitutes but a fraction of those who from time to time commit such acts. But over and above this obvious fact, we have found that there are variations in the ways in which different police forces administer these laws. In some parts of the country they appear to be administered with "discretion"; that is to say, in some police districts no proceedings are initiated unless there has been a complaint or the offence has otherwise obtruded itself upon the notice of the police, for instance by a breach of public order and decency. In other parts of the country, on the other hand, it appears that a firm effort is made to apply the full rigour of the law as it stands' (Report of the Committee on Homosexual Offences and Prostitution, Cmnd. 247, 1957, p. 46).

'For instance, in the whole of the Metropolitan Police District, in only 10 cases (each involving two men) were men over 21 convicted during the three years ended March 1956, of homosexual offences committed in private with consenting adults. In five of these cases, the offenders were caught *in flagrante delicto* by someone who reported the matter to the police. In the remaining five cases, the offences came to light in the course of an enquiry into other matters, for example, larceny or blackmail. It seems in some areas – it might be in most – the police deal only with such matters as obtrude themselves on their notice, not going out of their way to substantiate suspicions of covert irregular behaviour. What we have found is that there may, from time to time, arise particular local campaigns against this kind of offence, either as a result of a deliberate drive by the police or by reason of local public indignation' (Report of the Committee on Homosexual Offences and Prostitution, Cmnd. 247, 1957, p. 48).

That the situation has not changed is shown by a report in the *Police Review*:

'Vice is of greatest concern to the Police when it is of a kind which can lead to crimes such as grievous bodily harm, robbery and blackmail. This is why most Forces keep a close watch on importuning by men, in spite of the current demands that homosexual acts between consenting male adults should no longer be regarded as offences against the criminal law. Manchester is evidently one of the Forces which believe that the law should be strictly enforced, and some figures included in the Chief Constable's annual report in fact reveal a radical change of policy during the past few years. In 1955 there was one prosecution for importuning, in 1956 and 1957 there were none and in 1958 there were two. Mr J. A. McKay was appointed Chief Constable at the end of that year, and the number of prosecutions rose to thirty in 1959 and 105 in 1960, to 135 in 1961 to 216 last year. The inescapable conclusion to be drawn from these figures is that until 1958 a blind eye was turned on importuning and that prosecutions were not encouraged by the Chief Constable' (*Police Review*, 3-8-63, p. 721).

In this case the 'cause' of the increase of this crime is clearly police activity.

Variability also occurs in institutions directly under the control of the Home Department and the Scottish Home Department.

'Our attention has been called to some of the difficulties experienced by headmasters and managers of approved schools in dealing with indecent acts among boys committed to their charge. Since boys in approved schools cannot, like boys in ordinary boarding schools, be expelled or removed by their parents, the sanctions available to those responsible for the management of these establishments are limited. Indecencies of a trivial character can quite properly be, and usually are, dealt with within the establishments as breaches of school discipline. But there arise occasionally more serious cases – for instance where boys are being persistently bullied or victimized by another boy or boys – where some more severe action against the offender is called for.

This is another matter on which there is some divergence of practice as between England and Wales on the one hand and Scotland on the other. In Scotland the managers of approved schools are given discretion to deal with all indecent or homosexual acts by pupils and are free to decide whether or not to report particular incidents to the police. The action taken in such cases must, however, be recorded in the punishment book or log book of the school, whichever is appropriate. But in England and Wales, the managers of approved schools, while they are given discretion to deal with indecencies of a minor character as breaches of school discipline, are required to report to the police and the Home Office not only cases of victimization but also all cases in which buggery or attempted buggery is detected or alleged' (Report of the Committee on Homosexual Offences and Prostitution, Cmnd. 247, 1957, p. 53).

If the behaviour of the police was consistent, universal, and automatic in its action, police activity as a cause of crime could be held constant in the analysis and disregarded while other causes were investigated. Although it is not possible to relate police action to behaviour, it is possible to compare police action over time and between areas.

THE EFFECT OF POLICE POLICY IN
DIFFERENT AREAS

The Wolfenden Committee has shown that the police, when confronted by sexual activity between men, have a wide discretion in deciding into what category to place an offence. This discretion not only lies in classification, but also derives from the point in time in the behaviour at which the police intervene. Thus quite different consequences arise where police activity is confined to the public section of a convenience compared with those which arise where the private compartments are under surveillance: here policy may be critical.

Criminal statistics make only part of this matter open to examination, because it is possible to class such behaviour, if the intervention is early, as importuning, a non-indictable offence for which there is no record in the reports of crimes known to the police. Three indictable offences however exist. The divisions are ill-defined, and the element of time may be crucial. They are:

16 Buggery
17 Attempts to commit buggery (including assaults with intent to commit buggery, indecent assaults upon male persons, and male persons soliciting for immoral purposes)
18 Indecency between men.

With such offences there is no reason to expect large variation from year to year, or large local differences except perhaps for naval towns where homosexuality is part of the naval subculture.

The returns for England and Wales may be taken as a basis.

DISTRIBUTION OF OFFENCES BETWEEN CATEGORIES 16, 17, AND 18 : ENGLAND AND WALES

Offence	1953 No.	%	1957 No.	%	1959 No.	%
16		12·3		12·7		12·3
17		58·2		57·0		59·7
18		29·5		30·3		28·0
Total	5680	100	6327	100	5732	100

From these data it would be surprising if there were differences from year to year in individual police districts, but the Home Office returns show some quite remarkable variations.

DISTRIBUTION OF OFFENCES BETWEEN CATEGORIES 16, 17, AND 18 : MIDDLESBROUGH

Offence	1953		1957		1959	
	No.	%	No.	%	No.	%
16		100		0		0
17		0		100		50
18		0		0		50
Total	37	100	27	100	12	100

DISTRIBUTION OF OFFENCES BETWEEN CATEGORIES 16, 17, AND 18 : WALLASEY

Offence	1953		1957		1959	
	No	%	No.	%	No.	%
16		0		6		0
17		61		75		90
18		39		19		10
Total	41	100	16	100	10	100

DISTRIBUTION OF OFFENCES BETWEEN CATEGORIES 16, 17, AND 18 : CHESTER COUNTY

Offence	1953		1957		1959	
	No.	%	No.	%	No.	%
16		14		24		6
17		53		44		48
18		33		32		46
Total	79	100	196	100	87	100

It is interesting that the very high number of cases in 1957 is accompanied by a high proportion prosecuted for the most serious offence.

In the adjoining county of Lancashire, the variation in the totals is similar but the distribution between the categories is different.

DISTRIBUTION OF OFFENCES BETWEEN CATEGORIES 16, 17, AND 18: LANCASHIRE COUNTY

Offence	1953		1957		1959	
	No.	%	*No.*	%	*No.*	%
16		19		10		5
17		53		52		79
18		28		39		17
Total	137	100	211	100	145	100

The differences between adjoining areas are very striking in some parts of the country.

From these data it would appear that the more liberal attitude of the Metropolitan Police resulted in migration of homosexuals from the County to their district. A comparison of large towns with similar populations is also illuminating (see over).

This evidence suggests a wide variation in police practice, a variation which Mr E. J. Dodd, Chief Inspector designate of Constabulary for England and Wales, confirmed: 'At the moment you may be prosecuted for an offence in one part of the country and get off with a warning elsewhere or the police may not bother at all' (*New Statesman*, August 1963, p. 164).

The purpose of this discussion is to show that police action is arbitrary in relation to types of offence and types of offender. This would not be important to the search for 'causes of crime' if police action were random, but it is reasonable to assume that there are a number of systematic factors at work. Police action is more certain in relation to crimes of property and certain crimes of violence than with most other crimes; it is more certain

111

DISTRIBUTION OF OFFENCES BETWEEN CATEGORIES 16, 17, AND 18:
BIRMINGHAM AND WORCESTER COUNTY

| Offence | 1953 | | | | 1957 | | | | 1959 | | | |
| | B'ham. | | W. Co. | | B'ham. | | W. Co. | | B'ham. | | W. Co. | |
	No.	%	No.	%	No.	%	No.	%	No.	%	No.	%
16		13		8		4		10		10		17
17		66		54		78		52		72		29
18		21		39		18		39		18		54
Total	115	100	52	100	126	100	62	100	128	100	72	100

DISTRIBUTION OF OFFENCES BETWEEN CATEGORIES 16, 17, AND 18:
THE METROPOLITAN POLICE DISTRICT AND SURREY COUNTY COMPARED

Offence	1953				1957				1959			
	M.P.D.		Surrey Co.		M.P.D.		Surrey Co.		M.P.D.		Surrey Co.	
	No.	%	No.	%	No.	%	No.	%	No.	%	No.	%
16		9		7		6		10		8		15
17		58		83		61		85		58		79
18		34		10		33		6		35		6
Total	576	100	218	100	645	100	84	100	640	100	173	100

DISTRIBUTION OF OFFENCES BETWEEN CATEGORIES 16, 17, AND 18:
LIVERPOOL AND MANCHESTER COMPARED

Offence	1953 Liverpool		1953 Manchester		1957 Liverpool		1957 Manchester		1959 Liverpool		1959 Manchester	
	No.	%	No.	%	No.	%	No.	%	No.	%	No.	%
16		3		9		14		4		10		2
17		72		20		64		68		67		39
18		25		72		22		28		24		59
Total	65	100	82	100	115	100	156	100	84	100	123	100

in relation to offences with some classes of vehicles than with others; it is more certain in relation to the working classes than the middle classes; and it is more certain in relation to men than women. In addition to these, fashions in public interest influence police activity by increasing the reporting of alleged offences and by increasing police action as a protective response. The enthusiasms of chief constables may likewise introduce systematic differences between areas. Thus one chief constable particularly sympathetic to the problems of children reduced the incidence of juvenile delinquency by introducing a new method of dealing with offenders outside the courts. Another devoted a considerable proportion of his resources to the tracking down of male homosexuals, especially those in the middle and upper classes, pursuing the trail into an adjoining police authority's area where a more liberal policy existed, with interesting results.

The police have the duty of preventing crime; indeed, the combination of regular police patrols and street lighting has constituted a major factor in the prevention of crime. Prevention does, however, conflict with the function of the police as agents for the apprehension of 'criminals' defined as persons who will inevitably commit crime. Where such people are concerned, it is argued, police patrols, street lighting, and other measures merely have the effect of changing the time and place but not the quantity of crime.

The implications of this have not been explored. It suggests, however, a number of dichotomies between 'spontaneous' and 'premeditated' actions and between those who are weak and liable to succumb to temptation and those who are permanently depraved.

From this proposition it is possible to consider another related issue. It is arguable that the success of a police force is measured by the number of convictions and, since these must bear some relationship to the number of actions, the police may therefore have a vested interest in concentrating their activities more on the detection of crime than on its prevention.

A variant of this situation is that, on the assumption that there is an inevitable amount of some kinds of crime, it is convenient to have it located in some place, institution, or area

115

where it can be controlled – the theory of the Red Light District.

The conflict between prevention and detection in its simplest form is obvious, but there are some aspects of the process that warrant further exploration.

In the simple case where plans to commit an offence become known to the police and the police allow the crime to take place, they are clearly creating crime, on the assumption that the criminals are continually engaged in crime and that *on balance* there will be less crime if the police set out to catch them in the act, rather than, say, ostentatiously patrol the area of the planned offence.

The issue, however, is more complicated, because it is necessary to discover how the police become aware of the intentions of the potential criminals. This is a matter upon which the police and the criminologist have had little to say, since it concerns those latent functions, the investigation of which may place the investigator in the kind of difficulty that Shils and Kingsley Davis discuss in their different ways (see above pp. 50-52 and 98).

In the Challenor case, King, who was sent to prison for two years for the possession of explosives planted by Challenor, claimed that he was 'framed' because he refused to become an informer for Challenor. He was later released and given a free pardon and compensation (Grigg, 1965, p. 38).

The case of Louciades is even more interesting:

'Louciades remained in prison, completing two concurrent terms of eighteen months. It was the first time he had ever served a prison sentence, although he had been inextricably involved with the police since 1956. On one occasion charges brought against him were later withdrawn. On another he was brought to trial on different counts and the charges were dismissed. It emerged in the autumn of 1959 that Louciades had been helping the police with information and that this was how he had found himself in a situation which had led to his being charged. He did not want to continue assisting the police, and he made a public statement to this effect. Challenor must have refused to accept the position because in May 1962 when he met Louciades casually, he said "You are in my territory now. You will have to help us" (Grigg, 1965, p. 47).

THE POLICE AND THE 'UNDERWORLD'

The essence of the matter is the social and functional relations between the police and the professional criminals and their associates. That is, in spite of the conflict that creates the existence of the police, police and criminals are for some purposes one society, this being especially so for the Criminal Investigation Department of the service. It is a picturesque detail of history that the founder of modern criminal detection, Vidocq, was himself a professional criminal.

It is sometimes thought that this relationship is a simple one of sustaining a small group of auxiliaries who, while retaining their amateur status, provide information on a piece-rate basis. Although this does happen, the writer has been informed by several chief constables that the amount spent by police forces in this way is very small; the symbiosis is of another kind.

The autobiographies of retired police officials and evidence in criminal cases show the dependence of the police on such informants as other criminals, prostitutes, club proprietors, and bookmakers.

Chief Superintendent Arthur Thorp gives this account:

'It is an extremely tricky and dangerous, but essential part of police work to keep in with potential informers. Every good C.I.D. man has his circle of such "friends", and the police authorities keep a constant close watch on the whole subject' (Thorp, 1954, p. 31).

A leader in the *Economist* describes the situation thus, in relation to the Hanratty, Ward, and Gordon cases:

'In each of the cases the police were operating in that dingy half-world of pimping, drug-taking, thieving and receiving, the band of shade where the actors depend on official sufferance for their freedom, and the guardians of the law must themselves maintain an uneasy fingerhold if they are ever to secure a conviction at all. In this world there must be some sort of two-way traffic: for information received there must be favours given. In the other direction, one must suspect, for evidence given in court there may also be favours given – or at least sometimes charges suspended' (*Economist*, 10-8-63).

In a case in Leeds where detectives were prosecuted on charges of perjury, conspiracy to pervert the course of justice, false pretences, procuring and shop breaking, receiving and stealing, it was revealed by a detective inspector that:

' "There is a recognised practice in the police force which enables a C.I.D. officer to make payment to informants for information." A special fund was maintained for that purpose. The officer concerned had to make a claim for payment.

"I feel sure," he added, "I have signed claims for payments by M. It is common practice for a detective to keep the identity of his informant to himself, but I knew that B was an informant." '

In this case a professional criminal claimed that he was given immunity in return for information and at the request of one of the detectives arranged crimes so that persons named by the detective would be caught in the act (*Guardian*, 14, 15, and 21-8-64 and 22-1-65).

In the same case another man with a record of convictions claimed that he agreed to admit to a crime which he had not committed in return for an undertaking that the woman with whom he lived would not be prosecuted for a crime to which she had confessed.

The practice of keeping the C.I.D., the plain clothes police, and the uniformed police separate can occasionally destroy a carefully organized source of information. Thus, in a case known to the author, the uniformed branch successfully prosecuted a club-owner for selling alcoholic drinks after time and closed his club, which had been under the 'protection' of a C.I.D. officer in return for information on larceny and narcotics.

The justification of this kind of activity depends on the theory of the balance of advantage, which, in turn, depends on the reliability of police predictions. The limiting case occurred in Liverpool, where police, having set up an observation post above a manicuring salon in an office building which was used for purposes of prostitution, observed the murder of the proprietress and were able to apprehend her murderer.

THE CREATION OF CRIME BY THE POLICE

An extension of the practice of intercepting criminals after they have embarked on an offence, rather than preventing them from beginning it, is that of laying traps for potential criminals. This assumes a threshold of opportunity separating the potential criminal from the non-criminal and lowers the threshold so that the former crosses it and will be caught. Clearly, by raising or lowering the threshold, more or fewer persons would be exposed to risk. One form of this is to select, create, or maintain a suitable locus for an offence, theft, or a sexual offence, such that if it were altered by open patrolling or improved lighting no offence would be likely to occur. Some of the methods employed are to have speed traps on open roads, to arrange for the doors of lock-up shops to be left unfastened, and, in one town, to have secret facilities for observation built into a men's public convenience.

To prevent crime where the police have placed a trap is regarded as 'obstructing the police in the execution of their duty', as motoring organizations found in their long feud with the police.

Thus, A. P., a metropolitan policeman who flashed his headlights to warn a motorist of a police trap in another police area, was fined £5 and dismissed from the force, having been found guilty of obstructing a police patrolman in the execution of his duty (*Daily Mail*, 4-1-62).

The case of the 'couple in the car' who were charged with outraging public decency in Ennismore Gardens, Kensington, on 10 April 1959, was a classic illustration of the police trap, and the report of the trial and the subsequent prosecution of the police should be read in full, since it includes such fascinating propositions as that one of the accused, who claimed to have been struck by a blow from a policeman's truncheon, obtained his injury by beating himself on the head with his hands.[1]

The essential facts were given by police constable D. M., who, with constable M., was concealed in the cul-de-sac to await couples who might make love in motor-cars. He stated, 'In the

[1] This is a variant of the claim made on occasions to account for the injury of the accused person while in the hands of the police.

18 months before April 10, 1959, he arrested 90 couples. Eighty-nine couples pleaded guilty, and the couple who pleaded not guilty were found guilty' (*Guardian*, 2-2-61). In this case, however, in actions which took some two years to conclude, the couple successfully defended themselves and were awarded damages against the police, and the officers were punished.

Several issues arise out of this. The first is that if, instead of two concealed policemen, there had been one visible policeman the crimes would not have taken place; moreover, there would have been one policeman free to prevent crimes elsewhere. Second, had the street lighting been adequate the crimes would not have taken place, and it might be thought that it was a part of the duty of the police to point out to the local authority where lighting conditions were likely to encourage crime. The third issue is that of the large numbers of couples who pleaded guilty. In cases like this, a plea of guilty almost certainly reduces the time taken over the case and the amount of detailed evidence given in court, and consequently the degree of publicity (none of the 89 cases where the defendants pleaded guilty was reported in the national daily newspapers), but if the case is defended the consequences may be immense. Moreover, since the police can claim, as they did in this case, to have witnessed an act of a 'lewd, obscene and disgusting nature', the pressure on the accused to settle for a plea of guilty can be very great. Here, in fact, is the ideal situation for the manufacture of crime by the police.

The question of the *agent provocateur* is more complex and ranges from intervention in political movements, in a series of suspected crimes, like fraud or confidence trickery, to intervention in a criminal process already in train, like blackmail, to deliberately provoking illegal acts in order to transform the potential criminal into an actual offender. Among recently reported cases, one may be noted where the police, disguised, attended a Bond Street night club and endeavoured to persuade hostesses to meet them after leaving the club, in an unsuccessful attempt to establish that the club was a disorderly house.

The Wolfenden Committee noted the employment of young police officers to trap potential homosexual offenders and clearly had some difficulty in justifying the practice. What is important in this issue is the fact that the Committee based its appraisal of the practice on interviews with the officers concerned but *not* on independent observation of their activities.

'This particular offence necessarily calls for the employment of plain-clothes police if it is to be successfully detected and prevented from becoming a public nuisance; and it is evident that the figures of convictions, both of importuning and for indecencies committed in such places as public lavatories, must, to some extent, reflect police activity. It has been suggested by more than one of our witnesses that in carrying out their duties in connection with offences of this nature, police officers act as *agents provocateurs*. We have paid special attention to this matter in our examination of the Commissioner of Police and other senior police officers, and we are satisfied that they do everything they can to ensure that their officers do not act in a deliberately provocative manner. We also made a special point of examining some of the constables engaged in this work. Those whom we saw were ordinary police constables, normally employed on uniformed duty but occasionally employed in pairs, for a four weeks' spell of duty on this work, between substantial periods on other duties. We feel bound to record that we were on the whole favourably impressed by the account they gave us of the way in which they carried out their unpleasant task. It must be, in our view, accepted that in the detection of some offences – and this is one of them – a police officer legitimately resorts to a degree of subterfuge in the course of his duty. But it would be open to the gravest objection if this were allowed to reach a point at which a police officer deliberately provoked an act; for it is essential that the police should be above suspicion, and we believe that if there is to be an error in the one direction or the other it would be better that a case of this comparatively trivial crime should occasionally escape the courts than that the police as a whole should come under suspicion' (Report of the Committee on Homosexual Offences and Prostitution, Cmnd. 247, 1957, pp. 43 and 144).

What is remarkable about this statement is that it asserts that an offence can be detected, before it occurs, by provoking it.

This activity is justified by assumptions that cannot be demonstrated: among them that no male is ever induced to consider a homosexual act for the *first* time by a disguised policeman and that no male is ever provoked who would not have committed a homosexual act with another person had he not first been provoked by the disguised policeman.

Had independent observations been made, the committee might have reconsidered its belief that the role of the disguised policeman was that of an innocent bystander. The most obvious difference is that of time – exposure to risk; only two classes of normally healthy persons frequently visit and long remain in those public lavatories which are known resorts of homosexuals: these are homosexuals and policemen. The other is an equally important issue. The homosexual subculture contains a wealth of signs, gestures, code words, details of dress and décor that would pass undetected by the heterosexual majority, but that convey information to the ingroup. It is by such means rather than by an overt verbal invitation that provocation takes place.

INTERROGATION AND THE PLEA OF GUILTY

The extent to which the plea of guilty creates crime is a matter upon which it is impossible to be certain. Other writers have drawn attention to the element of bargaining that goes into such arrangements, the essence of which is that the defendant foregoes the chance of acquittal in return for prosecution on a lesser charge or for favourable treatment by the prosecution with the imposition of a light sentence of imprisonment or a fine (Newman, 1962, p. 24).

The Wolfenden report commented on this possibility:

'Some of our witnesses have suggested that the offence with which a person is charged does not always correspond with the actual behaviour of the offender. We have seen one case, and heard of others, in which the facts would seem to sustain a charge of gross indecency, or attempting to procure the commission of an act of gross indecency, rather than a charge of importuning, though the offender was charged with the latter offence. It has been suggested that the police sometimes advise persons found committing acts of gross indecency in public lavatories to plead guilty at the magistrates' courts to importuning in order to avoid going for trial before a jury on a charge of gross indecency. How often this happens we cannot say: the statements of persons who plead guilty to offences which they subsequently deny must be treated with a certain amount of reserve. But if our recommendation that gross indecency should be triable summarily is accepted, there would be no encouragement to the offender to enter a false plea of guilty to importuning in order to avoid going to trial in respect of an act of gross indecency which had been committed, and no temptation to the police to frame a charge with a view to enabling the magistrates' courts to dispose of a case they could not otherwise properly deal with' (Report of the Committee on Homosexual Offences and Prostitution, Cmnd. 247, 1957, p. 44).

In this situation the accused is offered the positive inducement, if convicted, of a lighter sentence, less publicity, and a saving of time and money, in return for a confession.

Negative inducements may also be employed to extract confessions. The theory of police interrogation is well described by the former Attorney General, Lord Shawcross:

'From the moment that a criminal falls under suspicion to the moment of the eventual verdict, the suspected criminal is protected against any kind of inquisitorial examination before trial or even during trial' (*Daily Telegraph*, 6-11-63, p. 26).

A suspected person may not be detained without a charge, nor need he answer any question, and if charged may demand the presence of a solicitor before answering any question if he consents to do so. The manner of his questioning is strictly controlled by the Judges' Rules. Practice, however, differs considerably from theory.

'The police are scrupulous in their efforts to avoid persecuting whom they believe to be innocent, they are absolutely ruthless in pursuing whom they believe to be guilty. They let virtually nothing stand in their way. They become highly selective in their gathering of evidence, accepting anything that confirms the theories they have formed, rejecting everything that doesn't. They bully, threaten, plead, ingratiate, keep some people waiting for hours, interview others in the middle of the night, and use every kind of psychological pressure in order to obtain what they want. This is not something peculiar to this country. It is done by all police forces all over the world. There is evidence for it over and over again, in the histories of individual cases, in the articles and books of barristers and sociologists, in successive Reports of the Royal Commission on the Police' (Kennedy, 1964, pp. 226 and 227).

Lord Shawcross, in his lecture previously quoted, claimed that the police often know who has committed a crime but that for want of admissible evidence are unable to make an arrest. This is widely believed by judges, lawyers, and policemen and clearly confuses two quite different logical categories, knowledge capable of sustaining a belief in a policeman's mind, and evidence of a kind likely to sustain a conviction. Here is a fruitful field for investigation. Some preliminary inquiries show that the beliefs of judges, lawyers, and policemen are likely, in some cases, to predispose them to assumptions for which there is no evidence concerning the *class* of person about whom the assumption is made, and *a fortiori* no evidence concerning the individual about whom the assumption is made. Some assumptions that are common are that persons with Central European names are likely to be engaged in fraud, that homosexuals are politically radical or are security risks, and that pacifists are violent. The influence of these stereotypes can be seen in police evidence given about members of the Campaign for Nuclear Disarmament and the acceptance of such evidence by magistrates and judges.

Lord Shawcross comments:

'In the result, the police sometimes suffer, not unnaturally, from a sense of frustration and are occasionally led into using undesirable subterfuges, strong-arm methods, or even, sometimes but I believe most exceptionally, perjury, not against innocent people but against those whom they have good grounds to believe guilty though they cannot prove it otherwise' (*Daily Telegraph*, 6-11-63, p. 26).

Here the logical confusion is evident.

There is no satisfactory test of the extent to which the methods listed by Lord Shawcross are used by the police in the creation of crime, but of the fact there is ample evidence.

124

The most difficult situation is one where the case hinges on words alleged to have been spoken at the time of an offence.

The classic case is that of Bentley who was alleged by three police officers to have said, 'Let him have it, Chris', while in the custody of a police officer. Bentley was hanged, Craig – who fired the shots – being too young, was sentenced to prison and has since been released (Hyde, 1954, pp. 154 and 155).

A more recent case was that of George Clark, active in the Campaign for Nuclear Disarmament, who was sentenced to eighteen months' imprisonment on a charge of inciting a crowd to commit a nuisance by unlawfully obstructing the free passage of a highway – a common-law charge – on the evidence of two plain-clothes police officers, who, recognizing him, stood near him in a procession and claimed that he said 'Follow me'. The charge was dismissed on appeal, the police having failed to establish an unlawful obstruction (*Guardian*, Law Report, 19-11-63).

Statements alleged to have been made by accused persons while in custody are of two kinds: those claimed to have been made spontaneously and quoted by the police in evidence, and those taken down and signed by the accused as a true statement of their answers to questions or statements volunteered without interrogation.

The first category is often very damaging to the accused and occurs in stereotyped form – 'It's a fair cop' or 'Who has grassed?' or other phrases which are accepted by the public and juries as the language of criminals. Of a similar nature is the claim that 'the accused turned pale and adjusted his collar', damaging to the accused and impossible to refute.

Often the accused is in the custody of the police. The task of the police is to obtain a statement which can be used as a basis for a successful prosecution. In this process the police question, the suspect replies, the policeman records part of the replies, and in due course the suspect signs the statement as a true record. Attendance at a court will show that the statements signed by prisoners are rarely in their own language but in police jargon, except where a particularly incriminating phrase is employed (not all this translation is necessarily suspect – the author has had the experience of trying to find words that a policeman taking a statement could spell). The effects of this process have not been studied in Britain, but American records have shown the contribution it can make to crime (Arens & Meadows, 1962, p. 57).

There is a continuity in the process of questioning from a situation in which the questioner and the respondent are in a position of equality to one where, regardless of his interests or intentions, the respondent is under the control of the questioner and can be made to make any statement required of him.

Curiously, this matter has not been much studied by criminologists, in spite of the possible incentives offered by the inexplicable confessions of leading members of the Communist Party of the U.S.S.R. during 'treason trials' under the Stalin régime. There is, however, an extensive literature in the field of public opinion research and social survey which shows how the status of the interviewer and the form of the question may influence the answer.

A study of so-called 'brain-washing' and 'third degree' has suggested that social isolation, fatigue, hunger, fear, and strain imposed by confinement, bright lights, and the like, can cause acquiescence to propositions and attachment to such propositions after the interrogation is over. It has suggested also that the interrogation process is one of interaction and that the interrogator himself may be equally convinced of the truth of the results of his questioning.

It is not uncommon for suspects to be taken into custody late at night and to be questioned for many hours. The case of Timothy Evans has been quoted:

'Even in Great Britain today false confessions are sometimes elicited quite unknowingly despite the acknowledged integrity of the British police, especially when evidence is being collected by them which may result in a suspect's prosecution, trial for murder and his subsequent hanging. A good recent example of this almost certainly happened in the case of Timothy Evans. His trial is bound to become a medico-legal classic as it involved the hanging of a probably innocent man, because wrong third and fourth confessions were elicited from him and then quite genuinely believed in by the police. Evans was tried and hanged for

murder in 1950 after the dead bodies of his wife and child had
been found hidden in the house in London in which the family
rented rooms.

In 1953, another tenant of the rooms in the same house discovered human remains hidden behind the wall. A subsequent
police search of the house and garden uncovered the remains of
the bodies of six women, all of whom had been murdered. A man
named Christie was tried and convicted for murder and confessed
to the killing of all six. Christie had been a friend and co-tenant of
the Evans family at the time of the murder of Mrs Evans and her
child' (Sargant, 1959, p. 180).

It is of interest that the subsequent reports on the conviction
and execution, while providing abundant evidence of the emotional strain imposed on the defendant, did not consider that
the confession and its acceptance were the product of the social
interaction process of the questioning (Henderson, 1953). It is
also of passing interest that, like Bentley, Evans was unable
to read the report of his statement. On 18 October 1966 Timothy
Evans received a free pardon.

One aspect of questioning that criminals have described to
the writer concerns tobacco. The suspect is deprived of his
tobacco and questioned for many hours by an officer who smokes
– a cigarette becomes the reward for cooperation. To a person
addicted to tobacco, deprivation in these circumstances imposes
great strain.

The advantage of these methods is that the accused does not
display evidence of injury or pressure, so that if he wishes to
retract his statement on the grounds of duress he will find it
difficult to persuade his judges.

Information about the interrogation of suspects is notoriously
hard to obtain. It has not been the subject of academic study,
most evidence coming from reports of cases like that described
above, or from the statements of persons who have been in the
custody of the police. These reports deal with the ill-treatment
of suspects, or, as in the Evans case, the possibility of a mis-
carriage of justice. What is lacking is an account of the normal
procedures and their effects on the 'causation' of crime. There
are the Judges' Rules, which lay down the manner of conducting
interrogations, but there is no machinery for ensuring their

observance at the time of the questioning. In this situation the first offender, the illiterate, and the ignorant are likely to fare worse than the suspect with experience or the middle-class person who knows enough to maintain silence until his legal adviser has been sent for.

In contrast to the situation in Britain, the practice of one large American police force, that of Chicago, has been codified and presented as a textbook. It is a study that defends practices many would find surprising, criticizes legal limitations on interrogation, and offers an impressive explanation of the role of the confession in criminal connection. In many of the examples discussed it shows not that the prisoner's confession was extracted by the demonstration of overwhelming evidence against him, but that the confession was the basis on which other evidence was collected (Inbau & Reid, 1962).

The authors, who were formerly director and staff member of the Chicago Police Crime Detection Laboratory, offer this as the justification for interrogation.

'One completely false assumption accounts for most of the legal restrictions on police interrogations. It is this, and the fallacy is certainly perpetuated to a very considerable extent by mystery writers, the movies, and TV: whenever a crime is committed, if the police will only look carefully at the crime scene they will almost always find some clue that will lead them to the offender and at the same time establish his guilt; and once the offender is located, he will readily confess or disclose his guilt by trying to shoot his way out of the trap. But this is pure fiction; in actuality the situation is quite different. As a matter of fact, the art of criminal investigation has not developed to a point where the search for and the examination of physical evidence will always, or even in most cases, reveal a clue to the identity of the perpetrator or provide the necessary proof of his guilt. In criminal investigations, even of the most efficient type, there are many, many instances where physical clues are entirely absent, and the only approach to a possible solution of the crime is the interrogation of the criminal suspect himself, as well as others who may possess significant information. Moreover, in most instances these interrogations, particularly of the suspect himself, must be conducted under conditions of privacy and for a reasonable period of time; and they frequently require the use of psychological tactics and techniques that could well be classified as "unethical", if we are to evaluate them in terms of ordinary, everyday social behaviour.

To protect ourselves from being misunderstood, we want to make it unmistakably clear that we are not advocates of the so-called "third degree". We are unalterably opposed to the use of any interrogation tactic or technique that is apt to make an innocent person confess. We are opposed, therefore, to the use of force, threats, or promises of leniency – all of which might well induce an innocent person to confess; but we do approve of such psychological tactics and techniques as trickery and deceit that are not only helpful but frequently necessary in order to secure incriminating information from the guilty, or investigative leads from otherwise uncooperative witnesses or informants.

Our position, then, is this, and it may be presented in the form of three separate points . . .

1. Many Criminal Cases, Even When Investigated by the Best Qualified Police Departments, Are Capable of Solution Only by Means of an Admission or Confession from the Guilty Individual or upon the Basis of Information Obtained from the Questioning of Other Criminal Suspects (ibid, pp. 203 and 204).
2. Criminal Offenders, Except, of Course, Those Caught in the Commission of Their Crimes, Ordinarily Will Not Admit Their Guilt unless Questioned under Conditions of Privacy, and for a Period of Perhaps Several Hours (ibid, p. 206).
3. In Dealing with Criminal Offenders, and Consequently Also with Criminal Suspects Who May Actually Be Innocent, the Interrogator Must of Necessity Employ Less Refined Methods Than Are Considered Appropriate for the Transaction of Ordinary, Everyday Affairs by and between Law-Abiding Citizens' (ibid, p. 207).

The book describes every aspect of the process of interrogation, the room, its furnishings, its technical equipment, the social setting, and the variety of tactics to be employed with different types of suspect, with men and with women and with members of different social classes. A major aim is to create tension and emotional insecurity.

'The interrogation room should contain no ornaments, pictures, or other objects which would in any way distract the attention of a person being interviewed; and this suggestion also refers to the presence, within the subject's reach of small, loose objects, such as paper clips or pencils, that he may be inclined to pick up and fumble with during the course of the interrogation. Tension-relieving activities of this sort detract from the effectiveness of the interrogation, especially during the critical phase when a guilty subject may be trying desperately to suppress an urge to confess' (ibid, p. 8).

The tactics to be employed are described under two headings: those to be used where the suspect's guilt is definite or reasonably certain, and those to be used where guilt is in doubt This reveals an interesting situation, the belief by the police that they can be certain of guilt where the evidence to convince a court is lacking, the function of the interrogation being to produce this evidence.

The titles of the different tactics recommended give an inadequate indication of the nature of the processes employed, which are described in detail in the text, but space precludes all but a brief account. Here are some tactics to be employed where guilt is 'certain':

'A. Display an Air of Confidence in the Subject's Guilt.
B. Point out Some, but by No Means All, of the Circumstantial Evidence Indicative of a Subject's Guilt.
C. Call Attention to the Subject's Physiological and Psychological Symptoms of Guilt.
D. Sympathize with the Subject by Telling Him That Anyone Else under Similar Conditions or Circumstances Might Have Done the Same Thing.
E. Reduce the Subject's Guilt Feeling by Minimizing the Moral Seriousness of his Offense.
F. Suggest a Less Revolting and More Morally Acceptable Motivation or Reason for the Offense Than That Which Is Known or Presumed.
G. Sympathize with the Subject by (1) Condemning His Victim, (2) Condemning His Accomplice, or (3) Condemning Anyone Else upon Whom Some Degree of Moral Responsibility Might Conceivably Be Placed for the Commission of the Crime in Question.
H. Utilize Displays of Understanding and Sympathy in Urging the Subject to Tell the Truth.
I. Point out the Possibility of Exaggeration on the Part of the

Accuser or Victim or Exaggerate the Nature and Seriousness of the Offense Itself.

J. Have the Subject Place Himself at the Scene of the Crime or in Some Sort of Contact with the Victim or the Occurrence.

K. Seek an Admission of Lying about Some Incidental Aspect of the Occurrence.

L. Appeal to the Subject's Pride by Well-Selected Flattery or by a Challenge to His Honor.

M. Point out the Futility of Resistance to Telling the Truth.

N. Point out to the Subject the Grave Consequences and Futility of a Continuation of His Criminal Behavior.

O. Rather Than Seek a General Admission of Guilt, First Ask the Subject a Question as to Some Detail of the Offense, or Inquire as to the Reason for Its Commission.

P. When Co-Offenders Are Being Interrogated and the Previously Described Techniques Have Been Ineffective, "Play One against the Other" ' (ibid, pp. 23-81).

Under C the authors write:

'An offender who is led to believe that his appearance and demeanor are betraying him is thereby placed in a much more vulnerable position. His belief that he is exhibiting symptoms of guilt has the effect of destroying or diminishing his confidence in his ability to deceive and tends to convince him of the futility of further resistance. This attitude, of course, places him much nearer the confession stage.

This technique of calling attention to various physiological and psychological phenomena . . . is a reliable indication of guilt . . .

Although an accelerated pulsation of the carotid artery in the neck is experienced by some innocent persons as well as a certain number of guilty ones, such a phenomenon exhibited by a guilty subject can be commented upon to good advantage . . .

When a subject of the emotional offender type is being interrogated, it is advisable to remind the subject that he "doesn't feel very good inside", and that this peculiar feeling (as if "all his insides were tied in a knot") is the result of a troubled conscience' (ibid, pp. 29, 30, and 31).

Under I, an interesting tactic is described:

'To add to the effectiveness of the exaggeration or the nature and seriousness of the offense, the verbal statements of the interrogator

131

may be augmented by resorting to some documentary "evidence" in support of the interrogator's exaggerated statement of the amount of money or property stolen. For instance, in the interrogation of an embezzler of $500, the interrogator may arrange to have a letter or a memorandum typed (perhaps even on the employer's stationery) and addressed to the insurance company, or to the police department, in which a statement is made that since the loss was originally reported it now appears that the amount taken was not just $500 but rather $1500, and that some negotiable bonds worth $3000 were also taken. The letter may even name the subject as the one the company manager believes to be responsible for everything. After some repeated foldings and handling of the letter or memorandum, to make it look more authentic, it should be shown to the subject. At that point the interrogator should proceed to suggest that the reported loss may be exaggerated and he should then give the possible reasons for the exaggeration (e.g., trying to cheat the insurance company, or a company manager covering up his own thefts)' (ibid, p. 63).

Reference has already been made in Chapter 3 (p. 71) to a successful prosecution of a doctor in Penzance on a charge of having performed an illegal abortion. The following letter shows that some of the tactics described above are practised in England.

'With regard to the way police evidence was obtained in the case of the Penzance doctor charged with procuring abortions, readers may be interested to know that the police interviewed 45 women.
In most cases they drew a blank. One woman who refused to admit to having been to the doctor in question is the French wife of a local man. She was taken to the police station and questioned for four and a half hours as she was quite ignorant of the fact that this was contrary to the law. During her interrogation she was told that as a foreigner who had lived off the British for years, the least she could do was help and that had it been France she would have been made to talk.
Of the five women who gave evidence, four were very young and ignorant and again were not informed of their rights under the law. One was promised that her name would be kept out of the papers if she told all she knew. It was not, of course, and when I spoke to her she was talking of suicide. Another was told that "A girl had died" after an abortion and by giving evidence she would be

helping to convict someone guilty of manslaughter. No one had died' (*Guardian*, 20-8-64).[1]

Torture has been a normal method of increasing the willingness of suspects to disclose information and is widely employed by intelligence services in wars and against political enemies where struggles for power are in progress. The documentation of such practices is adequate for all countries except for one's own (Vida-Naquet, 1963). The social pattern is consistent. There is a hierarchy of officials; those at the highest level are socially acceptable and play no part in the actual interrogation but give orders in a general form, those at the second level give orders of a more specific kind, to obtain information (often with euphemistic references to the means of persuasion), and those at the third level actually carry out the torture and are trained to do so. In return they are protected if they break the law or offend against the norms, and the ideology describes them as an elite with a special role to defend the state, the army, or the party, thus relieving them of guilt.

This pattern, while achieving the necessary results, preserves the institution from attack, since the lowest ranks can always be sacrificed, the middle ranks can claim to be misunderstood, and the leaders can claim complete innocence.

It is a remarkable tribute to the consistency of human institutions that the pattern described by Vida-Naquet was also found in the Sheffield case.

The pattern of the Sheffield case was simple. From a group of persons with criminal records, four were selected late at night and beaten to persuade them to confess to crimes. As these events took place in the privacy of the police station, the facts are hardly likely to be fully known, and the events have been the subject first of all of the unsuccessful prosecution of the victims, then of the prosecution of their assailants, then of a public appeal by the assailants against their dismissal from the police force. However, the general principle underlying the behaviour of the police and other institutions of power in the matter of creating crime by inducing confessions may be deduced.

[1] See also Burt (1959, p. 29 *et seq*).

Before proceeding to examine the evidence in detail it must be said that there is no evidence upon which any judgement can be made as to the extent of these practices. They are, however, known to have occurred elsewhere at the present time and in the past, so that they may be regarded as 'a general tendency', in the scientific sense, of institutions with power. It has been argued against this that the Sheffield situation was a subcultural one, in that there had been a tough 'crime squad' in action at an earlier date.

Arising out of the beating of suspects to obtain a confession, two policemen, Streets and Millicheap, were dismissed from the force and they appealed against their dismissal. The following account and quotations are from the inquiry into their dismissal.

The first information concerns the establishment of a 'Crime Squad' or *corps d'élite*. Here it may be noted that this is a standardized and patterned response to conflict situations. A group of persons are selected from the rank-and-file and given special powers, including exemption from the mores, by those in authority. More is, of course, known about such formations in the police forces and armed forces of enemy or former or potential enemy countries, especially Nazi Germany and the U.S.S.R., but such groups exist in all armed forces, in espionage networks, and in political police. Their activities form a continuum from invasions of privacy such as telephone-tapping and intercepting and reading the mail (see p. 57), to torture and assassination. The establishment of the *corps d'élite* is accompanied by an ideology which describes the 'enemy' as alien, subhuman, or having cultural characteristics which place him outside the group in which the mores apply (Sheffield Police Inquiry, 1963).

'The Squad was addressed first generally by Detective Chief Superintendent Carnill, who then left, and then by Detective Chief Inspector Wells, the deputy head of the C.I.D., who related the success of a similar Squad under his command in 1957.[1]

There is a direct and important conflict as to what further Detective Chief Inspector Wells said at the Conference. Certainly he

[1] In October 1957 a boxer, who had been convicted of assaulting a youth, breaking his jaw, while serving in the Huddersfield police force, joined the Sheffield force (*Daily Telegraph*, 15-11-67). In November 1967 he was found guilty of assaulting a prisoner in custody and breaking a rib.

said that the Squad would be dealing with hardened criminals who might be expected to plead not guilty. Equally certainly he related (possibly with humorous touches) an incident when a member of the 1957 Squad was accused in Court of using a "lie detector". By this he certainly meant an instrument used to extract a confession by violence, and we do not accept those witnesses still in the service who say they thought the reference was to a scientific instrument or tape recorder. The conflict was between those witnesses (including himself) who maintain that he only referred to this incident as a warning of the false accusations that the Squad might have to meet, and the appellants who testified that by words and gestures he indicated that they might have to use a lie detector on occasions. Upon the whole we have come reluctantly to the conclusion that the admitted reference to a "lie detector", which had otherwise little point, did contain a veiled hint to those who wished to take it that force might have to be resorted to coupled, as we find it was, with references to "taking chances". We find it difficult otherwise to understand why, on hearing next day of the violence that had been used that very night, Detective Chief Inspector Wells, did not immediately round on the Squad for having disregarded his warning. Conversely, his mental attitude to the use of such methods is illustrated by his remark to the appellant Streets, which we were satisfied was made in the canteen next day, to the effect that he should be feeding on raw steak instead of milk, as also by his general attitude to the allegations and their investigation to which we shall refer later.

The minds of the appellants were already conditioned by the dangerous notion they had formed that a Crime Squad was a "corps d'élite" which could use tough methods to deal with tough criminals and take risks to achieve speedy results. Mr Streets, who we judged to be the stronger personality, told us that he held views that criminals are treated far too softly by the Courts, that because criminals break rules, police may and must do so to be a jump ahead, that force is justified as a last resort as a method of detection when normal methods fail, and that a beating is the only answer to turn a hardened criminal from a life of crime. These views must have infected Mr Millicheap. Otherwise it is impossible to understand how he came to depart, as he did, from the very clear tenets of the police training that both admitted they had received in the District Training Centres regarding the care and custody of prisoners and from the Judges' Rules and from his up-bringing by a policeman father.

After the Conference we are satisfied that a discussion followed between the members of the Squad as to whether they would be backed up if they followed the suggestion to use violence if necessary' (ibid).

The results of this meeting were that on the same evening

'There followed a series of interrogations at the C.I.D. Headquarters at Water Lane, during which the arrested men were moved from room to room and three of them were undoubtedly seriously assaulted by Police Officers.

As might be expected after this lapse of time and having regard to the circumstances and the quality as witnesses of the assaulted men, the accounts varied in precise detail: but we were satisfied that the appellants committed the following assaults, mainly in the upstairs Conference Room where chairs had been arranged for interrogation. At some stage the blinds were drawn to cover windows overlooked by flats.

We find that the appellants were guilty of the following assaults.

(a) On Kenneth Hartley

The appellant, Mr Streets, committed three separate deliberate and brutal assaults in the Conference Room to extract confessions, using an old-fashioned truncheon, the origin of which is obscure, and an instrument which was called a "rhino tail". Mr Streets had acquired this from among a collection of offensive weapons handed in to the police; and we accept his evidence that he carried it around on bank escort duties and in case of conflicts between coloured informants, that it acquired its name as a C.I.D. joke and that his possession of it was well known in at least the lower ranks of the C.I.D. It was described as being about eight inches long, the thickness of a finger, of gut-like material and with a loop of plaited string at one end. Both instruments were burned by Mr Streets on 15th March.

These assaults resulted in pronounced weals and bruising over the shoulders and buttocks, which were shown in the photographs that were taken the next day and were described in the medical report and the evidence of Mr Sharrard, a Consultant Orthopaedic Surgeon, who examined the two Hartleys and Bowman on the afternoon of the 15th March. The intensity of the bruising was borne out by the expert evidence of the photographer. Between the assaults, Mr Streets stripped to his vest in order to frighten Hartley.

(b) On Albert Hartley

In the Conference Room this prisoner was subjected to five separate and successive beatings; three by Mr Streets alone, mainly with the truncheon, one by Mr Millicheap alone with the rhino tail which he saw on the table and picked up, and one by both together. Albert Hartley's estimate of 60 or 70 blows may be on the high side, but his injuries were at least as serious as those of his brother, and again are depicted in the photographs and described in the medical evidence. Again the object of the beating was to extract confessions.

(c) On Clifford Bowman

Mr Millicheap initially assaulted Bowman in the Detective Officers Room downstairs, striking him with a gloved hand one or more blows, so as to make his nose bleed. At this stage it seems more likely that the assault was from loss of temper with an awkward and offensive prisoner than designed to obtain a confession (though it could have been a softening-up process): but in any event the assault was wholly unjustified.
In the Conference Room Mr Millicheap committed a prolonged assault on Bowman with the rhino tail, producing very similar injuries to those inflicted on the other two, again depicted by the photographs and described in the medical evidence. We are satisfied that Mr Millicheap was wholly responsible for these injuries and that Mr Streets left the room just as this beating started. The object of the beating was to elicit confessions as in the other cases.

(d) On George Hancock

He was not called as a witness but Mr Streets admitted slapping his face to see if he would confess' (ibid).

What follows is of interest. The suspects' solicitor, Mr Hewitt, produced evidence of the assaults in the case which was brought forward based on a 'confession' extracted from one of them. The solicitor then asked the Chief Constable if he would prosecute:

'At the interview of the 20th March, Mr Hewitt and Mr Barlow repeated the allegations already made in Court about the assaults with a cosh and a rhino whip, and showed the Chief Constable

137

photographs and told him there was medical confirmation of the use of some such weapons, and asked if he would prosecute, mentioning Section 18 of the Offences Against the Person Act, 1861: but the Chief Constable, though obviously shocked by the photographs, gave them the strong impression that if the matter was left to him he would take disciplinary proceedings only. The Chief Constable said that this impression was quite wrong; but it certainly accorded with the terms of a letter which the Chief Constable was about to send to Mr Hewitt and showed to him, and of which only a copy survives. The Chief Constable had left the drafting of this letter to Detective Chief Superintendent Carnill, as the reference CID/GAC shows, and whilst assenting to an identification parade and certain facilities if required, it concluded with the phrase that "whatever allegations your clients may make, they will be answered by the officers concerned at the appropriate time and place". The Chief Constable also told Mr Hewitt that he had no chance of succeeding in a prosecution under Section 18 – although he had by then no information on which to base that view, other than his confidence that no officer of his force could be guilty of such conduct and a vague suspicion that the injuries might be the result of flagellation between sexual perverts, which enquiries as to the records of the complainants quickly dispelled. He asked for and received by letter of the same date written confirmation of the formal complaint, naming the appellants and Detective Constable Rowlands and alleging that Detective Inspector Rowley was present during some or all of the assaults.'

Here the pattern of internal private justice with at least partial immunity is present.

The report then describes how one of the senior officers invented a story to account for the suspects' injuries.

What then happened can be interpreted as a process in which changes were made until public interest was satisfied. That is, until a state of equilibrium was restored. The two detective constables were prosecuted, found guilty, and dismissed from the force.

'On the 2nd May the appellants appeared before the Justices and pleaded guilty to the charges under Section 20. The prosecution were willing to accept the pleas, which Mr Hewitt insisted should be made in person; and after retiring the Justices consented to the pleas being accepted and to dealing summarily with them. A freelance journalist, Mr Harold Martin, reporting the case for "The Times", fortunately was able to produce a transcript of the shorthand note of the proceedings (Exhibit 19). From this it is clear

(a) that Mr Hewitt opened to the Justices the correct story of the assaults in so far as it concerned the appellants.
(b) that Counsel for the appellants put forward a mitigation based on the fight in the lavatory version.
(c) that the Justices seem to have accepted the prosecution rather than the defence version having, of course, seen the photographs.

The reasons why the appellants did not tell the true story to their Counsel were those set out in paragraph 16 with two additions:—

(a) they thought that the true story implicating senior officers would not be believed by the Justices, and that an appearance of trying to shift the blame and of disloyalty would only make matters worse for them.
(b) they said they had received advice to plead guilty and hints that they would not lose their jobs from Detective Superintendent Carnill, Detective Sergeant Oats and Detective Inspector Rowley.'

Once the officers had been found guilty the facts compelled further action by the Chief Constable, particularly with reference to their immediate superiors.

'Having completed his investigations, Superintendent Bowler served Notices in accordance with Regulations 3 of the Police (discipline) Regulations, on the three Officers concerned, setting out the allegations of which there appeared to him to be prima facie evidence, i.e. in effect:— agreeing that force would be used if the prisoners did not admit crime: being present at the assaults by the appellants involving the use of a trunchon and rhino whip failing to report these facts: and later making false or incorrect statements in the preparation of the case. Some of these allegations, of course, did or could amount to criminal offences and it was suggested with some force to the Chief Constable in cross-examination that they were founded, if anything, on stronger evidence than was available to Mr Hewitt against the appellants when he started his prosecution. All three elected to make no reply to the allegations at this stage.

139

The complete file would normally have been submitted to the Assistant Chief Constable, to whom the Chief Constable had delegated his powers under Regulation 5, but as he was on leave it was submitted through Superintendent Appleyard to the Chief Constable on Monday the 20th May, and then he exercised his discretion to peruse it.

On the 22nd May the Chief Constable went to consult the Director of Public Prosecutions as to what action he should take. He did not follow the normal practice in criminal matters of submitting the file in advance to the Director, but took it and Detective Chief Superintendent Carnill with him and orally outlined the facts and "put forward points". He did not show the Director the allegations drafted by Superintendent Bowler, nor tell him the form of them, though he told us he did mention aiding and abetting and the allegations generally. In the result, no doubt much to the relief of the Chief Constable who was most anxious for an end to publicity (a hope fore-doomed to disastrous failure), the Director advised orally that criminal proceedings should not be taken, that disciplinary proceedings should, that a multiplicity of charges was undesirable and that the matter should be dealt with under a charge of discreditable conduct under Paragraph 1 of the First Schedule of the Discipline Code.

We felt that public policy prevented us from delving more deeply into the Director's reasons for this advice, but we must record our view that the oral presentation of the problem to him was not the most satisfactory method for obvious reasons. It would likewise be quite wrong for us to criticise the advice or to speculate whether it might have been different if the Director had had the file.

As a result, charges of discreditable conduct were framed and included indisciplinary forms under Regulation 6 and were served on the three officers on the 15th May. In each case there was one charge of discreditable conduct, the particulars following the allegations originally drafted by Superintendent Bowler, i.e. there were no modifications of the allegations above set out' (ibid).

Once again the pattern of internal private justice is repeated at a higher level, that of the Director of Public Prosecutions. It is of interest that the authors of the report felt unable to delve more deeply for reasons of public policy, thus repeating the pattern of the Chief Constable's action.

What is important in all this is that everything described is patterned and predictable and that it forms a part of the normal behaviour patterns of institutions of power. The institution exists for crime, it is involved in the creation of crime, it has or develops an ideology of the 'hardened criminal', 'conflicts between coloured informants', and 'flagellation between sexual perverts', to quote the report of the appeal, and of sexual perversion, pederasty, and assaults on children, none of which was involved in this case, to quote the justifications given in television interviews. It conceals the violence used to obtain confessions in order to appear 'just' and 'moral' by systems of internal justice confirmed stage by stage through the whole hierarchy, including the Appeal Inquiry itself. Within the institution some members create wholly or partially fictitious accounts to protect themselves (the same behaviour has been observed in national administration) and these accounts are accepted by those at higher levels in the system, out of loyalty or because they accept the stereotype with which the institution operates. Once, however, the institution is found to be at fault, the pattern is to try to restore equilibrium between the organization and society by progressive sacrifices step by step up through the hierarchy. In this case, the process ended with the resignation of the Chief Constable.

The doctrine of ministerial responsibility, whereby the leader is sacrificed for the errors or misdeeds of his subordinates, is an interesting alternative pattern.

Here the process takes account of the fact that the Sheffield force is but a part of a larger institution, for these resignations protect the police as a whole and are accompanied by suitable expressions of indignation and statements of the uniqueness of the behaviours.

It is salutary to remember that the pattern of the Sheffield *corps d'élite*, the conflicts within the Sheffield Police Force, and the pattern of the public concern and the working of the tribunal were all described in 1950.

'The immediate task of those who create an irresponsible élite is the stabilizing of the individual's acceptance of his external conscience, and the direction of his aggressive and resentful impulses against the enemy (the "evil father-figure"). If this system breaks down, the paternal, guiding, protective, and propelling force of authority may become the object of these resentments. Such a change, while it is the first step towards a rational movement to displace or resist delinquent government, is predictably uncongenial to those who depend upon the executive to carry out their plans and fantasies' (Comfort, 1950, p. 63).

It is of theoretical interest to observe the operation of two moral orders in this situation, the 'natural' and the 'positive', to use the language of earlier criminologists such as Garofalo. In an hierarchical system with internal justice, the leaders can grant immunity from the law. There remains, however, the problem of 'natural law', conscience, or the superego – the same concept essentially. This is the universally diffused acceptance of pity and probity. It is dealt with in two ways, first, by depriving the intended victim of status, of humanity, or of nationality, making him a member of an outgroup; and, second, by describing all the prohibited actions in acceptable words, the inhibition of the actions being associated with the verbal symbols which represent them. The language written and spoken of the German concentration camps contains many examples of this, of which 'final solution' to describe genocide is one. Many nineteenth-century criminologists, including Lombroso, noted the inversion of the moral significance of words in the argot of criminals. Havelock Ellis, reviewing the literature of this subject, wrote: 'So that while the better things of life are degraded, there is a tendency to elevate those that truly indicate degradation (Ellis, 1914, p. 206). What was assumed to be a characteristic of the language of criminals is a general tendency.

The process has some affinities with that practised in concentration camps and prisons where the 'outcasts' are compelled to perform all the actions most disapproved in 'natural law', thus confirming their outcast status and providing a justification for their punishment and death. This process has the refined effect in prison of isolating the 'trusty' even from the society of his fellow prisoners.

Another technique employed in cases where the police are convinced of guilt, but lack proof, is the planting of incriminating evidence. According to informants who are retired police officers, this has sometimes been practised on club-owners.

There is substantial evidence that such practices occur without the excuse of a conviction of guilt in the minds of the police, but simply to advance a policeman in his career. Such practices depend on selection by the police of vulnerable subjects, that is, persons who conform to the stereotype of criminal and whose word is unlikely to be accepted by the court in contradiction to the evidence of the police. The conviction of such persons contributes to the cumulative body of evidence confirming the correspondence of the stereotype and the 'criminal'.

The Challenor case will become the classic example, since it confirms the operation of the stereotype both in the success of Detective-Sergeant Challenor and in his downfall (Grigg, 1965; James, 1965).

This officer, with an estimated six hundred arrests to his credit, was discredited only when operating outside his normal field. He planted evidence – a half brick – on a political demonstrator, a highly literate member of the middle classes, with a knowledge of the law and influential friends. Here was a person who conformed neither to the stereotype of the criminal, nor to that of the communist agitator; and, well defended, with the resources of good counsel and forensic science, he was acquitted. Almost as though an experiment had been set up to demonstrate the validity of the author's argument, another demonstrator in the same court, a Greek, was – in spite of the same defence – found guilty, and still others, who were not so well placed socially or so well defended, were found guilty at the same court. All were alleged to be carrying half bricks, and in spite of the fact that the various half bricks fitted together to form whole bricks, and that there was no evidence to connect the accused with each other, only one of them was acquitted.

Eventually the accused who had been found guilty were pardoned, and in the case of those who appealed, the case was not proceeded with. In the same case, to four of the accused, the Metropolitan Police paid – without explanation – the sum of £1,000 compensation.

What is of interest here is the association of criminality with politics: criminals are not only those who conform to the stereotype, but also those whose political views run counter to those of the 'Establishment'. This was a situation which, during the

143

economic depression of the thirties, created so much concern that the National Council for Civil Liberties was formed to see that justice was done to the unemployed demonstrator.

Mary Grigg, writing about the Challenor case, says:

'Demonstrators are also vulnerable. If a police officer claims that a demonstrator has obstructed him, insulted him, assaulted him, or incited others, it is very difficult to prove otherwise. Witnesses for the defence will probably be other demonstrators, and if by chance an impartial passer-by witnesses an arrest of this kind, the court's assumption may be not so much that the police must be mistaken as that the passer-by was perhaps not completely impartial. There is always an atmosphere in the courts which suggests, although the law says to the contrary, that demonstrations are not entirely legal. And, in fact, many political demonstrations are hedged around with by-laws, police regulations and incidental offences, so that police officers may begin to believe that all demonstrators arrested are guilty, to start with, not of obstruction or a breach of by-laws, but simply of demonstrating' (Grigg, 1965, pp. 166 and 167).

In due course some twenty-six people claimed that they had been convicted as a consequence of having false evidence planted on them and perjured evidence given in court. Of these the authorities admitted twenty-four, who between them had served thirteen years of imprisonment.

Challenor selected his victims with skill: they included, an Italian, a Greek Cypriot, and others with names denoting foreign origin; a coloured West Indian, Jews, and deaf mutes. Among them were a Covent Garden porter, a window cleaner, a waiter, and others all in the lower-status groups.

Mary Grigg describes his behaviour thus:

'Challenor was not entirely haphazard in his arrests. He usually selected people who, for one reason or another, were not in a position to answer back. They were not the sort of people who were going to make a public fuss about the charges: they didn't have the right kind of knowledge or connexions. Some of them, indeed, had previous convictions which effectively silenced them. Somehow a grotesque symbolism developed when he began to arrest deaf mutes – for the people who "matter" are, above all, extraordinarily articulate.

Definition of the people who "matter" would be difficult. There are too many factors involved, and clearly the old saying that there is "one law for the rich and another for the poor" no longer meets the case. The people-who-don't-matter, however, are far more easily distinguished and in framing ex-prisoners and political demonstrators Challenor was working to a general pattern. Complaints against the police in general suggest that these groups, among others, are prone to victimization.

A man who has once been in prison is, perhaps, the easiest person to frame. His record will tell against him in court, and his "criminal" background will lose him sympathy if he complains about being ill-treated. But, in addition, there is a scientific charge on which a person may be judged by his past record. This is the charge of being "a suspected person loitering with intent". A man walking home late at night may be arrested by a passing police officer who will only need to say that he saw the person concerned "looking at" cars and otherwise behaving suspiciously to get him convicted of an offence. Evidence of previous convictions may be used as evidence that the person concerned is a suspected person and the defence may narrow down to proving that the person accused was not thinking what the policeman says he was thinking. If, in a situation of this kind, the policeman is prepared to embroider the story, there is little hope of acquittal' (ibid, pp. 165 and 166).

The reference in this quotation to 'people who matter' was confirmed by one of the writer's informants, a police sergeant in a large county borough, who said that when training young police recruits he always warned them to make certain that their suspects had 'no strings attached to them' – that is, no connections with important or powerful people in the local community.

The Challenor case also throws an interesting light on pleas of guilty. In this affair it was revealed that, where persons had been accused of crimes they had not committed, and had had evidence planted on them in the form of offensive weapons or stolen property, faced with a magistrates court in which it was clear that their evidence would be disbelieved in favour of that of several police witnesses, or where it appeared likely that the judge and jury would be hostile, they pleaded guilty, often on the advice of their legal advisers. For example, the case of Gold, on whom stolen cigarette lighters were believed to have been planted:

'Wallace Gold pleaded guilty to receiving a quantity of stolen cigarette lighters. A plea of guilty would appear to mean that the person concerned had done what was alleged. What it can mean, however, is that if he had no way of proving that he is not guilty then he will antagonize fewer people and present a better appearance in court if he says that he is.

Mr Gold spoke to a number of lawyers before he appeared at London Sessions and all of them advised him not to attempt to contradict the prosecution. Challenor, they told him, could not lose' (ibid, p. 45).

The difficulty of the defendants in such cases is well illustrated by the cases of Patrick Albert Tisdall, Thomas Alfred Kingston, and Sidney Hill-Burton, who were convicted and fined for being in possession of offensive weapons and, upon the appeal by the defendants against this conviction, sentenced to twenty-eight days' imprisonment. This procedure is in itself crime-creating, since any innocent person wrongly found guilty but punished with only a small fine is under strong compulsion to let the matter rest and not to spend time and money on an appeal and risk imprisonment into the bargain.

In this case, the defending solicitor was so convinced of his clients' innocence that he kept up a determined campaign through Parliament to force an inquiry. Only after a series of internal police investigations – all of which confirmed the original evidence of the police – was an independent inquiry made by the Home Secretary.

The report of the inquiry shows clearly the *corps d'élite* process at work thus:

'(i) Detective Superintendent Radford was in breach of his duty in that he failed to carry out a thorough and impartial inquiry. It was not thorough because he was partial to his subordinates. He was partial because he possessed the admirable qualities of loyalty and consideration for his subordinates. It was impossible for him to fulfil the duty which was laid upon him' (Mars-Jones, 1964, p. 135).

The report is of interest in that it shows also the internal conflict between the C.I.D. and other branches of the police.

The inquiry, which disclosed violence, lying, the concealment of a witness from the court by a verbal trick, and a variety of breaches of police discipline, reached these conclusions among others:

'(*a*) If the evidence disclosed in the course of this Inquiry had been available at the trial or appeal of Mr Tisdall, Mr Kingston and Mr Hill-Burton, they would never have been convicted of being in possession of offensive weapons' (Mars-Jones, 1964, p. 135).

'(*c*) The evidence disclosed in the course of this Inquiry is not sufficient for me to be able to find, five years after the incident, that the allegations made by Mr Tisdall, Mr Kingston and Mr Hill-Burton that offensive weapons were "planted" on them by police officers are established beyond all reasonable doubt. But the bulk of the evidence so disclosed tends to support their allegations and points to their innocence' (ibid, p. 153).

'(*d*) If an honest, impartial and thorough inquiry into these allegations had been made in 1960, it would have been the duty of Assistant Commissioner Jackson, and failing him, Commander Townsend, to refer the matter to the Director of Public Prosecutions for his decision as to whether the five police officers concerned should be prosecuted for perjury, or conspiracy to pervert the court of justice, or both' (ibid, p. 133).

The time taken to clear the defendants is some measure of the effectiveness of the *corps d'élite* principle. The fortuitous nature of justice (that is the process whereby persons are designated as criminal or non-criminal) is shown by the fact that the key piece of evidence which disclosed the lying of the police witness was the discovery by a police investigator of the exact time of a telephone call through the Post Office. It is noteworthy that this information was not acted upon:

'Chief Superintendent Fieldsent did not suggest that the information about the time of the telephone call justified reopening that enquiry; nor did anyone else who saw the papers consider that this should be done or that this fresh information should be communicated to the Home Office' (ibid, p. 112).

147

Bearing in mind that a prison sentence is the crucial variable in the identification of a person with the stereotype of criminal, the fact (already referred to) that the police have a choice in bringing charges under legislation with different potential punishments and the courts have discretion in imposing penalties constitutes an important variable. During the period of mass unemployment in the thirties, and recently during demonstrations by pacifist groups, a tendency has been observed to bring prosecutions for conspiring and incitement under common law, which makes possible heavy prison sentences, rather than under statute or by-laws where only a fine, generally a small fine, may be imposed.

It has been argued that in such cases the executive may be influencing the police and judiciary to add its political opponents to the 'criminal' classes. Such an argument is probably a mechanical over-simplification. Informal discussion with politicians, judges, barristers, and senior police officers suggests rather that, as tension rises, a community of thought emerges which to the outsider looks like an attempt by the executive to influence the judiciary (Hannington, 1936; *New Statesman*, 13-9-63).[1]

THE INFLUENCE OF THE COURTS

Thus far, attention has been concentrated on the part played by the police in the creation of crime and the selection of potential criminals. A few observations will now be made on the working of the courts.

As has already been noted, there is a fundamental difference between the finding of guilt and the establishments of facts, so

---

[1] Kennedy's comments on the Ward case are relevant here:
'Since the trial many people have asked who it was who was responsible for Ward's persecution. I think the answer lies not in the specific orders of any one person but in the spontaneous actions of many. When the establishment closes its ranks, when authority takes arms against what it mistakenly believes to be a sea of corruption, there is no need for the posting of battalion orders. Within the hierarchy each member knows what is required of him, what he must do; and during the long investigation and trial each man did it. The proceedings against Ward had a certain inevitability. Once put into motion, they gained a momentum of their own which it subsequently became impossible to stop' (Kennedy, 1964, pp. 227 and 228).

that the organization of a trial becomes a ritual debate designed
to influence a magistrate, a judge, a panel of judges, or a jury in
their decision, whether or not a person's alleged offence is such
as to be punished by a monetary penalty, or some restriction of
liberty, or whether he should be put in the custody of an officer
of the court. Symbolically he has left civil society and is in the
keeping of the law.

The order of debate is not designed either to elicit truth or to
be just, the prosecution having the first and last words and
being under no obligation to disclose the basis of their case to
the defence.

In the process of the trial, in spite of the ritual oath taken by
witnesses to tell the truth, the whole truth, and nothing but the
truth, the witness may in fact only answer questions put to him
and these will be designed to extract from a matrix of information those parts most likely to prove guilt (or innocence). This
can introduce an element of chance into the process of finding
of guilt.

It is difficult to escape the conclusion that many trials by jury
are not so much inquests as to the fact but debates to decide
whether a particular person should go to prison. In this the bias
is against the poor and illiterate.

An interesting controlled experiment occurred when two men
employed on the same work in the same firm at the same time
were accused of the same fraud on a government department,
arising from the exploitation of the cost-plus system. Both admitted all the actions of which they were accused and both told
substantially the same story in evidence. One pleaded guilty.
The other pleaded not guilty on the interesting ground that he
was only doing what all other government contractors were
doing during the war and that, if they were not prosecuted, he,
by the same token, must be innocent. Thus fortified, he told his
simple story of the charging to the government department of
the wages of some two hundred imaginary operatives with the
addition of the appropriate percentage. The jury found guilty,
as they had to, the defendant who pleaded guilty – but the defendant who pleaded not guilty, his honesty having so impressed
the jury, was found not guilty.

The debating process places a high premium on the services of counsel with special skills, and the wealthy are in the position to obtain considerable advantages compared with the poor, who will be prosecuted by the state with limitless resources (this is particularly important where a criminal case may have political overtones, as in the Ward affair).[1] The poor may not be defended at all or may have to rely on Legal Aid, which may provide competent defence, but rarely the best. The exceptions to this pattern are the occasional spectacular or particularly bizarre or sordid murder trial where the defence is paid for by a Sunday newspaper in return for an exclusive 'confession' after the trial. In at least one case a woman successfully defended in this way admitted the charges in her 'confession' before departing for the antipodes to begin a new life with the balance of her literary earnings.

These and other similar issues are discussed by C. G. L. Du Cann in *Miscarriages of Justice* (Du Cann, 1960). The issue here is not that of justice or injustice, but simply that there is evidence to justify the hypothesis that the system of trial in Britain introduces other factors than the behaviour of an individual in determining whether or not he is a criminal. A second hypothesis it suggests is that these factors make it more likely that the poor person will be convicted and sent to prison than the rich.

An issue of a related nature that needs detailed examination is the relationship between imprisonment and the *popular* concept of criminality. Imprisonment often involves loss of employment as well as absence from family, neighbours, and friends, and these factors mark down the offender much more effectively than a fine or probation (Martin, 1962).

The issue becomes more complex on examination. Crimes against property and the person, which are believed to be characteristic of the poor, have a high rate of conviction and a high incidence of prison sentences; middle-class crimes like motoring

[1] 'Our courts of justice are still pervaded by the barbaric notion of the duel. We arrange a brilliant tournament, and are interested not so much in the investigation of truth as in the question of who will "win". We cannot hope for any immediate radical change in this method, but it is our duty to do all that we can to strengthen those elements in our courts which are concerned not with the gaining of a cause, but with the investigation of truth' (Ellis, 1914, pp. 360 and 361).

offences and offences against the revenue, on the other hand, have a lower rate of conviction and a low incidence of prison sentences. In some cases only monetary punishments are provided in the legislation applicable; in others, where prison is an alternative punishment, it is rarely employed. Where the possibility of a fine or a term of imprisonment exists there is presumably an idea in the minds of the legislators that these are equal – so much money equals so much time, but also that one kind of punishment is more suitable for some persons than for others. It can be assumed that the legislator believes that a prison sentence is the appropriate punishment for the poor, whereas a fine is appropriate to the rich, for the rich have plenty of money but are short of time, whereas the poor are by definition short of money and, if unemployed, have plenty of time.

Where a poor person is legally aided it is clear to the judge that he will not be able to pay a large fine, his financial status having already been investigated, so a prison sentence is the only possible one. There is, therefore, a higher possibility that the poor will be given a prison sentence and the rich a fine.

The sentence of a fine as an alternative to prison has two forms: a fine with time to pay and a fine without time to pay it. It is likely that the rich are more likely to be able to raise money, given time, than the poor.

That this is not a negligible matter can be judged from the return of the Prison Commissioners (see table on p. 152).

This table shows a continuous increase in the numbers who go to prison (and thus become identified as criminals) because of inability to pay a fine and a continuous increase in the proportion who, even though given time, are still unable to pay. The role of poverty in the designation of the criminal of popular stereotype is clearly displayed.

The intention of this discussion is to call attention to the causal role of the police and of the courts in the designation of criminals and to add to the evidence already accumulated that the process is selective, in that the poor and the illiterate are more likely to be thus designated than the well-to-do and the well-educated.

It is not the intention, however, to suggest that all the police are brutes, perjurers, or conspirators, or that the courts consciously select their victims in some kind of class war. Such considerations are irrelevant to this study. What is important is the hypothesis that the behaviours described constitute part of the normal workings of institutions of social control and not the aberrations of tired or wicked or foolish men.

RECEPTIONS UNDER SENTENCE OF IMPRISONMENT IN DEFAULT OF PAYMENT OF A FINE[1]

Year	Time to Pay (a)	No time to Pay (a)	Total	Ratio a to b
1951	1,919	3,085	5,004	0·622
1952	2,333	3,181	5,514	0·733
1953	2,320	2,759	5,079	0·841
1954	2,377	2,538	4,915	0·938
1955	2,102	2,537	4,639	0·829
1956	2,370	2,426	4,796	0·977
1957	2,825	2,714	5,539	1·041
1958	3,072	3,057	6,129	1·005
1959	3,333	3,105	6,438	1·073
1960	3,677	3,191	6,868	1·152

[1] Source: *Report of the Commissioners of Prisons in the Year 1960*, Cmnd. 1467, p. 149.

CHAPTER FIVE

The Role of the Victim in Crime

The popular stereotype of crime assumes that the relationship between the criminal and his victim is one in which the victim has no knowledge of the criminal and his intentions. The occasion of the crime is one in which the victim takes all possible legal measures to protect his person, his morals, his rights, and his property against the actions of the criminal. The victim is assumed to support the police and the judiciary in the pursuit and conviction of the criminal and will gain in reputation by so doing.

This formulation describes, in fact, only a small portion of the total of crime and mainly a minority of those offences which take place in public.

Nevertheless, even where the victim has contributed to a crime, by carelessness, neglect, or provocation, his behaviour tends to diminish the offence of the criminal rather than to bring censure upon himself.

In many cases the victim plays an important, often a crucial, role. The behaviours of which this is true range from the commonplace to the bizarre and take in the legal categories of crimes of violence, including murder; sexual offences; and crimes concerned with property, including theft and fraud.

A major category of victim-provoked offences comprises situations where criminal and victim, and often other persons, are engaged in a continuum of behaviour of an aggressive or sado-masochistic type that at some point passes a threshold of intensity and results in the serious injury or death of one of the group. These behaviours are intense interpersonal relationships in which chance may decide which person in the situation will be

153

criminal and which will be victim. Many crimes of violence, including sexual offences like rape, carnal knowledge, and indecent assault, manslaughter, and murder are of this kind (Von Hentig, 1948).

A second category of crime in which the victim is causally involved covers the situation where the criminal exploits the cupidity or criminal intentions of the victim. This occurs in cases of fraud, both petty and large scale, but is seen at its best in the classic confidence trick. When such frauds are discovered by the police, it is common for them to ignore the illegal acts of the victim in order to concentrate on the greater evil of the criminal, especially where he is a professional. This contrasts with the practice of the police in cases where homosexuals have been the victims of blackmailers.

A third category of victim-provoked crime is one where the victim deliberately follows a course that will provoke some person to commit a crime, or some members of a larger population to commit crimes, because on balance the total results will be advantageous. One type of situation of this kind may involve not crime, but simply an offence that would be a crime if known to the police. In this category are sexual offences against women and men (by men) which are provoked and then exploited for financial gain or power; or the situation in which a provoked, or contrived, or an unprovoked offence may be exploited: the act of larceny by a servant who may then be persuaded to give extra service or accept a low wage in return for not being prosecuted, for example. The most common situation is, however, that of open display in retail trading.

A fourth category refers to crimes where the victim deliberately places himself or herself in a situation where he or she is likely to be the victim of an offence. Such behaviour is often associated with mental disturbance, as in hysteria, where the behaviour is a form of attention-seeking.

A fifth category is one in which 'Society' attempts to protect the citizen from his own follies and from the exploitation of his weaknesses. In such situations the criminal and victim are united in hostility to the law and its enforcement. In this class of offence the victim is usually treated as innocent or, if punished at all, treated with relative leniency. Such offences are numerous in the field of crimes against morals, prostitution, the supplying of pornography, the presentation of obscene entertainment, the supplying of drugs of addiction, the provision of alcoholic liquor in illegal circumstances, and the like. The fact that in many such behaviours the victims are willing to pay very large sums of money for the gratification of their interests indicates the crucial role played by the victim.

The role of the victim is perhaps most dramatically displayed in crimes of homicide. Marvin E. Wolfgang, in his essay, 'Victim-Precipitated Criminal Homicide', shows how this has been recognized in American law, thus:

' . . . the law of homicide has long recognized provocation by the victim as a possible reason for mitigation of the offense from murder to manslaughter, or from criminal to excusable homicide. In order that such reduction occur, there are four prerequisites.

(1) There must have been adequate provocation.

(2) The killing must have been in the heat of passion.

(3) The killing must have followed the provocation before there had been a reasonable opportunity for the passion to cool.

(4) A causal connection must exist between provocation, the heat of passion, and the homicidal act. Such, for example, are: adultery, seduction of the offender's juvenile daughter, rape of the offender's wife or close relative, etc.' (Wolfgang, 1962, p. 388).

The position in Britain revealed in the case histories given by Morris and Blom-Cooper is similar (Morris and Blom-Cooper, 1964).

In homicide and other crimes of violence there are patterns of relationship which occur with great frequency and patterns of interaction in which violence of speech and action are found with regularity in many social situations.

In the same way there are many environmental, temporal and social patterns that occur frequently. In many, third parties may play a causal role.

The first matter that warrants attention is the discovery of the nature of the relationship between the victim and the criminal. This may be of kinship, marriage, work, residence, or religion. Such relationships may be of cooperation or conflict.

The Home Office study *Murder* describes part of the situation but does not attempt to show the role of the victim in the event (Gibson and Klein, 1961, p. 16). It shows that where children under sixteen are the victims the proportion of cases where a relative is the subject is in the range of 70 per cent to 90 per cent year by year. In cases where the victim is a female over 16, the largest group, about 40 per cent, is of wives killed by their husbands, followed in order of importance by females killed by other relatives, boy friends, and acquaintances, and by a small group of prostitutes killed by their customers.

In contrast, most men are killed by strangers in fights or in furtherance of theft. Murder by acquaintance, friend, or neighbour is not uncommon. There are some murders of husbands by wives or of lovers by their mistresses, but the most common pattern of murder of males by relatives is the Oedipal pattern of father murdered by son.

No systemic study of the victim-precipitated homicide exists in the British literature, but Wolfgang's study showed that 26 per cent of homicides occurring in Philadelphia between 1 January 1948 and 31 December 1952 would be regarded as victim-precipitated (150 out of 588) (Wolfgang, 1962, p. 392).

In *A Calendar of Murder*, Morris and Bloom-Cooper give brief accounts of all cases of persons prosecuted for murder in the years 1957 to 1962; many of these accounts are in sufficient detail to show the victim's role and that of other persons in the homicide situation. There is also evidence indicating the part played by other social and environmental factors (Morris and Blom-Cooper, 1964). The accounts are brief and in many cases, inevitably incomplete, so a statistical analysis of the kind attempted by Wolfgang was not possible.

Among the many relationship and social relationship patterns which are revealed are the following:

1. Murder of wife by husband
2. Murder of husband by wife
3. Murder of child by mother
4. Murder of child by father
5. Murder of mother by child
6. Murder of father by child

7. Murder of child by parent substitute
8. Murder of parent substitute by child

A refined analysis of categories 3 to 6 would distinguish the age and sex of the child, and of categories 7 and 8 the varieties of parent substitute and the age and sex of the child.

9. Murder of mistress by lover
10. Murder of lover by mistress
11. Murder of partner by male homosexual
12. Murder of partner by female homosexual
13. Murder of female prostitute by customer
14. Murder of customer by female prostitute
15. Murder of male prostitute by male customer
16. Murder of male customer by male prostitute
17. Murders which arise in the course of interaction between persons of different social classes, colour, ethnic groups, culture, or religion
18. Murders of neighbours
19. Murders of fellow workers
20. Murders that occur in the course of sexual assault or theft

This list by no means exhausts the range of kinship relations, relationships by marriage, and social relationships within which murder occurs, but it includes the major categories and in so doing emphasizes Von Hentig's observation that homicide should be regarded for the purpose of analysis as a 'duet frame of crime' (Von Hentig, 1948, pp. 383 and 385).

Some examples given by Morris and Blom-Cooper will show the part played by the victim in some of the commonest categories of murder.

'Carter (30) was accused of the non-capital murder by manual strangulation of his wife (24) at their home. It was alleged that he had become very suspicious of her having an affair with a neighbour, for which there was some evidence, and that recently she had refused to have sexual relations with him (the accused). After the wife had insulted him and hit him, Carter lost his head and killed her (Morris and Blom-Cooper, 1964, p. 6).

Carter was found not guilty of murder, but guilty of manslaughter; which illustrates the effect of the part played by the victim in reducing the responsibility of the accused.

157

Malice is not always present, as is shown in the Buckland case. 'During a "sexual adventure", in which Buckland (31) bound and gagged his wife, Mrs Buckland (22) died, presumably from asphyxiation. It was stated that the couple were "devoted to each other" and that the gagging and tying had undoubtedly been done with the wife's consent; she had evidently been drinking heavily during the evening' (ibid, p. 39). Buckland was found guilty of manslaughter.

The pattern of sexual gratification which is associated with violence, and the restriction of movement by binding, confinement, and, on occasion, partial suffocation, is found in both heterosexual and homosexual relationships. In situations thus contrived, violence, through misjudgement or in excitement, may pass beyond the anticipated degree and lead to the death of one of the partners. Several cases in which male homosexuals have been involved have occurred in Britain in the period 1961-1963.

Cases of murder of a husband by his wife are less common, but when they occur often arise out of quarrels and fights instigated by the victim. Thus: 'Wignall (42) pleaded the defence of provocation to a charge of murdering her husband (38) at their home by stabbing him with a vegetable knife. It was alleged that the marriage had been a very unhappy one – husband gambled and drank heavily, constantly beating, insulting and threatening his wife, the accused. During one fight, while he was twisting her foot and throwing her from chair to chair, she grabbed a knife and cut her husband on the arm in order to make him stop. But he became more infuriated and lunged towards her, she stabbing him by accident.' Wignall was found not guilty (ibid, p. 34).

In this case the provocation was by the strong of the weak – a very common occurrence (ibid, p. 32). A general pattern also found in many relationships is one where the relatively weak partner exploits his or her weakness by defying the stronger partner with insults or blows, relying on the social pressure exerted by others to control the reactions of the stronger partner. Misjudgement leads to retaliation in which the weaker is injured or killed.

A possible hypothesis, prompted by domestic quarrels overheard, is that the victim, the weaker partner in the conflict, sees in provoking the other to such violence as will result in death the possibility of the major and macabre retaliation of trial, conviction, and life imprisonment, or, until recently, hanging: the final triumph of the weak over the strong.

This situation has a resemblance to suicide. Suicide and attempted suicide, when these were offences, were perhaps the alternative forms of attention-seeking where the victim and the perpetrator of the offence are one person, and the objective – according to psycho-analytic theory – is to call attention to some plight, or to create a situation in which some other person is blamed or punished.

The example of the Hannah case, in which a father killed his son, displays the role of the victim in this pattern.

'Hannah (61), a fitter's labourer, the father of 19 children, *pleaded not guilty to murder but guilty to manslaughter (on grounds of provocation)* of his son (23). This plea was accepted by the prosecution at *Liverpool Crown Court*, 13-2-1958, and he was *sentenced to six years' imprisonment*.

Hannah's wife refused to let her son (who was very drunk) bring his girl friend in to sleep with him for the night – it was Christmas Day 1957. A quarrel then arose between the father (who was also drunk) and Thomas Hannah, which led to the son attacking his father. Hannah picked up a knife which he used in his work, and stabbed his son. No intention to kill, but used knife in trying to defend himself' (ibid, p. 53).

In the case of Street and Boddington, the Oedipal pattern is displayed, with the victim playing a considerable causal role.

'Street (23) was a forestry labourer. After his mother (48), Mrs Love, had been living with Boddington for 25 years and had borne him 7 children, she decided to revert to her married name of Love and the children took her maiden name of Street. There were a series of domestic quarrels during which Boddington turned out the mother and children from his cottage without any money. There followed a number of fights on the same evening between the accused and his father; the latter died from injuries received from blows from a motor-car hand-pump. . . . Street . . . found guilty of non-capital murder and sentenced to life imprisonment, Leicester Assizes, 6-2-1958' (ibid, p. 74).

Disputes leading to fights which end up in death are common between persons of different ethnic, national, and religious groups. Such disputes often occur over women and are commonly associated with heavy drinking. Morris and Blom-Cooper list cases in which Irish, Cypriots, Maltese, Hindus, Pakistanis (Moslems), Somalis, Jamaicans, Hungarians, Poles, and Ukrainians have been concerned with other groups.

In the case of Awad and Rees, the victim Rees clearly contributed to his own death.

'Awad (29) a Somali, was attacked by Rees (age not reported) and six others in the street; Rees hit him on the head with a bottle, and one of the others produced a clasp-knife. Awad grabbed the knife from him, opened it and showed it to the group in order to frighten them off. Cooze, the owner of the knife, attacked Awad and was wounded; then, as Rees tried to hit Awad again, he was stabbed. Rees died 10 days later. Awad . . . was found not guilty at Glamorgan Assizes, 10-4-1957' (ibid, p. 1).

In some cases both religion and the ethnic factor were involved, as in the case where a deeply religious Jamaican was 'mercilessly tormented by two Hungarian workmates', one of whom was killed as the outcome of an attempt to get money from the Jamaican by intimidation.

In a high proportion of murders, the fact that drink or drunkenness is involved suggests that not only are victims important in the violence pattern but also publicans. Publicans have a legal responsibility to refuse to sell alcoholic beverage to persons who show signs of approaching intoxication. The police have the responsibility of enforcing this and the licensing magistrates have the power to deprive a publican of his licence to sell liquor. It is obvious from the accounts given by Morris and Blom-Cooper that this responsibility is frequently neglected by all parties. This is confirmed by studies which show the frequency with which heavy drinking is a factor in road accidents and may be checked by a few visits to licensed premises in the late evening. *A large industry with the tacit approval of the police and the magistracy is causally involved.*

Sexual offences present extreme difficulties when an attempt is made to discover the role of the victim, for the 'duet' nature of the situation is one in which powerful drives exist in both partners, but in which the expectations of each partner may not be known to, or even understood by, the other. In addition there are many forms of sexual relationship which are either taboo or prohibited by law, and a further complication exists in the prohibitions on sexual relationships before the 'age of consent', between certain relatives and between males, and between humans and other species.

Morris and Blom-Cooper write: 'Where certain young children are concerned "innocence" is probably a misplaced term, for while little girls cannot be classed directly with adult prostitutes, by no means all of them are lacking in sexual curiosity. It is invariably a drive they dimly perceive but one which may draw them into situations where they may become the victims of crime' (Morris and Blom-Cooper, 1964, p. 323; and Morris *et al.*, 1963, p. 190).

The part that children of both sexes play in initiating 'crime' of which they are the victims is to some extent concealed by the fact that, when their activities become known, they are often dealt with by probation officers without going through the court, or by social workers on the initiative of parents or clergy or club leaders, or appear in the courts as 'out of control' or as 'care and protection' cases.

The evidence in some cases of indecent assault, incest, and rape suggest that the victim has made a substantial contribution to the offence, which is, after all, the product of a stimulus-and-response situation. In some instances they have created the situation to obtain power, and in others have exploited a situation in which they were not so much victims as active agents, to escape subsequent guilt or punishment.

In a case described to the writer in detail by social caseworkers to whom the 'victims' were well known, two labourers were convicted and sent to prison for the rape of two girls who were known to the social workers to be part-time prostitutes and who had spent several evenings in the company of the young men. One of the girls offered the explanation of 'rape' to her mother, who unexpectedly intercepted her coming in very late at night with her clothing soiled and in disorder.

The stereotype of the innocent female and the predatory male

161

fits the pattern of police prosecution. In cases where youths and men are accused of offences with girls under the age of sixteen the contribution of the victim may be crucial. The Boston Case illustrates the situation.

The appeals of a man aged twenty-two who had been sentenced to eighteen months' imprisonment and of two youths eighteen-and-a-half and nineteen years of age who had been sentenced to Borstal training were dismissed by Lord Chief Justice Parker in the following terms:

> 'The Lord Chief Justice, giving the judgement of the Court, said that their appeals disclosed an extraordinary situation in a part of Lincolnshire. They involved sexual intercourse with girls under 16, and the Court had been told that in this whole sorry story there were no less than eighteen young girls and forty male persons involved.
>
> The girls in question were school girls, or girls just leaving school . . . The probation officer in her report stated that all the girls "were willing participants in what took place, and one gains the impression from the girls themselves that this behaviour arose from the fact that this particular group of youngsters were bored and desperate for some form of excitement and kicks, and sexual adventure became the 'vogue' amongst them." The offences took place mainly at the weekends when the girls and youths met at dances' (*The Times*, Law Report 2-12-63).

Fraud, in which the behaviour of the victim plays an important part, occurs in a wide range of situations from the customer of the mail-order firm who falls for a misleading description, hoping to do better than he can by shopping locally, through the victim of a confidence trick, large or small, to the customer of the clip joint and strip show and the patron of the after-hours drinking saloon, the pornographic cinema or theatre, or the brothel, all of whom, by placing themselves in a vulnerable position, invite exploitation.

This list shows that in almost all cases the behaviours with which this discussion is concerned are behaviours in which the difference between the legitimate form and the proscribed form is a matter of degree rather than kind, and in which the victim is almost always regarded as innocent at law. Thus it is the

keeper of the shebeen and the brothel, the prostitute rather than
the customer, who is prosecuted. This is consistent with the un-
stated theory that the victims are innocent, but are corrupted
by the criminal, this in spite of the evidence of the specialized
tracts of great cities where the 'innocent' victims can be seen in
large numbers seeking gratifications that can only be provided
by someone's breaking the law. Because many of these gratifications are contrary to the mores, the victims expose themselves
to dangers which range from gross exploitation in the 'cabaret'
or night club to blackmail and violence in places less well conducted.

The most obvious kind of crime in which the victim has a
crucial role is the confidence trick, which in essence is believed
by the victim to be a conspiracy to defraud, but a conspiracy
with only a small element of risk. The process is facilitated by
the fact that most confidence tricks resemble very closely certain
kinds of legitimate activities, the distinguishing characteristic
being that they are confined to an elite or other ingroup from
which the victim is normally excluded.

One common form is the fraud in which the victim believes he
will be able to avoid customs duty, purchase tax, or other taxation. This fits the common stereotype that 'businessmen' avoid
taxation, and in the ideology and in practice is regarded as less
serious than, say, theft of similar value.

Sutherland adds the following gloss to this comment:

'A professional confidence man, after reading this manuscript,
wrote:

"The statement that if there was no larceny in a man and if he
were not trying to get something for nothing and rob a fellow-man
it would be impossible to beat him at any real con racket is unqualifiedly true. This remark is often made by professionals."

Another confidence man wrote:

"These suckers ought to be trimmed. It is a hard thing to say,
but they are a dishonest lot and the worst double-crossers in the
world."

Another confidence man wrote:

"A confidence game will fail absolutely unless the sucker has got
larceny in his soul. One of the first questions asked of a prospective
sucker after the build-up is developed is 'have you got larceny in

your soul'? This question is asked outright and a 'yes' or 'no' answer is necessary. If he answers 'no' and the mob believes he is telling the truth, he is dropped immediately. If he answers 'yes' they can go on with him. A certain business man, deacon in church and a respectable citizen, was asked whether he had larceny in his soul and answered: 'No, I would not do a dishonest thing for any reason.' But the proposition was developed a little and involved depriving Jim O'Leary, who was then the biggest gambler on the South Side in Chicago, of his money. The sucker sat and thought several moments and then said, 'I have always hated gambling, I think it is ruining hundreds of people. I would be willing to go a long way to injure the gambling business. If this proposition will assist in putting down gambling, I am willing to help. And after we get O'Leary's money can't we go down to Hot Springs and ruin some of the gamblers there?' I have never heard of a prospective sucker who turned down a proposition which was built up properly, on the grounds that it was dishonest . . . Of course, we select our prospects. We look over his bank account, his family life, the way he spends his money. Bankers, for instance, are very good prospects. They engage in a lot of speculative business, and anyone who speculates is a good prospect. We try to find someone who is living beyond his means, who has social ambitions, or whose wife has social ambitions which are beyond their income. The banker who is speculating is probably short in his accounts already, and a chance at big profit will generally appeal to him as a way out of his difficulties."

The method used by the confidence men who swindled Norfleet involved purchase of stock on advance information and was a form of surething gambling, in which he had no possibility of losing, and the other party to the transaction had no possibility of gaining. Furthermore, he knew that, if he participated in this with the representative of the concern (who was actually the confidence man), he would be assisting this representative to violate the orders of the concern for which he was working. These two forms of dishonesty in which Norfleet was willing to participate are described in his own account of the confidence game in which he was beaten, and the thieves report that he concealed other aspects of the techniques. The method used by confidence men in the attempt to swindle Norfleet in Denver does not involve dishonesty on the part of the victim, according to the account Norfleet gives of the techniques, although it does involve an effort to get something for nothing (see Norfleet, op. cit., Van Cise, op. cit.).

The truth of the assertion that the victim of confidence games cannot be beaten unless he is himself dishonest depends on the definition of 'confidence game'. It seems to be impossible to make a logical differentiation between confidence games and other dishonest practices. They merge gradually into one another. Study courses for civil service jobs, the puff racket, the sale of dentifrices and real estate, and thousands of methods described in the literature of consumers' organisations are like the confidence games except that they involve stupidity on the part of the victim, while confidence games are on the somewhat higher level and involve cupidity on the part of the victim' (Sutherland, 1956, pp. 89 and 70).

Sutherland's 'Professional Thief' stated that 'It is impossible to beat an honest man in a confidence game' (ibid, p. 69).

The rapid growth of the number of offences of shoplifting which has accompanied the opening of supermarkets (accompanied presumably by changes in E.E.G. patterns in housewives) illustrates the causal role of the victim.

The aim of the display system of the supermarket is to make the taking of goods as easy as possible, and to stimulate demand by every possible device up to the limit of the customer's capacity to pay.[1] Since this capacity varies and customers' susceptibility to theft is not always a function of their incomes, these techniques increase thefts and sales together.

Informal discussions with retail-trade executives have revealed a tendency to approach the problem first of all as an economic one. Open display and its accompanying sales promotion will pay up to the point where the increase of loss from theft exceeds the increased profit from higher sales. Further, the employment of store detectives is now almost universal, and policies of prosecution will be extended up to the point where their costs balance the saving due to the decline in losses from theft. The causal role of the victim is clear.

In the contrary direction it is of interest that Marks & Spencer gave up elaborate systems of stock control because the costs of control were much greater than the losses by pilferage (Thaw, 1963, p. 38).

[1] Compare Lacassagne, *Les Voleuses des Grands Magasins*, Lyons, 1903. Quoted in De Quirós, 1911.

In the first case, higher profits are made as a result of open display accompanied by an increase of crime, so the normal commercial objective of the supermarket is a cause of crime. In the second case, commercial interest is seen as reducing crime. Both are causal in that a variation in one factor, profit, results in a variation in another factor, crime.

This discussion has concentrated on the extreme case where the victim has played a large part, even the crucial part, in the situation which produces the crime. Every crime that involves a victim can be considered from the point of view of the *degree* of responsibility that the victim has for the event.

In contrast to the situation in civil law where the concept of liability, for example in the form of contributory negligence, is well established, criminal law only takes account of the victim's role as mitigating the offence of the criminal. The punishment of the victim, the householder who leaves his home unlocked, for example, is confined to public disapproval expressed by the judge or magistrates.

This by no means exhausts this topic, which under the title 'Victimology' is emerging as a self-contained discipline. It is intended simply to suggest that a criminology which concentrates almost exclusively on the 'criminal', and neglects almost entirely the causal role of the victim, is unlikely to establish a satisfactory theory: that is, one from which reliable predictions may be made.

CHAPTER SIX

Behaviour and Approval

THE NATURE OF CRIME AND ITS RELATION TO MORALS

The nature of criminal and delinquent behaviour may be regarded in terms of the action in itself, the consequences of the action, and the degree of approval or disapproval excited by knowledge of the act in different persons or groups of persons and in different institutions.

The importance of isolating these different aspects of a disapproved action arises from the attempts of criminologists to discover the 'causes of crime'. These are sought in the physical nature of the individual, in his personality as determined by his nurture, his physique, and his environment.

It is common for studies of criminality to assume that a behaviour that is condemned occurs only in a minority of the population – the subnormal or abnormal, referring to the frequency distribution of attributes. Some design their sample of cases on this assumption; thus Andry (1960) writes:

> 'The majority of boys in the Remand Home and in the two modern secondary schools were from working class families. It was decided to eliminate all the boys from middle and upper class homes from the two samples . . .'

From the initial assumption of abnormality it is argued that some changes in the persons or their environment can lead to their behaviour changing in the direction of normality. In some countries and in some states of the U.S.A. sterilization and castration are prescribed to this end. Experiments have also been conducted in which drugs have been administered that change personality and are believed to modify the propensity to crime (Eysenck, 1964).

167

If, however, it can be shown that certain basic categories of behaviour such as aggression are generally distributed in the population and that social factors lead to their designation as criminal when they are performed by certain minorities in certain situations, then it becomes necessary to inquire into the social processes which lead to the selection of these minorities and situations.

Doubt is also cast on the validity of proposals to change behaviour by surgical or chemical means if it can be shown that the election of subjects for such treatment is arbitrary or if the behaviours designated as criminal could acquire new designations by, for example, changes in legislation or *ex cathedra* pronouncement.

Some studies regard criminal behaviour as a failure of socialization and look for its source in experiences in the family and in education. This failure results in the subject's seeking gratification regardless of the effects on others or on himself. It is, of course, evident that many such behaviours are not disapproved of. A second type of failure in socialization is indicated where the criminal behaviour arises through ignorance. The treatment of such behaviours is ambivalent: on the one hand, ignorance of the law is not accepted as a defence – presumably the offender is expected to have a general capacity to distinguish right from wrong; on the other, first offenders are usually treated with leniency, and ignorance is often advanced as a defence.

If all actions that are pursued by individuals without regard to their consequences to others or themselves are studied, it becomes possible to isolate those that are disapproved of from those that are regarded with neutrality and those that are approved, that is legitimate. If this is done, then socialization appears to be not only the process whereby the individual becomes aware of the pattern of rights and duties he has in relation to others but also of the means to achieve selfish goals and escape retribution. Knowledge may likewise be not only the means of avoiding the forbidden but also the means of achieving it. For example, the range of permitted homosexual and heterosexual behaviour is limited, and behaviours outside the permitted range are heavily punished. Yet in nearby cultures in Europe as well as cultures in Africa and Asia, practices that are condemned in Britain are permitted. Thus knowledge of the sexual mores of other countries and possession of the means to travel may allow the practitioner to transform a criminal into a non-criminal behaviour and, incidentally, avoid the danger of being subject to certain treatments believed to be curative.

In the area of sexual mores as opposed to criminal behaviour proper, the role of the metropolitan city is of interest. As city size increases, the range of permitted sexual behaviour changes, not only in the approval-disapproval patterns, but also in the tolerance-intolerance patterns of the police, a pattern which is displayed at the limit in the West End of London. This situation permits a wider range of sexual behaviour for the wealthy and for certain groups in the working class – those in transport and the marine, salesmen, and migratory workers in building and construction. It is of interest that in Germany prostitution is an offence only in towns of less than 20,000 inhabitants.

The simplest model of the moral order is that it consists of rules of behaviour associated with a system of rewards and punishments, discovered empirically, which may ensure regularity and predictability in social life, and which may, by reducing conflict, conserve energy and resources. The reward-punishment system bears a direct relationship to the social costs of nonconformity or the social product of conformity. The word justice and the symbol of the scales both express the underlying concepts of adjustment, balance, and input-output ratio, as does the idea of retribution.

Such a model goes far to account for much of what exists and provides a suitable analytic structure for the examination of a parliamentary debate on proposed legislation.

A more complete model must, however, take account of the cumulative tendencies of all institutions to adapt, not by changing functions, but by adding to them; thus there is an inherent resistance to the repealing of law, associated with a continuous process of making new laws. To some extent this process is associated with the concentration of political power and has the effect that, from a reservoir of obsolete legislation, a government has at any time the power to make any act a crime and the option to prosecute a particular action under different legislation depending on the political desirability of a heavy or a light sentence or on the estimate by the prosecution of whether a jury or a magistrate is more likely to give the desired verdict.

Political power is also important in that interest groups such as landed proprietors, huntsmen, motorists, brewers, cyclists, and the professions may succeed by pressure in directing or modifying legislation to favour their interests.

Thus many persons are forbidden by law to do things for which they are competent because they are not 'qualified' or, if permitted to do them, may not use the name which describes their occupation and has done so for centuries. The control of professions by legislation not only ensures the minimum qualifications of the members but serves to exclude certain able persons (those trained abroad for example) and to limit numbers on economic, not social, grounds. It also tends to reduce the possible division of labour by confining even routine semi-skilled operations to the members of the profession. Moreover, 'private' legislation often gives to corporate bodies and private companies such as municipalities and dock and railway undertakings powers to make actions criminal in certain places that are not criminal elsewhere.[1] Thus it is an offence to be a 'nightwalker' on Swansea docks, or to play pitch and toss there, or to throw snowballs, and a snowballing nightwalker could easily, by walking a few yards, pass from an area of innocence into one of crime.

Legislation may also reflect broad conflicts of interest in society, between workers and employers, for example.

Having said this, however, it must also be said that there is much legislation for which there can be no explanation in terms of primary rationality, social control, or group interest: the law concerning sexual behaviour, for example, unless the vested interests of certain religious sects in certain prohibitions are regarded as a group interest. It is observable that dominant religious groups endeavour to obtain and often succeed in securing legislation which reinforces their precepts in such matters as contraception, divorce, and homosexuality (Friedmann, 1959, p.

[1] For example, prior to the Street Offences Act 1959 (7 and 8 Eliz. 2, c. 57), there were considerable differences in local by-laws governing soliciting by prostitutes. See *Current Law Statutes Annotated* (1959).

205 *et seq.*). It is characteristic that some of the sexual mores and the laws controlling sexual behaviour restate taboos which are recorded from very early times and may be accounted for, without necessarily having recourse to psychoanalytic explanations, as likely to lessen conflict within the family or small group, or to have done so at some time.

Once, however, a taboo exists in folk tradition and becomes, in Freud's term 'latent in the culture', the explanation given in *Totem and Taboo* becomes plausible and would be possible of verification.

Freud wrote:

'The earliest moral precepts and restrictions in primitive society have been explained by us as reactions to a deed which gave those who performed it the concept of "crime". They felt remorse for the deed and decided that it should never be repeated and that its performance should bring no advantage. This creative sense of guilt still persists among us. We find it operating in an asocial manner in neurotics, and producing new moral precepts and persistent restrictions, as an atonement for crimes that have been committed and as a precaution against the committing of new ones. If, however, we inquire among these neurotics to discover what were the deeds which provoked these reactions, we shall be disappointed. We find no deeds, but only impulses and emotions, set upon evil ends but held back from their achievement. What lie behind the sense of guilt of neurotics are always psychical realities and never factual ones. What characterizes neurotics is the fact that they prefer psychical to factual reality and react just as seriously to thoughts as normal persons do to realities' (Freud, 1913, p. 159).

It is illuminating to consider, in the light of this, the events preceding the setting-up of the Committee on Homosexuality and Prostitution, the Committee's Report, the subsequent discussion, and the resulting changes in legislation which brought additional restrictions on and penalties for heterosexual intercourse while doing nothing to relax the prohibitions on homosexual relationships until 1967.

It is possible to add to Freud's explanation of legislative restrictions on sexual behaviour some sociological factors. Many taboos may be explained in terms of the functional necessities of earlier societies. Thus the restriction of marriage (and sexual intercourse) between close kin derives from the restriction of marriage between distant as well as close kin imposed in Northern Europe by early Christian missionaries as a means of weakening the power of the family and clan by compelling exogamy. Such sociological explanations and the scientific approach to social problems are relatively unknown to politicians and conflict with the supernatural explanations of the priest; thus two major influence groups in the field of social control are unlikely to respond to proposals to change legislation in response to the situation as it is displayed empirically in the light of human needs.

The part played by divine revelation in morals raises considerable difficulty, since the fragmentary documentary records of a nomadic tribe and later of the same society as a subject people under the Roman Empire are regarded as the substantial basis for a complete system of regulation for complex industrial societies. It is true, of course, that in the Anglican Church precept changes as the 'will of God is made manifest through the minds of his priests'. Reference to the contribution of bishops in the House of Lords to the debates on such issues as capital punishment, social legislation, and the like, would suggest that their attitudes could also be predicted from a knowledge of their educational background, wealth, and social status.

The presence of institutions of religion introduces complexities in the model of the moral order in many ways. Religious observance plays a small part in the lives of adult civilians, although it is a regular part of military life.[1] It influences the very young through the universal religious observance in state schools, through the considerable part it plays in denominational schools, and through Sunday Schools. There is thus for many a sharp differentiation between the Christian ethic acquired in early childhood in song, parable, analogy, and myth

[1] See Naval Discipline Act 1957 (5 and 6 Eliz. 2, c. 53). Under Part I Articles of War, '1. All officers in command of Her Majesty's ships shall cause public worship of Almighty God to be solemnly, orderly and reverently performed in their respective ships, and shall take care that prayers and preaching, by the Chaplain of those ships, be performed diligently and that the Lord's Day be observed.'

and the 'rational' organization of adult social and economic life in a competitive society. The ethic thus acquired is 'latent' to use Freud's term and corresponds to conscience as generally understood.

Thus in many everyday situations conflict develops between socially approved means and ends and the ethic learned in childhood and gives rise to emotional disturbances not controllable by logical argument; that is, to feelings of guilt.

The problem of the approval or disapproval of behaviours is further complicated by the confusion over means and ends. In general it may be said that an approved end may not be achieved by a disapproved means, but this is not universally true and in some cases, provided the end is successfully achieved, the nature of the means may be overlooked.

This could be of relevance to a theory of occupational selection, including the selection of crime as a profession. Merton has called attention to the structural barriers to socially approved goals, and crime could be considered as a special case of a disapproved means to socially approved ends. It is possible to grade means of earning or gaining wealth in a hierarchy of approved means (Merton, 1957, p. 132 *et seq.*). Low in the hierarchy is a continuum of occupations in the field of public entertainment – prostitute, boxer, wrestler, dancer, singer, actress, ballet dancer, and so on – a hierarchy corresponding curiously to the extent to which the gratification offered is 'real' or symbolic. In the making of money the hierarchy would run through the varieties of thief and swindler, again dependent on the degree to which the transfer of property was in real or symbolic form, through bookmaker, shopkeeper, merchant, insurance broker, up to banker, at the head of the symbolic process. The social status of the crime also reflects the status of those most likely to commit it; thus robbery has a lower status than fraud and tends to be punished differently.

The existence of structural barriers has certainly acted to direct persons of talent from certain urban areas, Glasgow, Leeds, Liverpool, Cardiff, and the East End of London into the fields of public entertainment. This applies particularly to persons with social disadvantages – Jews, Negroes, and the Irish. It could apply to professional criminals.

173

Jack Dempsey, the former world heavy-weight boxing champion, in his autobiography describes the situation thus:

'You get your good fighters mainly out of families and racial groups that are poor, underprivileged and without much schooling. Just look back in the record books. When the Irish were poor in the country, fresh off the boat, the ring was filled with good Irish fighters. Then as the second generation and the third generation came along and got better schooling, better living conditions, they began disappearing from fighting. They were followed by the Italian fighters, then by the good Jewish fighters. The Jews were replaced by the Negro fighters and now the Puerto Ricans are coming along real strong – because they're the new under-privileged class' (Dempsey, 1960).

This concise statement suggests a valuable framework for the examination of the social composition of many occupational groups.

To return now to specific behaviours, the situation for any action is extremely involved.

An act may be approved or disapproved in the mores and/or in the law. This approval or disapproval in rare instances may have the universality and generality of a commandment like 'thou shalt not kill' and refer to the act performed by any person, at any time, in any place, and in any circumstances.

The context of the commandments suggests that the precept 'thou shalt not kill' did not apply to tribal enemies or to murderers within the tribe, a circumstance which is held to justify capital punishment and participation in wars declared just by the hierarchy of the church (Book of Common Prayer, 1662).

This illustrates a general principle operating through the culture that actions can become good or evil, or criminal or legal, if certain persons say so. For many actions this takes place as the result of a debate taking years or even centuries, but in some cases the change may take place overnight, as, for example, upon the declaration of war.

In practice, for most behaviours, there is a range with a large number of variables.

Thus an act might be disapproved of by some, many, or all of the people to whom it was described or by whom it was seen.

This disapproval might be expressed by an action to prevent the behaviour or an action to invoke actions by others. Or the act might be disapproved of by certain classes of person, the young or the old, men or women, ministers of religion, justices of the peace, schoolmasters, or policemen. The disapproval might take the forms described above. It might be that the act would be disapproved of if performed by the young or by the old, or by a man or by a woman, or by day or by night, or on a weekday or on a Sunday, or on a beach or in a street, and again the disapproval might take any of the forms described above. The crucial role of privacy is obvious here.

In that behaviour in conformity with the mores and/or in contravention of the mores and the law involves so many variables, themselves subject to varying influences, it is unlikely that any simple theory of crime causation will be found.

Moreover, it suggests that an appropriate form of sociological investigation would be into the origins of the disapproval complex and associated actions. This is the field of the sociology of law, a discipline which plays a surprisingly small part in discussions of crime.

It could be argued that the principles underlying the moral order, the tendencies to predictability, regularity, security, and peace are discernible as long-term tendencies, and many of the complexities and contradictions listed above arise from the institutionalization of the moral order with the continuous accumulation of relics of earlier systems of social control. This is tantamount to recognizing that much crime is caused by differences in the rates of change of different social institutions, especially those of public justice and religion, on the one hand, and socio-economic institutions, on the other. Curiously enough, in spite of the attention that this problem has received from Weber, Marx, and Tawney, the literature of criminology appears to deal with this only as a problem of rationality, of legal reform, and not as a problem of dynamic institutional theory.

The Boston case referred to earlier illustrates this issue. In this, young men were charged with and found guilty of sexual intercourse with girls under the age of sixteen.

There is substantial evidence that the age of menarche has declined since 1859 from over seventeen years to an average of

175

thirteen-and-a-half in the general population and to twelve-and-three-quarters in the middle classes, and that this trend is continuing at the rate of about four months per decade (Watson and Lowrey, 1962).

Cone, writing in the *Journal of Pediatrics*, discusses this in the context of the acceleration of the rate of growth in height and weight and comments:

'As a corollary to this trend, should one not take this speed-up of growth into account when dealing with the adolescent because all of us tend to consider them in terms of their chronologic rather than biologic age? If growing up has been hastened, perhaps some of the difficulties encountered by parents, teachers, and even physicians, in dealing with adolescents may result from the failure to appreciate that their earlier biologic maturation may cause them to develop emotional, social and heterosexual interests at an earlier chronologic age than did their parents and grandparents' (Cone, 1961, p. 740).

In the light of this it is relevant to note the changes in the legal 'age of consent' from 10 years in the time of Elizabeth I to 12 in the nineteenth century and to 16 in 1885, this age corresponding then to the age of menarche, and to reconsider the remarks of Lord Chief Justice Parker quoted in Chapter 5.[1]

This matter is complicated further by the fact that institutions change not only at different rates, but also at different rates in different places.

As has been described, several boys and young men of Lincolnshire have served prison sentences for illegal sexual intercourse, had they lived in Hampshire they might never have reached the courts at all.

In Hampshire the Chief Constable has become aware of the physical and social changes and has directed the actions of his officers to meet these changes.

'In his annual report, Mr Osmond, discussing cases of unlawful sexual intercourse with girls under 16, said, "These cases are taken so much for granted by the courts and the public that no useful purpose is served by bringing them to trial."

[1] Criminal Law Amendment Act 1885 (48 and 49 Vict., c.69).

Later he added: "The law was designed to protect innocent young girls. Today the girl is often as responsible as the boy. The law was made to protect the innocent, not to make rulings on morals." He said the police might warn youngsters, or consider a care and protection order, or talk to the parents, or put the matter into the hands of a child guidance clinic.

Mr Osmond in his report emphasized that proceedings were initiated when there was deliberate seduction and corruption of young girls by mature men.

Mr Osmond said: "I think one uses the law in the light of social conditions. I have not given my forces any explicit instructions, but if we took every unlawful sexual intercourse case before the courts they would be overloaded. The moral welfare people prefer things this way" ' (*The Times*, 25-4-65).

This quotation illustrates also the causal role of the police in crime.

If social and environmental causation were the only types of explanation offered to account for crime, it would not be necessary to consider the 'behaviour in itself', but many writers argue that psychophysical factors are involved (Gibbens *et al.*, 1963).

Such 'biological' explanations account for the tendencies to certain behaviour regardless of the degree of approval or disapproval. In their simplest form, they are, for example, that muscular boys are more likely to be aggressive in sports such as boxing and wrestling and in interpersonal relationships than are physically weak boys (ibid). The literature of this subject goes far beyond the field of criminology.

The prevalence of the term 'psychopath', the frequency of the reference to psychiatrists of certain classes of criminal and criminals of certain classes, and the volume of psychiatric studies of criminals confirm this point of view.

THE VALUE OF THE OPERATIONAL DEFINITION

What is required is first to present behaviours without their moral referrents, which can be done by means of operational definitions, and then to account for the disapproval or approval of behaviours in certain circumstances.

Theft, burglary, larceny, embezzlement, fraud then become:

177

'The transfer of goods or rights from one person to another without the former's full knowledge and consent'.

The particular form would include references to the time of day, the employment of symbols, and so forth.

Assault would become: 'actions which cause pain and/or injury to the health of the subject'.

When, however, this is done, two things become evident. The first is that for any behaviour thus defined there exist condemned, neutral, and approved forms, the valuation of each depending on factors independent of the action. This model would be useful in discussing the general case; for example, the professional specialist criminal. It is clear, however, that some disapproved actions arise in highly specific circumstances, for example those where technically inefficient means to obscure ends are employed with an inevitability of discovery. Here a more complex model is needed.[1] The second is that many disapproved behaviours may be institutionalized as socially approved means to ends, and certain persons exempted by political and religious authority from disapproval. War, capital punishment, and corporal punishment are examples of this.

It is worth noting that institutions of religion are functionally involved in the punishment system, including hanging.

A few examples will suffice to make the point. Under the first rubric, the transfer of goods or rights without full knowledge and consent: this would include theft and fraud but also those forms of speculation where one person profits by secret or superior knowledge. Many coups on the Stock Exchange and some property deals are of this kind. It is recognized that some of these activities are 'immoral' and from time to time cases are investigated by a committee of the London Stock Exchange, but even where such findings are adverse the action does not become a crime. Within the middle classes confidential information of a profitable kind about the future prospects of public companies is frequently made available to selected members of small social and professional groups, which allows some persons to gain at the expense of others. The obtaining and imparting of such information is highly regarded and status-conferring and is a frequent

---

[1] Gibbens, in his study of borstal lads, discusses the case of the boy who steals from the prepayment gas meter in his own home (Gibbens *et al.*, 1963).

source of financial advantage to a part of the higher professional and business classes.

The 'Ferranti Affair' of 1963 is relevant because it falls precisely under the operational definition: 'the transfer of goods or rights from one person to another without the former's full knowledge and consent'.

The essential facts are simple: The Ministry of Aviation entered into a fixed-price contract for the supply of missiles with Messrs. Ferranti on the assumption that costs would be £12,013,720 and profit £810,353, a rate of 6¾ per cent on cost. A subsequent inquiry revealed that costs had been £7,051,109 and profits £5,772,964, a rate of 82 per cent on cost. The agreement specified a 'fair and reasonable profit'. It is pertinent to record that the price for the contract was negotiated while production was proceeding and the price was not finally agreed until more than eight-tenths of the missiles had been delivered. Sir John Lang (the Comptroller and Auditor General) in his report makes it quite clear that the company knew that the wage bills they were paying were only a fraction of the Ministry's estimate (upon which overheads were in turn calculated). He noted that 'emphatic instructions were given to estimating staff that they should be careful not to agree estimates on a basis that might lead the firm to a loss. Their estimates were very cautious'. It was a situation in which inexperienced junior civil servants were dealing with 'estimators who have every opportunity both of gaining experience and keeping up to date'.

After a period during which spokesmen for the company attempted to justify their actions it was agreed to return £4,250,000, leaving the company a profit of 21 per cent, about three times that originally allowed for in the Ministry's estimate.[1]

What is interesting here is that the question of whether or not the law was at any time broken was not discussed and that the discovery of the discrepancy was largely accidental, so the possibility that similar transactions have taken place cannot be overlooked. The Bristol-Siddeley affair in 1967 confirms this.

[1] First Report of the Inquiry into the Pricing of Ministry of Aviation Contracts: Cmnd. 2428 (1964).

In that large numbers of persons were involved in the negotiations on the company's side and that they must have had knowledge of the situation, a psychiatric study of them might well yield useful material for comparisons with psychiatric data about criminals whose offences were not merely disapproved but also punished as illegal.

Some aspects of trade have similar characteristics and it is highly unlikely that prices for the same commodity with a range of 12 to 1 could survive in the face of 'full knowledge'. The report of the Monopolies Commission on motor accessories is relevant here.[1] The practice of selling commodities ranging from motor spirit to medicine using demonstrably false claims is too well known to warrant further discussion.

The actions of corporate bodies present issues of some complexity. Corporate bodies can initiate actions and often have great power; where their actions and power give rise to a conflict of interest, this is generally regulated by civil law rather than by criminal law, although the laws relating to fraud, the Companies Acts, the Forgeries Acts, and much other legislation, do bring corporate bodies within the scope of criminal law. In some fields there is a continuum of behaviours which range from offences under civil law, such as the supply of goods not being of the required standard, to offences under the criminal law, such as fraud. The threshold where the offence changes from one punishable by a fine charged to the assets of a company to one punishable by the fining or imprisonment of a director or manager would be determined by a study of cases. In other cases the offence is not against an identifiable person but against the community. Here the element of moral disapproval is small and such offences are usually dealt with under civil law.

When, however, actions are defined operationally the distinction between some actions which are dealt with under civil law, where corporate bodies are involved, and under criminal law, where individuals are concerned, disappears.

The infringement of a patent deprives the owner of rights and often property; to establish this he must initiate and win a civil action against the person or corporate body whom he believes

[1] Report on the Supply of Electrical Equipment for Mechanically Propelled Land Vehicles (1963).

to have wronged him. In many cases, of course, the infringement is accidental but in some it is a deliberate and calculated action based on an assessment of the patentee's capacity to conduct proceedings in the courts. In some cases the weakness of the patentee may make him willing to sell his property under duress, for example he may not be able to afford the cost of an action. The decision to infringe a patent is not only operationally identical with theft but when carried out by a corporate body is operationally identical with conspiracy, a very serious crime.

The law of treason as it affects individuals may be compared with the law controlling the export of strategic goods as it affects individuals and corporate bodies. The punishment for treason in peacetime is imprisonment, usually long-term imprisonment, but the Export of Goods (Control) Order 1960 provides only financial penalties for offences under this order. If, however, the laws of the country are contravened by forgery, fraud, or conspiracy, then other penalties, including imprisonment, may be imposed. Yet the export of strategic goods may be operationally identical with some forms of treason and has been so described by some of Britain's allies in diplomatic exchanges concerning certain permitted exports.

In general, the actions of corporate bodies tend to lose any moral significance, a process which increases the power of corporate bodies in society and weakens the effect of mores on the behaviour of individuals.

One other important issue must be considered. An individual or a group of individuals may form a company or other corporate body and by so doing take many of their actions into the area of civil rather than criminal law. Moreover, if they form a Limited Liability company they may share any financial penalties with their shareholders, thus reducing the effects of the penalties designed to control their actions. The facts of power in modern business are well documented; decision-making is in the hands of a very small number of persons, liability, to the extent of their shareholding, is widely spread. The operational definition of disapproved actions to this situation reveals another major area of middle- and upper-class immunity.

Writers on punishment have drawn attention to the skill and ingenuity that have gone into the techniques of causing pain, and with the growth of public knowledge and mass communications the development of techniques that do not leave physical signs has been important. What has not been recognized is the number of such processes which are available to those with authority in hierarchical administrative structures.

In many such structures, membership is compulsory, as in the case of the armed forces and primary and secondary school education. It is not compulsory, but there is difficulty in escaping from membership in an industry where there is unemployment, in professions and trades where the skills are highly specialized and the employment opportunities limited, as in university teaching or in religious institutions, or where the financial penalties in a change of occupation are high. There is also difficulty as age increases.

In such authoritarian structures power exists to deprive subordinates of status, role, and reward, and such power is frequently exercised, sometimes in order to protect the status of the office-holder, sometimes for no objective reason.

Such actions, in some cases, *appear* to result in mental and physical breakdown and, in instances known to the writer, death (to test such evidence scientifically presents difficulties). These actions evoke some disapprobation but carry little stigma and no punishment.

In institutions of hierarchical form, role deprivation occurs not only as the arbitrary act of one person with power towards one or more persons without power, but as a pattern of social structure in which whole classes of persons are subject to deprivations and adverse discriminatory treatment. This is especially true in the armed forces, which are the limiting case, but it is found even in institutions ostensibly concerned with enlightenment and rational thought like provincial universities (Shartle, 1957).

In determining whether an action is a crime or not, capacity to distinguish the end from the means, to avoid proscribed means, is crucial. This is a special case of a more general pattern in which the differential distribution of knowledge and resources determine the social distribution of criminality. In many fields of business and commerce the existence of a legal prohibition on some line of action merely introduces another parameter into a problem. The function of the legal adviser is to discover a procedure or often simply a formula of words that will permit the prohibited goal to be reached without a penalty. This suggests another area for psychiatric study.

The determination of whether an action is criminal or not is complicated. To take an example in the matter of personal injury: in most circumstances a premeditated attack upon a person is a crime, a spontaneous attack arising out of some situation may be a crime but is generally regarded as being less serious, but an injury arising from the random effects of an action is not criminal unless an element of negligence can be shown.

In spite of this, it can be demonstrated that if certain actions are repeated frequently a predictable incidence of injury or death will occur. The carrying out of such actions is not regarded as criminal and if challenged is strongly defended. Such cases present an interesting subject for study, since the consequences of the behaviour are known, the disapproval in the mores (but not in the law) is clear, but the behaviour is persisted in. Once again, persons who carry out such actions could have applied to them the familiar tests of social pathology. Examples would include those engaged in the tobacco trade, in the trade of alcohol, and in many industries and services where lives and health are risked for profit. The role of insurance is of interest here, since where the risk is relatively low, as it is in some industries, it is cheaper in money terms to allow death and injury to occur rather than for all the employers to prevent death and injury by modifying the environment of work. In some 'test' discussions arranged within an institution concerning the employment of window-cleaners without safety belts, contrary to a by-law, it was found that the moral dilemma was resolved in the case of direct employment by insurance, and in the case of subcontracting by the insertion of a clause in the contract transferring the legal responsibility to the subcontractor, who in turn insured against the consequence of risk. Such actions, described in operational terms, are killing men to make profits or to save money.

An example from recent history will make this clear.

If a profit of £x per unit could be made from the sale of the

183

eyes of schoolboys, and if some entrepreneur set about obtaining them by violent assault, it is probable that such an activity would be disapproved and would be found to be criminal. Studies of accidents to children involving fireworks show that two major sources of danger exist: the cheap explosive (the 'penny banger') and the tendency of fireworks to ignite each other because of the unprotected fuse. In face of a high casualty rate and publicly expressed indignation and even the remote threat of legislation, the manufacturers gave the impression in 1962 that the major hazards would be met for November 1963 by the discontinuance of the 'penny banger' and the provision of plastic safety caps on other fireworks, a decision in effect to reduce profits to reduce injuries, or perhaps to forestall legislation which might have been more commercially harmful. However, in November 1963 it appeared that this decision, if it had been made, had been reversed and the dangerous toys were again on sale with results operationally identical with profiting from the sale of schoolboys' eyes. Current theories of criminality would lead one to expect that the directors of firework companies would possess the stigmata of psychopathology. Further examination of the industry reveals, however, that a major product of the pyrotechnic industry is the production of flares, parachute signals, and rockets for use in saving lives at sea and that these have reached a high degree of perfection and are in a continuous state of improvement under the direction of the same persons. In these circumstances it would be reasonable to expect evidence of psychopathology only in those directors whose activities under the first heading were not compensated for by those under the second.

This topic is dealt with by legal theorists in their discussion of the Law of Tort; it is observable that the influence of insurance has changed the function of the law so that only gross, criminal, and wanton negligence are recognized as deriving from fault. In this regard, negligence is rated by reference to what is 'fair and reasonable', and guilt is apportioned on this basis. Friedmann points out that 'in those fields of tort which are socially most significant – traffic accidents, responsibilities of manufacturers and other controllers of properties and enterprises – the fault principle has either been superseded by strict

184

liability or *lost its moral significance* and become barely distinguishable from so-called strict liability'. He continues that a basic dilemma is the 'immunity for the tortfeasor', and suggests that this may not be objectionable since he may pay his share of compensation in some other capacity, as tax payer for example, and because the 'moral significance of fault liability . . . has become restricted to a very few situations' (Friedmann, 1959, p. 164).[1] Not all lawyers would accept a statement as categorical as this; although some would accept the proposition that this is a general tendency in the legal system, they would argue, however, that there are some countervailing pressures.

It will be of interest to observe the results of the recent scheme to compensate the victims of violence since it could, on analogy with the Law of Tort, reduce the moral significance of violence.

Not only does insurance provide absolution through corporate involvement, it is symbiotically associated with crime in another way.

Insurance companies faced with heavy claims for stolen valuables employ professional intermediaries to assist them in the recovery of such goods. The function of these intermediaries is to discover the thieves or their agents and to buy back the stolen property at a low price, the 'reward' for the recovery of

[1] G. H. Mead, in his 'Psychology of Punitive Justice', explains the situation in which the criminal law has ' become the ponderous weapon of defence and attack' and expresses his point of view thus:

'I am referring here to criminal law and its enforcement, not only because respect for the law and the majesty of the law have reference almost entirely to criminal justice, but also because a very large part, perhaps the largest part, of civil law proceedings are under-taken and carried out with the intent of defining and readjusting social situations without the hostile attitudes which characterize the criminal procedure. The parties to the proceedings belong to the same group and continue to belong to this group, whatever decision is rendered. No stigma attaches to the one who loses. Our emotional attitude toward this body of law is that of interest, of condemnation and approval as it fails or succeeds in its social function. It is not an institution that must be respected even in its disastrous failures. On the contrary it must be changed. It is hedged about in our feelings by no majesty. It is efficient or inefficient and as such awakens satisfaction or dissatisfaction and an interest in its reform which is in proportion to the social values concerned' (Mead, 1918, p. 586).

Here is an alternative explanation of the change in the moral significance of torts.

the 'lost' property. This reward, described in discreet advertisements, as the 'usual' percentage, is in effect the limiting lower price in the market for stolen property. The need to have and maintain business relations with the professional criminals requires independence of the police and demands that the criminals shall have 'safe' dealings with the 'Loss Adjustor'. In effect, this profession corresponds to that of a licensed receiver of stolen property; it provides for the professional thief the desideratum of all business, a guaranteed market, and as such is as causal in the creation of crime as is the activity of any other 'fence' or receiver.

VOCATIONAL OPPORTUNITY AND CRIMINAL CAREERS

The identity of much business with crime when the activities are described in operational terms suggests that similar skills and interests may determine the choice of both pursuits, a thesis which is elegantly supported in the memoirs of Arthur Thorp.

> 'And so in March, 1953, about fifteen months after his original arrest, Mr X was sentenced at Gloucester Assizes to eight years' preventive detention. He was found guilty on sixteen out of seventeen charges involving share-pushing and fraudulent conversion. And he agreed in court, that besides the five years' penal servitude in 1933 for stealing money, trunks and other articles, he had been sentenced in 1939 to twelve months' imprisonment for fraudulently obtaining valuable securities and in 1943 to three years' imprisonment (with a fine of £300) for obtaining cheques by false pretences.
>
> It was a pity that Mr X couldn't keep straight. With that brain, he should have been able to do well in legitimate business' (Thorp, 1954, p. 187).

In the light of this discussion it could be argued that in certain cases the choice of criminal rather than non-criminal careers depends mainly upon the availability of vocational opportunity or vocational guidance. So far this discussion has been concerned with the identity of criminal and non-criminal actions when these are operationally defined. It is now appropriate to consider actions identical with crimes, both as operationally defined and as described in the common language, but specifically approved in law and/or in the mores.

The behaviours are those which injure humans or animals. Since such behaviours are especially interesting to specialists in psychopathology and arouse much emotion in judges and magistrates, an examination of them seems justified.

Attention to this matter was first given by the writer when he was serving as a private soldier in the Home Guard. During his service he was on many occasions compelled to carry out the following actions and expected to experience the accompanying phantasies:

1. To imagine that a stuffed and suspended sack was a German soldier or in some cases an officer. Attempts were made in the instruction to reinforce hostility to the Germans with class antagonism (in that the N.C.O.s were always of the working class and many of the privates were gentlemen this was not uniformly effective).
2. To imagine that the German had just been interrupted in the act of raping the writer's sister, daughter, wife, fiancée or mistress. Freedom of choice was given here, but no allowance for the disadvantageous situation of the enemy was to be made.
3. To shout a number of unfamiliar obscenities – presumably prescribed in a military manual to which privates did not have access.
4. To show the teeth and growl (the James-Lange phenomenon).[1]

---

[1] The psychologist William James and the physiologist C. Lange put forward, at the same time, theories of the emotions which are so similar that they are known as the James-Lange theory. The theory asserts the connection between emotion, changes in the body, especially the secretions of the endocrine glands, and a stimulus. The essence of the theory was that emotion was the sensation of the visceral and vasomotor changes. In its crude form James stated the theory thus: we do not cry because we are sorry; we are sorry because we cry. The founder of the Boy Scout movement had the same idea when he made the rule that the Boy Scout smiles and whistles. The argument here is that the weak stimulus, an imaginary German, would not produce the emotion of anger, but, reinforced with the vocal and facial expressions of anger, a cyclical process was initiated in which the emotion and the culturally determined behaviour associated with it were created.

5. To thrust the bayonet into the bowels of the German, to twist and withdraw it.
6. To attack the genitalia of the German with additional obscenities.
7. To subject the German, then presumed to be dead, to superfluous surgery with the bayonet if military circumstances permitted.

It will be understood that the author, being familiar with the literature of psychopathology, developed an intellectual interest in the proceedings.

The persistence of this practice is displayed in the following account:

'An Army major and a Royal Marines lieutenant are to be censured by their commanding officers after a board of inquiry into how a young Marine was bayoneted in a military demonstration at the Devon County Show.

This was revealed today by a Royal Marines spokesman at Plymouth who said: "The board decided that the officers made an error of judgement in an effort to please the crowd at the expense of normal safety regulations." The names of the officers are not being disclosed.

The bayoneted man, Marine X of Milton, Portsmouth, was back on light duties today at the Royal Marines infantry training centre at Lympstone, near Exeter. Marine X, aged 20, received a bayonet wound in the right side of the chest in the demonstration. He was in hospital for three weeks.

The Royal Marines spokesman said: "Service teams from various units were invited to enter a competition at the show which involved a race over obstacles and finished with the bayoneting of some dummies. The two teams left in the final of the competition were from the infantry training centre and to increase the public interest it was suggested to the Army officer in charge that one team should provide a comic run using live dummies who would run off when the teams approached.

One of the live dummies was unfortunately placed in the wrong position and Marine X failed to receive the command to get up and run. He was lying on the ground and didn't see the man with the bayonet coming." The board of inquiry considered that the injury was accidental and that there was no wilful neglect of any orders but the two officers were in error to permit the demonstration in a live form. The officers concerned are to be censured and this could affect their prospects of promotion' (*The Times*, 19-7-62).

What is particularly interesting in this account is that the dummies to be bayoneted were supine and thus could only represent helpless and injured enemies, the killing of whom is contrary to international conventions governing the conduct of war. This fact was not apparently worthy of comment nor was the appropriateness of this as a form of public entertainment discussed. In passing, it should be noted that the Military Tattoo studied historically is a rich source of data on the ideology of violence and the stereotypes of the external enemy.

Another rich source of data of this kind as yet unstudied by sociologists is training methods for soldiers and especially special troops, marines, commandoes, and paratroopers.

A list of occupations where violence in different degrees is approved, permitted, or prescribed includes:

public executioner
special service soldier
member of the armed forces
policeman[1]
prison officer
teacher, especially in Scotland and in public schools
boxer and wrestler
slaughterman
butcher
medical, and other experimenter with living animals
huntsman and gamekeeper

An interesting ideological detail is the practice by game-keepers of exhibiting the bodies of vermin on a gibbet in imitation of the crucifixion.

There are in addition to these general practices similar practices permitted on special occasions or to particular persons. Such occasions are: during the interrogation of suspects in times

[1] A recent advertisement for a career in the West Riding Constabulary contained no description of the work, conditions, or salary, but simply a drawing of a helmet with badge, a truncheon, and handcuffs, the symbols of authority and violence. See also footnote on p. 134.

of political conflict, including civil war, and the later stages of colonial domination as in Aden, Nyasaland, Kenya, Palestine, Cyprus, and Algeria; during the questioning of spies or captured enemy believed to have information, political prisoners, for example political conscientious objectors in World War I, and leaders of unemployed workers in the interwar period; and in the detection of crime.

The recognition of assassination as a permissible technique of war in World War II appears to have led to its extension as a legitimate technique of political change in countries where the interests of another state are involved and as such has become for some countries a part of the work of intelligence agencies.

If it is argued that there is a propensity in some persons to inflict pain on other persons or on animals, that this propensity is associated with certain psychological variables or psychophysical variables, and that these are detectable or measurable with tests or with apparatus, then a solution of some of the problems with which the criminologist is concerned appears possible.

Many individuals find themselves in occupations as a result of chance factors or special circumstances outside their control: the army, for example, has generally been recruited from the unskilled unemployed. It is likely, therefore, that in so far as choice or aptitude has played little part in their vocational placement, many of them are maladjusted.

At the same time many persons with a propensity to, a liking for, or in other words a vocation for, violence, lacking a legitimate outlet, find themselves designated as criminal.

Civil war in Africa at the time of writing and the recruitment of mercenaries to the Foreign Legion in the French armed forces and to other armies makes available occupations in which violence and killing are a part of the duties.

These employments present certain problems. It may still be an offence under British law to kill a foreigner in his own country; it may be an offence under Canon law to kill as a member of the armed forces of a foreign power or in the service of a rebellion; it is an offence under international law to kill prisoners of war in cold blood.

Nevertheless, citizens of the United Kingdom are engaged in warlike activities without censure or prosecution and without being the subject of psychiatric study or chemical treatment, which suggests a recognition of the validity of the argument above.

'A Liverpool man who fought with the 5th commando group of Major "Mad Mike" Hoare's Congo mercenaries, has returned to the city – with malaria.

Mr X, aged 29, formerly with the Queen's Dragoon Guards for seven years, said he could see no end to strife in the Congo.

"It looks as though it's going to go on for a very long time, with brother fighting brother," he said. "And that's why I left."

Mr X was in the country for over three months and took part in the relief of Stanleyville. He confirmed newspaper reports about there being no prisoners.

"Often we would hand over our prisoners to the National Congolese Army and they would be tortured. Sometimes we would shoot them ourselves," he said.

He added: "But there is no truth in some of the rumours that we were shooting civilians. All our operations were very carefully planned, and Major Hoare is a very careful man" ' (*Liverpool Daily Post*, 10-12-64).

Confirmation of these behaviours was provided by another British mercenary, G. Forrest, who wrote to the *Observer* thus:

'First, most people, certainly those who have been in the forces, know what a nuisance and embarrassment prisoners are. In the Congo, moving quickly as the mercenaries do, it is impossible to take and hold prisoners without endangering your own lives. You cannot take them with you, as space on the trucks is very limited, and you cannot leave them behind as they might cut off your retreat, or ambush subsequent vehicles. They must be put out of action immediately, and the only solution, brutal as it might seem, is to shoot them. This is what happens in any jungle war, not only the Congo. . . .

. . . As for torturing them, this was done only where it was necessary to get information, not, as has been implied, for sadistic reasons. If they divulged their information freely, they were never tortured' (*Observer*, 5-9-65).

A person with a capacity for violence who becomes a criminal thus appears to be the product of unsatisfactory vocational guidance or maldistribution of vocational opportunities, and the social problem can be taken out of the field of criminology and psychiatry and resolved as one of social administration.

That this is not a new idea can be deduced from an earlier practice of offering certain convicted criminals the alternative of prison or enlisting in the armed forces, and the recruiting of certain classes of criminal into specialist units of the armed forces in wartime.

Alex Comfort expresses the same idea thus:

'When, therefore, scientific psychiatry is deliberately invoked, as it is to-day, to deal with individual crime, it must inevitably become widely involved in the study of the non-criminal forms of delinquency upon which patterns of centralized society have come to depend, since both the demand and the supply of delinquents may be held to be products of that society. The convicted criminal represents, to this extent, not so much an eliminable by-product of our culture as a divergent surplus of one of its manufactures' (Comfort, 1950, p. 9).

Dr Comfort has developed this general argument in a very elaborate form. He has been concerned with the extent to which the institutionalization of authority stimulates and creates behaviours which in other circumstances would be considered criminal, and the extent to which persons whose behaviours would in civil society bring them into conflict with the law are free to act in similar ways inside the institutions of government (ibid, p. 9). He argues that the concentration of modern states on mass destruction is a direct outcome of such processes.

The trial of Adolf Eichmann, Mau-Mau, the Hola Camp in Kenya, events in Algeria and South Viet Nam, all of which have taken place since Comfort wrote, give substance to his main thesis:

'The object of this study is to relate the elements in the behaviour of modern governments which lead to the international equivalent of crime to those with which we are already partly familiar in individuals. Society has throughout its history treated crime as something hostile to itself, to be abolished by punishment or prevention. At the same time it has arbitrarily delimited the conduct which is criminal, while depending to a greater or lesser extent on the presence within itself of potential delinquents. No society based on centralized power has been able to dispense with large groups of people whose make-up is in no way different from that of punishable delinquents – it has abolished private, but tolerated public, executioners, for example. Some of these mechanisms will be examined here. While some such toleration has always been present, its study to-day gains urgency from the alarming growth of delinquent acts by states and by organs of power during the last fifty years' (ibid, p. xi).

Many other criminal actions besides violence find a counter-part or accommodation in permitted occupations; thus the voyeur may become a bath attendant, the exhibitionist a strip-tease artiste, and the pyromaniac an airman in charge of an incendiary raid or a soldier with a flame-thrower. 'Bomber crews during the war got great satisfaction when they saw the incendiary blaze below them, but got no revenge urge' (Schrain, 1964, p. 1189). The author of this statement discusses in a most enlightening essay the problem of firemen as fire-raisers, showing the identity of approved and disapproved behaviours in one situation. He quotes one who said, 'I wanted to get the nozzle in my hand' (ibid, p. 1189), as illustrating the Freudian hypothesis on incendiarism.

This discussion is, however, concerned with the lesser problems described earlier; its argument is, simply, that for any behaviour there are approved, neutral, and disapproved forms and that the selection of the form may be accidental or deliberate and if deliberate may depend on knowledge or aptitude. Where the end of a behaviour may be distinguished from the behaviour itself, both the end and the behaviour may be approved, neutral, or disapproved. In that the object of many behaviours is the acquisition of wealth, the issue of the means to the end may be crucial, and it has been shown that there is much similarity between legal and illegal means to wealth and that the choice of means may well depend on chance, opportunity, or intelligence. In the case of violence the same situation obtains, so in both these broad areas of behaviour it is possible to suggest a theory of criminality based on knowledge and opportunity as it determines vocational choice. Such a theory would be consistent with the ideas propounded by Robert K. Merton in his discussion of adaptations to *anomie*, to which reference has been made, namely that for many persons there are structural barriers preventing them from achieving the culturally approved goals in society and leading them to the selection of careers of a disapproved kind (including crime). Thus the profession of crime can find a place in the general theory of vocational choice and opportunity.

One further point remains. The criminologist is much occupied with the persistent criminal, the recidivist. The writer, from his acquaintance with professional criminals and members of other groups over a broad spectrum in the approved, neutral, and disapproved continuum of occupations, finds no difference in this matter between the dedicated thief with a vocation and the persistent plumber or incorrigible undertaker, in fact sees no reason why the tendency of most persons to remain in one occupation should not apply to criminals as much as to lawyers or policemen.

A recent study by Mack based on a small number of case histories suggests an important theoretical distinction between the successful and the unsuccessful criminal. The first group he calls 'habitual criminals':

'The habitual criminals give the impression of psychological normality. Although their behaviour deviates sharply from the norms of the wider society, which favour law-abiding and property-and-person-respecting behaviour, the reasons for this deviance are not psycho-pathological; they refer to the social as distinct from the personal history of the criminals in question' (Mack, 1964, p. 50).

This conforms with the experience of the author in his dealings with the criminal organization described in the preface, although the author believes that the distribution is a continuum rather than bimodal.

Mack's second group are distinguished as 'habitual prisoners', who are, as he points out, the subject of most studies of criminals.

His investigation is remarkable for the conclusion that he draws from his knowledge of the successful criminal, which is:

'that criminality is a normal aspect of the social structure, a per-manent feature of any complex society, an ongoing social activity like the practice of medicine or police work or university teaching or stevedoring. It is sustained, like these other activities, by a subculture of people and groups most of whom are tolerably well-adjusted to their subculture and most of whose leaders are not only socially and personally competent but are also exceptionally able individuals. It is the latter, the successful criminals, who maintain and keep up to date the criminal system of activities. They thereby render it the more able to receive into its flinty bosom that less successful miscreant, the habitual prisoner, who is often of lower intelligence, who is often propelled into crime by pathological drives, and who is by the nature of the case more continuously accessible to clinical observation than is his abler colleague'.

He continues:

'One remaining and ever-recurring question remains to be con-sidered. How do these so-called able and non-pathological crimi-nals come to take up a criminal way of life? It is clear from all the existing evidence, which is derived mainly from the study of delinquent neighbourhoods, that even a minority of the young learners enter into the criminal subculture as life members. What is it that propels into crime those of them who are not crime-susceptible on pathological grounds but who nevertheless become full-time criminals? It is almost invariably assumed in discussion of this point that the propellant or selective factor must be patho-logical, or at least derivable from some special developmental circumstances in the personal history or family group-environment of the person concerned. But this simply begs the question at issue. It is perfectly feasible to hold that the same process is at work in the production of normal criminals as operates in the manning of the ranks of sociologists, or policemen, or decision makers, or any other more respectable occupational group. It is simply that process of social selection which is to be found in all social systems and which in our particular social system works by a combination of chance, choice, and paternal cheque book' (ibid, pp. 52 and 53).

Mack does not, however, consider that in a complex society most persons can find occupations which match their attributes of physique, intelligence, and personality and that his 'psycho-pathically propelled individuals' are equally a part of normal society who have first of all failed to find a satisfactory vocation and, having once fallen into the hands of the police, become socialized and adapted to intermittent prison life and in due course become identified as the 'criminal' of stereotype, and, as such, are material for the functional role of scapegoat.

CHAPTER SEVEN

The Prison, and the Criminal as Scapegoat

THE QUALITIES OF PRISON

Of all human institutions prison is the most remarkable. It has been developed empirically, almost accidentally, and although it is in a state of continuous change it is one of the few institutions that exist in an almost identical form in all modern cultures.

It is of interest to list the functions that prison is believed to perform better than any other institution.

1. It makes the dishonest honest.
2. It makes the aggressive docile.
3. It makes the perjurer truthful.
4. It makes the contemptuous respectful.
5. It makes the bigamous monogamous.
6. It makes the homosexual heterosexual.
7. It makes the traitor loyal.
8. It makes the debtor willing to pay his debts.

This is a brief epitome of a list which could run into thousands of items.

Not only does prison perform these functions for prisoners, but it does two other things. It prevents some persons from being dishonest, homosexual, etc., and it also gives pleasure or satisfaction to the honest, the loyal, and the heterosexual, etc., when they become aware of the imprisonment of the dishonest, the disloyal, and the homosexual, etc.

The development of new variations of prison is a continuous preoccupation of criminologists, priests, voluntary societies, and bodies created especially for the purpose. One such body, a committee of the Home Department, has presented its views in a document *Penal Practice in a Changing Society*. The main lines of this report are set out in the following paragraphs.

'Existing penal methods have of necessity been developed piecemeal and empirically in response to experience and to the pressure of current problems. Experience is always a valuable guide and the immediate problem often an inescapable one, but in a society which changes as rapidly as ours something more is needed if penal methods are to be related effectively to the purposes which they are required to serve. We need periodically to consider whether existing methods are the best that can be devised for dealing with crime in the context of society as it is at a given time. As crime is related to the pattern and outlook of the society in which it occurs, so penal methods may need to be adapted to the society in which they must operate' (*Penal Practice*, 1959, p. 6).

What is implied here is not a criticism of prison as such but a recognition of the need to adapt to new kinds of offence created by social change and to adjust the régime of prison to keep the degree of relative deprivation under control as social change occurs, more specifically, to adjust to the rising standard of living outside prison.

The report does go on to consider fundamentals.

'A fundamental re-examination of penal methods, based on studies of the causes of crime, or rather of the factors which foster or inhibit crime, and supported by a reliable assessment of the result achieved by existing methods, could be a landmark in penal history and illumine the course ahead for a generation. Such a re-examination, though based on practical studies, need not – and indeed should not – be purely pragmatic. If it were not merely to assess past progress, but also to point the way forward, it must concern itself with the philosophy as well as the practice of punishment. It must consider the fundamental concepts underlying our treatment of offenders, and examine not only the obligations of society and the offender to one another, but also the obligations of both to the victim. The basis of early law was personal reparation by the offender to the victim, a concept of which modern criminal law has almost completely lost sight. The assumption that the claims of the victim are sufficiently satisfied if the offender is punished by society becomes less persuasive as society in its dealings with offenders increasingly emphasises the reformative aspects of punishment. Indeed in the public mind the interests of the offender may not infrequently seem to be placed before those of his victim' (ibid, p. 7).

The report discusses the function of punishment by making reparation as a part of the social relationship between the victim and the criminal, but seems curiously unaware of the way in which strict liability has replaced the concept of fault in civil law and has had exactly the opposite effect to that intended here.

'This is certainly not the correct emphasis. It may well be that our penal system would not only provide a more effective deterrent to crime, but would also find a greater moral value, if the concept of personal reparation to the victim were added to the concepts of deterrence by punishment and of reform by training. It is also possible to hold that the redemptive value of punishment to the individual offender would be greater than if it were made to include a realisation of the injury he had done to his victim as well as to the order of society, and the need to make personal reparation for that injury. The realisation of this concept could, however, be considered only in the context of such a general re-examination of penal philosophy and practice as is suggested above' (ibid, p. 7).

'Until we are ready for the more fundamental examination, there is still much to be done, as this Paper illustrates. Existing forms of penal treatment, continuously adjusted to the light of deeper insight and greater information must be developed to the limit of the good we believe to be in them. Only when their potential power to turn men from crime has been fully tested can we judge how far other methods may be required to reinforce and, if need be, to replace them' (ibid, p. 7).

The statement of the general aim of prisons is given a more precise formulation in a later paragraph, thus:

'The constructive function of our prisons is to prevent the largest possible number of those committed to their care from offending again. Since the report of the Gladstone Committee in 1895, it has been accepted that this end will not be reached by a regime designed simply to deter through fear. The object should be, in the words of that Committee, to send the prisoners out " 'better men and women, physically and morally' than when they came in".

For a generation past our prisons have sought increasingly to give practical effect to this concept of the function of imprisonment, which was specifically endorsed by Parliament in Rule 6 of the Prison Rules made under the Criminal Justice Act, 1948, which runs as follows:—

"6. The purpose of training and treatment of convicted prisoners shall be to establish in them the will to lead a good and useful life on discharge, and to fit them to do so" ' (ibid, p. 11).

The methods by which prison achieves its objects are various, but in all a few central elements are found.

Thus it is believed that 'The deterrent effect of prison must finally lie in the loss of personal *liberty* and *all that this involves.*'

The term 'liberty' is used here, probably, in apposition to 'slavery' and has political overtones: it is rarely discussed in sociological terms.

The assumption implied here – that 'all that this involves' is known, that its effects are understood, and that it has general approval – is interesting and quite false.

It may well be useful, therefore, to consider the social characteristics of prison life and civil life in order better to perceive the therapeutic value of the former.

What will be attempted is, first, a general discussion of the social system of the prison, using the evidence of the prison commissioners themselves, and then an examination of the sociological literature of the prison using three classic studies, *The Prison Community* (1958) by Donald Clemmer, *The Society of Captives* (1958) by Gresham M. Sykes, and *Pentonville* (1963) by Terence Morris, Pauline Morris, and Barbara Barer. All these studies have to a greater or lesser degree the defect that they are concerned with reform, *Pentonville* perhaps most of all and *The Society of Captives* least. In spite of this, the studies have added enormously to knowledge and *Pentonville* in particular is of great importance because it describes English conditions and confirms many of the general findings of the American studies. What is perhaps most striking is the contrast between the 'prisoner-centred' approach of the Home Office and the 'total society' approach of the social scientist, which recognizes the prison officer as a part of the social system. In this discussion an attempt will be made to extend this concept further and to include the wider society, which, by political actions, based on a system of beliefs, determines the nature of prison society.

First, the general social characteristics of prison must be considered. In civil life the citizen is generally a member of a family, a working group, a neighbourhood group, and a local community that has a wide range of interest groups, a complete age range, and an infinite variety of social relationships. Most adults have socio-sexual relationships of a permanent, continuous, and, usually, heterosexual pattern. In prison, in contrast, the social relationships are temporary (for the duration of the sentence) and compulsory (generally based on residence in a cell, cell block, or landing and on work, though in some prisons interest groups can arise). The age range is narrow, and socio-sexual relationships are exclusively homosexual. The segregation of the sexes has been considered a major achievement of prison reform.

The situation may be judged from the report on the local prisons in the report to which reference has been already made.

'These local prisons, holding more prisoners than they have ever held before, now have to house some 6,000 men sleeping three in a single cell. Moreover they are in themselves quite unfitted to modern conceptions of penal treatment, built as they were 100 years or more ago to serve the purposes of solitary confinement, treadmill hard labour and brutal repression. They stand as a monumental denial of the principles to which we are committed' (*Penal Practice*, 1959, pp. 13 and 14).

In the *Report of the Commissioners of Prisons for the Year* 1960, the number sleeping three in a cell in all prisons was given as 7,200 and in 1962 it was over 8,000 (*Prison Officers Magazine*, Vol. 52, No. 4, p. 91, 1962).

It is interesting that the pattern of accommodation adopted is either of one in a cell or of three in a cell designed for one, for, although physical conditions would be more comfortable with two in a cell, it has been argued that homosexual relations are less likely to occur with three men rather than two. However, the evidence for this assumption has not been published.

There is some evidence of social isolation of some groups of offenders, notably certain classes of sexual offender.

The socio-political structure of civil society is democratic and largely permissive, although authoritarian elements are found in industry.

In prisons the systems found range from simple authoritarian patterns with military analogies (it is still common to find high military personnel as prison governors, as it was formerly among chief constables) to authoritarian-paternal systems.

Morris in his Pentonville study described the previous careers of fifty-two prison officers, all of whom had served in the armed forces. He did not distinguish between conscripts and volunteers, but the majority must have volunteered for part of their service since they had served over seven years. It is apparent that, for many, prison service is a form of authoritarian total society, like the armed forces, to which the former soldier, sailor, or airman readily adapts. Fifteen of the fifty-two had come direct from the forces, and Morris comments of those who had had other work that 'these jobs had been held for only a very short time, and had represented the ex-serviceman's attempt to find a niche in civilian life; dissatisfaction had initiated the man's application to join the Prison Service' (Morris *et al.*, 1963, pp. 76 and 77).

In a written answer to a question in Parliament on 24 April 1967, Mr Roy Jenkins, then Home Secretary, stated: 'Thirty-seven per cent of the men and nine per cent of the women in the prison service were formerly regular members of H.M. Forces: the overall percentage is thirty-six.' He concluded his answer by saying: 'Applications to join the prison service by former members of the forces are welcome: we already have close liaison with the army resettlement centres at Aldershot and Catterick, and are currently in touch with the War Department to see if there are any other ways in which members of the services expecting to be retired can be made aware of the opportunities available in the prison service.'

This is a subject which deserves attention from two points of view: the influence of the norms of military society on the prison system and the effects of total social systems on the capacity of their members to adjust to civil society. The problems of adjustment facing the prisoner and the prison officer are of the same nature.

Goffman discusses these problems with great perception. He shows that the same fundamental behaviour problems arise in all total institutions. He gives examples from the merchant navy, mental hospitals, reformatory institutions for children, prisoner-of-war camps, concentration camps, prison, the armed forces, and religious orders. He shows that socialization is an interaction process affecting the prisoner and his guard and the patient and the doctor. Of particular interest is the pattern in which the inmate takes over some of the treatment, punishment, and custodial roles (Goffman, 1961, p. 4 *et seq.*).

There are, in addition to the official social systems, unofficial systems. These arise from sexual exploitation, trading in tobacco, (the supply of which is left well below the demand by the authorities), and unofficial relationships between prison officers and prisoners. These systems are secret and conspiratorial in nature and have few counterparts in civil society.

The status system of civil society is based on income, occupation, education, and participation in community affairs. Very little of this carries over into the prison system, and the limited range of job opportunities in prison favours the unskilled labourer and the craftsman rather than the professional man. The plumber can always establish a functional status, but the marine underwriter (with the disappearance of the prison hulk) can aspire only to a position in the library at best. The provision of work and training in prison is controlled by the external influence of the trade union movement, which is opposed to work done by prisoners (at small wages) that might reduce the employment or earnings of its members, and does not always recognize skills acquired in prison as equivalent to apprenticeship. The bulk of the work done by prisoners is in the running and maintenance of the prison and its ancillary institutions, including farms; in 1960 rather less than half of all prisoners, 11,694 out of 24,514, were engaged in manufactures; of these, 3,785 were making or repairing mailbags (Morris *et al.*, 1963, pp. 23 and 24).

In that status in civil society is closely related to earnings, it would be expected that the prisoner's status would also be so affected within the prison system itself and within his family, since on his earnings depends his capacity to continue to support them. In a money economy, income can also determine the expression of interest or affection through gifts: although prisoners often make contributions in kind to children, hospitals, and other sections of the civil community their capacity to give is greatly limited by their low earnings. The situation is illustrated in the report from the governor of a local prison: 'One may speak generally of the "type" but I never cease to be amazed at the individual in the type. At Christmas, two of the biggest scallywags and ill-behaved rogues I have ever had in my service bought Christmas cards at the canteen with their own money and sent them to me. Another, of little better conduct, made applications to send a pound of his own cash to the Congo fund for the children (*Penal Practice*, 1959, p. 87).

The report on *Penal Practice in a Changing Society* describes the situation thus:

'In this country before the war the system had been adopted of making payments known as "earnings", which though trifling in themselves were found to serve as a substantial incentive to prisoners to work faster and better. This system, with minor adjustments, has continued to the present time with occasional increases in the average level, which is now about 2s. 8d. a week. It not only provides an incentive to effort, but also allows the prisoner to have something to spend which he has earned and to think about how he shall spend it. This has a training value in more than one way. It does, for example, allow the prisoner the opportunity, rare in a prison, to do something unselfish for somebody else. It is remarkable how much of these small sums is spent in the canteens on Christmas and birthday cards, or on chocolates for the children when they visit' (ibid, p. 17).

It should, however, be mentioned that a prisoner in the last months of a long sentence is sometimes allowed to work outside prison in normal industry for normal wages, out of which he pays for his keep, maintains his dependants, and pays his national insurance contributions. The number of such prisoners is very small.

Another contrast between civil, social life and prison life is in clothing and personal possessions. The prisoner has few personal possessions, and his uniform clothing is his only on a temporary basis and may or may not be new when it is issued to him. In civil life the personality is to a large extent organized around possessions which express in a tangible form interests and emotions. Variety in clothing is likewise important. The question of dress is particularly important to women and the quotation from the report of the Prison Commissioners for 1961 is revealing.

'Plans to improve the women's and girls' clothing have progressed during the year. An experimental trial of nylon stockings was carried out at Cardiff prison and borstal. It was successful and these stockings will shortly be introduced generally. New pattern dresses, in three styles, have been made and tried out at Hill Hall. This was also a success and general production will begin next year. These dresses are of modern design and less institutional in appearance than the old pattern. Plans are well forward for issuing every woman serving a sentence over three months with her own personal kit of knickers and vest, as has been done for the women with long sentences. Nylon hair brushes, also on a personal basis, have already been issued. These measures are the beginnings of a comprehensive plan to make the clothes more stylish, more adult, and with the introduction of a winter uniform, warmer in cold weather' (p. 51).

Morris describes the very poor quality, ill fit, and shortages of clothing in Pentonville. His comments on footwear are sufficient to illustrate the subject:

'Footwear is very solid, and although initially satisfactory, is frequently inadequate owing to the fact that the reception issue is almost wholly second – or sometimes third or fourth-hand. Shoes worn originally by one man day after day for several months tend to distort to the shape of his feet, which is unlikely to coincide with that of the subsequent wearers. A few men, with acute foot trouble, do complain and are allowed on medical grounds to wear their own shoes. The prison does not, however, undertake to repair these shoes when they wear out and does not permit their replacement' (Morris *et al.*, 1963, p. 35).

It is worth observing that every year the government disposes of large quantities of a wide range of clothing and footwear from service stores at very low prices. It is unlikely, therefore, that the system of self-maintenance in clothing in prison is economically justified.

Morris also comments on the very high standards of clothing of young people committed to prison and on the fact that they are often conscious of fashion. The wearing of second-hand clothing not only destroys individuality, but in our culture is reserved for the poorest and most degraded. There are, in addition, residual taboos against things that have been in contact with the bodies of others.

Another element in the social system of prison that distinguishes it from civil society is institutionalized religion. In prison there is a higher level of attendance at religious services and greater contact with the clergy. Finally, there are training and general educational facilities for which there is no exact equivalent in social life (Morris *et al.*, 1963, p. 39).

As in civil society, there is a problem of social control and there are offences and punishments. This raises an interesting question: if prison is designed to fit a man for civil society, what can be derived from 'education' using the word in its broadest sense to fit him for prison?

The morale of the male prison can be deduced from a consideration both of offences and of punishments; the list of offences includes:

Violence against officers
Violence against prisoners
Damage to property
Escapes, attempts to escape, and breaches of parole
Idleness
Trafficking in and being in possession of unauthorized articles
Insubordination, which includes disobedience of any order
Disrespect towards any officer or authorized person visiting the prison
Abusive, insolent, violent, threatening, or other improper language
Leaving a cell, place of work, or other appointed place without permission
Meeting or incitement to meeting, and indecent language, act, or gesture

Communication with another prisoner without authority, committing any nuisance, repeated and groundless complaints, false and malicious allegations against an officer, offending against good order and discipline in any other way.

The punishment system takes the main quality of prison, social isolation, even further. The list of types of punishment includes corporal punishment, cellular confinement, restricted diet, exclusion from associated work, forfeiture of remission (or postponement of eligibility for release), forfeiture or postponement or suspension of privileges, stoppage or reduction of earnings, and cautioning.

In both borstal institutions and detention centres extra work or fatigues are imposed as punishment, thus helping to establish in the young mind an association between work and punishment. In borstal institutions an additional punishment not found in other institutions is the forfeiture of letters and additional visits, the reduction of communication with the outside world.

In prison a number of different punishments are often awarded together.

Corporal punishment is very rare and can be given only upon the recommendation of the Visiting Committee or Board of Visitors and confirmed by the Secretary of State for the Home Department. Strokes of the birch are thought to be appropriate punishment for gross personal violence to prison officers and incitement to mutiny, and in recommendations by Visitors to the Secretary of State such explanations as the following are given:

'The offence was vicious and unprovoked and corporal punishment was the only punishment likely to deter other attacks.'

'Corporal punishment was necessary in view of the prisoner's record and for the maintenance of discipline.' [1]

It is noteworthy that the murder, by any method, of a prison officer or his assistant (and of policemen) was until 1965 one of

[1] Corporal punishment in civil prisons was abolished by Section 65 of the Criminal Justice Act 1967 (c. 80).

the worst offences known to English law in peace time and was punished by hanging. The murder of any other person, unless it was in furtherance of theft, or by firearm or explosive, or in attempting to escape from custody, or unless it was a second murder, was punished by imprisonment. The offence ranked with high treason, piracy with violence, and setting fire to the Queen's ships or naval stores but not aircraft (Du Cann, 1960, pp. 246-249).

This description of the prison system must be extended to cover the classification of prisoners and their distribution in prisons of different types. The first division is into untried persons, criminal prisoners, and civil prisoners. The convicted persons may be sentenced to imprisonment, corrective training, or preventive detention.

Classification takes place with the following aims.

'First the separation of the sexes, of young prisoners from adults, of untried prisoners from convicted prisoners, and of civil prisoners from criminal prisoners; second, among convicted prisoners, the prevention of "contamination" of the better by the worse [the possibility that the worse might be contaminated by the better appears not to have been considered – D. C.]; third, among those convicted prisoners for whom positive training is possible, the provision of training appropriate to their needs' (*Report on Prisons*, 1960, p. 11).

Convicted prisoners are then divided into classes:

'1. Prisoners under 21 years of age are placed in the Young Prisoners' Class.
2. Prisoners of 21 years of age and over who have not previously been in prison on conviction are placed in the Star class unless the reception board considers that, in view of their record or character, they are likely to have a bad influence on others. The reception board may also place in the Star class a prisoner of 21 years of age and over who has previously been in prison on conviction if it is satisfied, having regard to the nature of the previous offence, or to the length of time since it was committed, or to the prisoner's general record and character, that he is not likely to have a bad influence on others.
3. Other prisoners are placed in the Ordinary class' (ibid, p. 111).

The importance of this system is that the Star prisoner is much more likely to go to a regional training prison: 'the population of a regional training prison is made up of 70 per cent of "stars", with 30 per cent of "ordinaries" whose records suggest some hope that they are not beyond rehabilitation (ibid, p. 112). Moreover, only Stars go to the open prisons where the prisoner is not wholly cut off from the social life of the community.

The full consequences of this multiple filtering system have not been fully examined, but two effects are apparent. The kinds of offence for which the middle classes are found guilty appear to lead to training or open prisons, while a small group of working-class criminals who receive a second sentence are likely to be subject to processes that reduce their connection with normal social life.

This group, known to the criminologist as the recidivist group, is regarded with special interest, and the question is posed: How is it that such persons return to prison again and again; that is, why does prison 'fail'?

It is now proposed to change tack and examine some of these data in the light of sociological theory.

The sociology of prison, as distinct from the criticism of prisons by social scientists, derives from two sources: the American studies, of which the works of Clemmer and Sykes are the most important, and on which the study of Pentonville was largely modelled, and accounts by political prisoners of their experiences in many countries. This latter source has an experimental quality, since political or racial prisoners are not considered evil (or in some cases are not so considered) as are criminals, and often, if they move to another society, are regarded as virtuous or even heroic. The effects of prison can in these cases be separated, intellectually, from innate wickedness (Taylor, 1960, pp. 65-69). This is true also of prisoners of war.

The central issue is the effect of prison on the prisoner's capacity to adjust to civil society. In adopting this approach, the sociologist largely abandons the idea of the prisoner's consciously accepting punishment as a just retribution and resolving to behave differently upon release, and concentrates on the problems of the prisoner in adapting and adjusting to a new social system.

Prisons are examples of total social system: that is, social systems in which the members are to a greater or lesser degree isolated from the society in which the total system exists.

The degree of totality is measured by the hours of the day, days of the week, and years of life that the member spends in the system, and the extent to which the system meets his needs. Another measure is the degree to which communication is restricted within the system and between the system and the external world.

In most total systems the design is intended to achieve certain ends and can be appraised in terms of its success or failure – thus the monastic system isolates its members from those features of normal life which conflict with the precepts of religion, and communication with man is reduced, but communication with God is increased. In the case of the armed forces, separation from civil society, including the stationing of units away from home, permits the use of the military in politics, which incidentally presents a constant danger to the civil administration. It also allows the use of troops in labour disputes. The armed forces are likewise isolated from the normative order which might conflict with their military role, in the taking of life, for example. Religious teaching and worship are separated from that of civil society, the clergy having the status of officers. The mental hospital isolates the patient from hostility and discrimination during his sickness, and the boarding-school permits a level of social training, learning, and indoctrination which would be impossible in the conflicting situation of normal life, which is spent in part at home and in part at school.

Total social systems can be subdivided according to whether they are systems in which the members spend their whole lives or only part of their lifetime, and, in the latter case, according to whether they adapt the member on leaving the system to the world outside.

The public school in Britain may be considered as a system of the latter type, since it prepares its members for an elite within the larger society; in it, but not wholly of it.

Prison has all the qualities of a total institution. The maximum security establishment and the practice of solitary and close confinement exemplify its most extreme form. Compared with some total institutions, there is confusion in the design of the system, so that, unlike the public school boys, who live in isolation from which they join society as members of a socialized elite, prisoners emerge as desocialized outcasts (Goffman, 1961, p. 74 *et seq.*).

The studies of Sykes, Clemmer, and Morris identify the goals of the custodians and then show the social processes which arise when the prisoners attempt to meet their own needs within the framework imposed. The equilibrium reached is a form of socialization quite unlike anything in the outside world.

Clemmer locates the 'prisonized man' on a scale indicating the degree to which he has been affected by the social system of the prison – from least to most. This schema he expands chapter by chapter until he has built up a complete picture of a total culture. His 'schemata of prisonization' epitomize the social factors and their effects on the inmates.

'With knowledge of these determinants we can hypothetically construct schemata of prisonization which may serve to illustrate its extremes. In the least or lowest degree of prisonization the following may be enumerated.

1. A short sentence, thus a brief subjection to the universal factors of prisonization.
2. A fairly stable personality made stable by an adequacy of positive and "socialized" relationships during pre-penal life.
3. The continuance of positive relationships with persons outside the walls.
4. Refusal or inability to integrate into a prison primary group or semi-primary group, while yet maintaining a symbiotic balance in relations with other men.
5. Refusal to accept blindly the dogmas and codes of the population, and a willingness, under certain situations, to aid officials, thus making for identification with the free community.
6. A chance placement with a cellmate and workmates who do not possess leadership qualities and who are also not completely integrated into the prison culture.
7. Refraining from abnormal sex behaviour, and excessive gambling, and a ready willingness to engage seriously in work and recreative activities.

Other factors no doubt have an influencing force in obstructing the process of prisonization, but the seven points mentioned seem outstanding.

In the highest or greatest degree of prisonization the following factors may be enumerated:

1. A sentence of many years, thus a long subjection to the universal factors of prisonization.
2. A somewhat unstable personality made unstable by an inadequacy of "socialized" relations before commitment, but possessing, none the less, a capacity for strong convictions and a particular kind of loyalty.
3. A dearth of positive relations with persons outside the walls.
4. A readiness and a capacity for integration into a prison primary group.
7. A blind, or almost blind, acceptance of the dogmas and mores of the primary group and the general population.
6. A chance placement with other persons of a similar orientation.
7. A readiness to participate in gambling and abnormal sex behaviour' (Clemmer, 1958, Ch. XII).

Whereas Clemmer tends to separate the organization of the prison from the social processes, Sykes adopts a more specifically functional analysis with results that are not less illuminating.

In his study Sykes (1958), like Morris, deals with a maximum security prison and considers it from the point of view of the administration. In 'The Regime of the Custodians' he describes the hierarchy of functions of the prison thus: 'The task of Custody', 'The task of Internal Order', 'The task of Self Maintenance', 'The task of Punishment', and last and least, 'The task of Reform'.

This list displays the incompatibility of the many functions of prison and the order of priority controls the extent to which prison reduces the capacity of the prisoner to lead a normal life outside.

The importance of custody has been underestimated in the British literature, although in his study of Pentonville Morris gives the facts about, but does not fully display the influence of the task of custody on, the ideology of prison life. To some extent this is the result of an ambivalence, one of the many such, in the general ideology of prison.

The details of detention, the walls, the locks, the stripped and padded cells, the canvas suits, and the rest of the artifacts of detention are repugnant, yet the effectiveness of custody is a measure of the efficiency of the system (Morris *et al.*, 1963, pp. 15 and 16, and pp. 123-160).

The situation was demonstrated in a dramatic form in 1964, when a highly successful train robber, who had been sentenced to thirty years' imprisonment, was rescued by friends from Winson Green Prison in Birmingham. The event was the subject of very wide comment, in the press, on the radio, and on television. The opposition in Parliament used it to mount an attack on the Home Office and the prison service. The Home Office in turn carried out an inquiry into the escape.

In such circumstances the external pressures on the prison service are very great and are the cause of conflicts between the needs of custody and those of rehabilitation. The fact that a failure in custody becomes known to the public and is made the subject of recrimination makes it unlikely that the needs of rehabilitation will come first (ibid, p. 131).

The consequences of the escape of some of the train robbers have confirmed this observation. Those remaining are now in conditions of maximum security in close confinement, and have been under military guard. In view of their ages and the length of their sentences, the likelihood of their becoming completely desocialized is perhaps of academic interest only.

It could be argued that the evidence of the deterrent effect of prison depends largely on the number of prisoners who find prison so unpleasant that they make efforts to escape, risking further punishment if they fail in their attempt. If this argument is accepted, then an index of the deterrent effect of prison could be calculated using, with other factors, the annual number of escapes. Such a statistic might relieve the Home Office and the prison officer of much opprobrium and hostility, since the evidence that is now produced as an indication of failure would become a measure of success.

In addition to the use of mechanical restraints, prison uses punishment and above all creates a moral order to control the general tendency to escape. It is this socialization or prisonization which conflicts most obviously with the function of prison to rehabilitate.

P

The punishment system for the prisoner who prepares for an escape, for example by making a key, or who attempts to escape and fails, demonstrates in an extreme form the underlying ethics of the prison system. The offender loses remission of sentence, may be put on to a restricted diet, may be put into solitary confinement, may be denied association with other prisoners in work or at other times, may be compelled to wear clothing with identifying patches, and may be moved to another prison which is believed to be more secure. All these are processes which reduce the normal socialization of the subject (ibid, pp. 131-135).

The general ethic of the prison is one in which the 'good' prisoner, from the point of view of both the prison officer and the prisoners, is one who conforms to the rules and to the informal system so that his behaviour is predictable and life can run smoothly (ibid, p. 301).

The escapee does, however, perform a symbolic function for the conforming prisoner and provides the opportunity by which other prisoners may gain favours or status by informing. This pattern, which is found in some monastic institutions and in some political organizations, contrasts with the more common pattern of total social systems like the armed forces and the public school, where tale-bearing is disapproved of by leaders and followers alike. It is of interest that this carries over into civil life; the police depend to a considerable extent on 'information received' in the detection of crime.

More important than the system of restraints and punishments is the prison regime itself. This operates on the one hand to create an identity of the prisoner with prison and on the other to reduce the attraction of civil society. To this latter end, letters and visits are restricted and press, radio, and television are censored (ibid, p. 301). At this point the 'Task of Custody' merges with the task of internal order, and it follows that the more the prisoner resembles a docile animal, the easier this becomes. Clemmer, Sykes, and Morris all describe the process by which the life of the prisoner is so taken up by detailed regulation and supervision that he is deprived of personal autonomy and reduced to the status of a child, even to the use of a chamber pot (ibid, p. 262).

Of the other tasks of prison little more need be said, since the evidence given earlier is merely repeated in these studies. It shows that self-maintenance provides a minimal opportunity for the development of normal social relationships, status, or interest; and that punishment is seen as the function preventing apparently obvious changes in the routine that would permit the development of social relationships or raise status. The task of reform is little understood, since by previous experience mainly military, by education mainly elementary, and by personality mainly authoritarian the prison officer is fitted for his task of custody and order by the very qualities that unfit him for the task of reform.

The prison system is the product of the intentions of the Home Office, controlled by its resources made available by Parliament, interpreted by prison governors, and executed by prison officers and prisoners, all heavily influenced in a period of rapid change by former patterns of administration. In that the prison population – governor, prison officers, and prisoners – are primarily concerned with the day-to-day working of their community, it is likely that their concern will be fundamentally different from that of those outside the service, and in situations of policy conflict the interest of the internal community may be more pressing than that of civil society.

In general, the issue is expressed in terms of hard versus soft practices. The prison officers appear to play a very small part in the overall design of prison administration, so the conflict often takes place on the ground of 'theory' versus 'experience' (ibid, p. 254 *et seq.*).

The conflict between the humane intentions and the reality of prison can be detected in the articles and letters in the *Prison Officers' Magazine*, which not only expresses discontent with almost every aspect of prison service – housing, pay, hours, even the material from which the officers' gloves are made – but also exhibits a widespread opposition to prison reform. This opposition is not simply negative; alternative policies are proposed, some of which would make conditions in prison harder for the inmates.

Pauline Morris has described the conflict between the humane intentions of the Home Office and the socio-administrative system of the prison which arises from the rigid hierarchical system of control and the elaborate rules governing the prison officers' conduct. Her observations are particularly important from the point of view of the sociology of social change.

'In the main it would seem that fundamental problems originate from the ambiguities of the prison system itself, and the emotive and intellectual conflicts that they impose on the prison staff. There is not only the apparent dichotomy of containment and re-form, but a further divergence between the idea of "social service" (which occupies a significant place in the recruiting literature) and the requirements of the discipline code for officers. In one context the officer is expected to use his initiative positively, to do his job well, and to expedite the process of reform; while in another he is required to adhere to a complex system of rules devised for the day-to-day administration of the prison. This conflicting situation seems to arise partly because Rules and Standing Orders have never been fundamentally altered to keep in line with modern policy, and partly because of the hierarchical structure of the staff which inhibits those in the lower echelons (and often more senior staff too) from taking initiative and accepting responsibility. The majority of officers *prefer* a simple system of clear and unam-biguous objectives and they are reluctant to accept new ideas because of the increased flexibility of the regime which frequently accompanies them. On the other hand there is a large minority of officers who languish under the rigidity and "dependency" which many of the senior uniformed staff impose upon them and would prefer a greater degree of autonomy which would, incidentally, accelerate the move of prison officers towards professional status.

The Discipline Code to which the prison officer is subject is as com-prehensive in its details as that part of the Prison Rules which governs the conduct of prisoners. To take but one example, trafficking is considered one of the most serious offences against the Discipline Code, but there is no differentiation made between the officer who systematically supplies goods for financial gain and the officer who gives a cigarette spontaneously as part of a genuinely warm relationship with a prisoner. Similarly, whilst officers are encouraged to take an interest in the personal prob-lems of men whilst they are in prison, and to work to the ideal of Rule 6, which states that "the purposes of training and treatment of convicted prisoners shall be to establish in them the will to lead a good and useful life to do so", at the same time they are ex-pressly forbidden to have any communication whatsoever with a man after discharge' (Morris, P., 1963, pp. 5 and 6).

One of the fundamental issues is that the behaviour required of a good prisoner – one approved of by his prison officers and likely to gain full remission – is that of complete and rapid adaptation to the social system of the prison (not necessarily conforming to the rules) (Goffman, 1961, p. 87 *et seq.*).

The social structure of the prison is distinguished by the basic hostility of the prisoners to the aims of prison, combined with a unity of interest of prisoners and prison staff in securing tranquillity. This is the general moral order, but subsystems arise around individual leaders and predators, traders, bookmakers, tobacco merchants, and others.

Morris, Morris, and Biely discuss the conflict thus:

'The function of leadership also varies. It can provide a kind of long-term solidarity expressed in emotional terms – the "we" continually opposed to the "they". In so doing, inmate leadership helps to lessen the pains of imprisonment; it keeps a picture of the arbitrary injustices of the prison regime constantly in the forefront of the prisoner's mind and continually reasserts those unchanging values of inmate culture – "doing your own bird", never grassing – which, come what may, cannot be eradicated by the staff. Alternatively, the function of leadership may be merely to enable individual inmates to combine in order to exploit their fellows whom the prison authorities are generally unable (and sometimes unwilling) to protect. This type of leadership tends to disrupt the unity of inmate society, for it gives rise to the development of "protective" associations which frequently exploit in their turn. To the extent to which feuds and factions develop, inmate solidarity and resistance to custodial authority is diminished' (Morris *et al.*, 1961, p. 3).

This social system, as the authors most clearly display, presents problems to both the staff and the prisoners.

Sufficient has been written already about this system to suggest that the prisoner, particularly the first offender, is faced with a major problem of resettlement, the more rapid the adjustment the greater being the degree of approval (and the shorter the length of the sentence which is served). On the other hand, the greater the success of the adjustment to prison, the more difficult the readjustment to civil life, unless the two systems are similar. Terence Morris expresses the dilemma thus: 'men cannot be trained to accept social responsibility in conditions which, at their most extreme, reduce them to a state of near infantile dependency (Morris *et al.*, 1963).

W. F. R. Macartney, describing his own experience in Dartmoor, devotes a chapter to a particular but central problem of the difficult process whereby a heterosexual adjusts first to auto-eroticism and then to homosexuality (Macartney, 1936, pp. 481 and 426; Morris *et al.*, 1963, p. 184 *et seq.*).

As has already been described, docile acceptance of the system is the norm; inciting the major crime and attempting to escape, that is to return to civil society as quickly as possible, is heavily punished and the whole design of the prison is based on the need to prevent this.

The situation can perhaps be best appreciated by considering the position of prisoners of war or of concentration camp inmates. The question is frequently asked as it was at the Eichmann Trial 'Why did they not revolt?', 'Why did they not attempt to escape?'. The answer must be the same for all prisons, that the social system, the moral order, and the administrative system are designed to induce conformity and make the prisoner acquiesce in the demands of his captors.

The security prison recognizes the possibility of failure in the moral order. The open prison demonstrates the superiority as well as the economy of psycho-social techniques over physical ones: the prisoners are deprived even of the wish to run away.

The literature of prison, except that referred to here, including the reports of the Commissioners of Prisons and such special reports as *Penal Practice in a Changing Society*, displays an ambivalence and a 'rationality' that takes little account of sociological knowledge.

The 'reasons' for this are many. The prison system is an historical accident, prison reform arose out of the gross economic and physical exploitation of prisoners by gaolers. Among those most responsible for this reform were the Quakers, whose centuries-old campaign has been crowned with the appointment of a Quaker as Chief Director of the Prison Commission and of another as a Commissioner. One of the triumphs of Quaker influence has been the segregation of the sexes in prison, although this might equally be attributed to the general hostility to sexuality in nineteenth-century ideology. Rationality is associated in prison design with Bentham and with the Quaker system from Philadelphia, which imposed total isolation and total silence on the prisoner. Prison practice in the nineteenth century was accompanied with appropriate social theory:

'The du Cane regime, far from following public opinion, was successful in directing it to some extent. Men and women went into prison as people. They came out as Lombrosian animals, shorn and cropped, hollow-cheeked, and frequently, as a result of dietary deficiencies and lack of sunlight, seriously ill with tuberculosis. They came out mentally numbed and some of them insane; they became the creatures, ugly, and brutish in appearance, stupid and resentful in behaviour, unemployable and emotionally unstable, which the Victorian middle classes came to visualize whenever they thought of prisoners. Much of the prejudice against prisoners which remains today may be due to this conception of them not as the commonplace, rather weak people the majority of them really are, but as a composite caricature of the distorted personalities produced by du Cane's machine' (Howard, 1960, p. 105).

The ambivalence in the ideology of prison expresses itself in such practices as preventive detention, maximum security prisons, the discipline system, corporal punishment, and hanging on the one hand, and classification, the star system, the Norwich system, open prisons, after-care, the psychological service, and the like on the other.

Other features of the situation are that, owing to low pay and poor housing, there is a shortage of prison officers, a situation leading to overtime, fatigue, and a tendency to hostility to the service which is sometimes projected onto the prisoner. The *Prison Officers' Magazine* gives a continuous commentary on the effects of wages and conditions on the morale of the force. These facts have been acknowledged too in *Penal Practice in a Changing Society* and in the Report of the Committee on Remuneration and Conditions of Certain Grades in the Prison Service (Cmnd. 544, 1958).[1]

[1] It is revealing that when the physique of the population generally has shown a dramatic improvement the physical standards for prison officers has been reduced from 5 ft 7 in to 5 ft 6 in and the requirement that they should weigh at least 133 lb and have an unexpanded chest of 33 in was withdrawn. However, this change was accompanied by the introduction of training courses in judo. (*Report on Prisons*, 1961, p. 8 and p. 10.)

Morris, in a most illuminating account of the relationship between the prisoner and the staff, describes how the ambivalence of the system affects the prison officer in the lower ranks in both attitude and behaviour. He writes:

'A view expressed by many officers at Pentonville was that "an officer who runs his feet off for the sake of prisoners is a bad officer. A good officer sees that a prisoner gets exactly what he is entitled to, no more, no less". Statements like, "there should be a treadmill here", and "prisoners should be sterilised to prevent them breeding children who will come to prison", can often represent bewilderment and confusion as much as outrage or moral indignation towards the offender.'

He goes on:

'Those who have served long years in Pentonville, or prisons like it, tend to settle for a degree of tolerance beneath which lies an impenetrable layer of cynicism' (Morris *et al.*, 1963, pp. 255 and 256).

The physical condition of prisons displays the state of ambivalence even more dramatically. The only institutions that can compare with the prison system for its attachment to ancient and unimproved buildings are the churches with their great investment in sentiment and ritual.

The following description of conditions in local prisons may be added to what has already been written:

'The evil of overcrowding seems now to be accepted as inevitable, even by the prisoners, and to their credit they do not create much difficulty despite the inconvenience caused which must be particularly trying when last minute alterations have to be made in their accommodation due to late receptions, which are not infrequent, especially at Session and Assize sittings. On one day in November last year we soared to our highest populations figure ever. This called for the stoppage of classes, as the rooms were needed, and our having to borrow equipment from other establishments. The overcrowding has given me much interest from one angle – the nearly complete lack of desire for men to exercise the privilege of association. The Stars generally do but the recidivists do not. Of those eligible, less than 1 per cent participate' (*Report on Prisons*, 1961, p. 78).

'Frequent transfers to relieve overcrowding – high numbers of receptions and a record number of men for trial produced an atmosphere which resembled an extremely busy transit centre. More frequent Quarter Sessions – extra number of courts sitting to clear the Calendars at Assizes – constant changing of location to cope with the problem of three in a cell – shortage of staff within the prison – closing of workshops and inadequate facilities gave little opportunity of individual treatment. Methods of security were severely tested. Many attempts to escape were detected and prevented and the officers' patience was sorely tried. Their firmness coupled with a sense of duty and understanding succeeded in maintaining a good standard of discipline' (ibid, p. 79).

'Overcrowding has produced the problems which are now expected and familiar in large local prisons. As in previous years this prison slowly but steadily became more overcrowded as the year wore on, but it seems that this very gradualness of increase is the one factor which allows it to be tackled. As it becomes clear that complete saturation can never quite be reached, standards and methods are constantly adjusted, and the approach to consequential problems becomes more elastic and flexible as the difficulty increases.

It has, for example, been difficult to find full employment for all in the association shops – not from lack of material, but from sheer lack of elbow room. Hence for some superfluous men, jobs have to be created in production shops.

Cellular accommodation is severely affected. Fortunate indeed is the prisoner who occupies a single cell, whether due to a weak heart or to misbehaviour, for there is little likelihood of his acquiring one otherwise. This means that often a man cannot be granted a single cell for social or personality reasons and this kind of problem is at best met by a change of treble cell' (ibid, p. 69; and Morris *et al.* 1963).

Briefly, the facts reveal on the one hand a continuous preoccupation with humanity, improvement, and reform and on the other a situation that would not be tolerated by a farmer for his cattle.

Most human societies have in their culture a moral compulsion, a tendency to accompany all actions with symbolic expressions, designed to fit them into a complex moral order. Wars are fought for virtuous ends, peoples are destroyed to protect the purity of the race, and prostitution is tolerated to

221

protect the virtuous woman. It is to be expected, therefore, that the prison system should have its accompanying moral justification.

For the sociologist, it is not of interest, except incidentally, to discover how efficient the prison system is in terms of its moral justification; as Merton has pointed out, this would miss the point as much as teaching meteorology to the participants in a rain-making ceremony. What is of interest is the function of the prison system in society.

The theoretical problem to be solved is to find out why, with an intelligent and humane Home Secretary, a parliament of wise and cultured men, an upper house including sociologists, criminologists, judges, and bishops, this situation persists. More particularly, why it persists since the publication of *Pentonville*, which has dispelled for all who have read it ignorance about the physical, social, and psychological nature of prison.

A facile answer would be that the sheer size of the problem is beyond the capacity of the economy to solve. The total prison population for 1961 was a little over 30,000 and the total cost of the prison service was £18,595,100.

In a country with immense resources this position is not tenable. A second explanation not openly expressed, but implied, is that somewhere within the state apparatus is a body of wicked men who control the money and it is they who prevent reform. Although the 'wicked men' explanation is the most frequently employed concept in human affairs, the evidence upon which this theory is based is not available.

A solution which fits the facts would be one which argues that there are at least two groups in society competing for power and influence in this field. There are those who want reform. They are on the whole weak politically, but literate, and for these a few modest reforms and an extensive literature are provided. There are those who believe in punishment and social deprivation as reforming influences, and they are politically powerful. The political history of the campaign to abolish capital punishment supports this thesis (Tuttle, 1961, and Christoph, 1962).

This conflict must not be regarded as a life-and-death struggle or a contradiction, but as a symbiosis. Each party is as essential to the functioning of the system as the other.

The Prison, and the Criminal as Scapegoat

The division thus described has another side in that it is reflected in and reflects different beliefs about the efficacy of prison as a technique of reformation.

Outside the official literature of prison, punishment is seen as having a number of social functions: prevention, both by terror and by restraint, retribution as well as reform. But within the administrative system reform is almost the only criterion by which success is judged, although the internal system of discipline still contains many retributive elements. The issue is discussed in *Penal Practice in a Changing Society* thus:

'A second question, which is very pertinent at a time when crime is increasing is whether these more humane and constructive methods of treatment may have been applied at the expense of the deterrent effect of imprisonment. So far as concerns general deterrence, that is, the effect of the fear of prison on all who may be minded to commit offences, it is not possible to distinguish fear of imprisonment as a particular form of punishment from fear of the totality of the legal and social consequences of being found out. There is at least no evidence that fear of imprisonment in itself has any less effect than it may have had in the past on those who have not yet been in prison. As for those who have already served a first sentence, it must again be noted that the great majority do not in fact return to prison. For those who do return, there is no reason to believe that an increasingly repressive regime would have a better effect. The deterrent effect of imprisonment must finally lie in the loss of personal liberty and all that this involves under any kind of regime, and that effect is not reinforced if the period of loss of liberty is used in a merely repressive and punitive way. This was the conclusion reached by the Gladstone Committee, after long experience of a system firmly based on punitive deterrence, and nothing in the experience of the last sixty years has pointed to a different conclusion' (*Penal Practice*, 1959, p. 13).

There is an implicit admission in the quotation above that, in spite of the conclusion reached by the Gladstone Committee, imprisonment has continued to be repressive and punitive for sixty years!

The difficulty that arises for the sociologist is the need to account for the persistence of an institution, for which it would be

223

easy to design tests of efficiency, but which has never been so tested, that continually claims, on evidence without validity, that it is successful. A quotation from *Penal Practice in a Changing Society* makes this issue quite clear.

'Although steady progress has been made on these lines, the question may legitimately be asked: how far are the prisons effective in their declared purpose? The answer to this cannot, and could not in the present state of knowledge, be given on any scientific basis. It is possible to say that such and such a percentage have not, over a given period of exposure to risk, returned to prison. But it is not possible to say whether that result is because of their treatment in prison, or in spite of it, or whether it would have been the same if they had never come to prison' (ibid, p. 12).

The report then goes on to make claims for which there is no evidence whatsoever:

'One test at least of the results of a prison system is its effect on those subjected to it for the first time. Statistics published in the Annual report of the Prison Commissioners for 1957 show that some 87 per cent of men and 89 per cent of women of the Star Class discharged from all prisons during 1953 and 1954 had not returned to prison under sentence by the end of 1957, i.e. after a period of at least three years' exposure to risk. These figures, encouraging though they may appear, underline the crux of the prison problem, that is, the treatment of those who do come back, and especially the hard core of persistent recidivists. The proportion of prisoners received each year with six or more previous proved offences has slowly increased over the last five years.

It is not possible to give for prisoners of the Ordinary (recidivist) Class reconviction figures on the same comprehensive basis as are given above for Stars. Figures are, however, published by the Prison Commissioners for discharges of this class from certain specialised prisons. These suggest that some 66 per cent of men discharged from central prison had not returned to prison within three years; for closed regional prisons the percentage is 74 and for regional prisons of minimum or medium security it is much higher. These results, again, are not discouraging in themselves. But the great majority serve their sentences in the local prisons where they cannot receive the training available in the specialised prisons' (ibid, pp. 12 and 13).

There is a logical confusion here, the assumption that if a person is not reconvicted he has not committed another offence.

It is possible that the Prison Commissioners and the Home Office and all those concerned with criminology do not know how to test whether or not a certain procedure is effective or not. What other explanation can be offered for the justification of these paragraphs than that the Prison Commissioners while paying lip-service to 'any scientific basis' are not prepared to use it in their practices?

The justification of more and longer prison sentences for second and subsequent offences is based on a curious belief in the 'hardened criminal', and much attention is given to him as a psychological type.

Mays displays the attitude common among criminologists, thus:

'It seems to me that both kinds of delinquency are genuine but they are of different types. The first type is deep-seated and often intransigent to treatment; the second type is more benign in nature and more amenable to retraining and educational techniques. In one case, the usual complex is rooted in the psychology of the individual offender, in the second case, the delinquency is largely a function of the local environment. This simple diagnostic distinction is to my mind crucial for any understanding of crime *en masse*. It is simple yet fundamental and is the starting point for any worthwhile classification, and classification, in turn, is the beginning of sophistication in both criminology and psychology. The difference between the mainly socially and the mainly psychologically motivated delinquents might also be described in terms of the other-directed and the inner-directed personality. One offends, in the main, because his pals do; the other because he is psychologically disturbed. One is driven by the desire to conform; the other is compelled by inner necessity. One is normal, the other is abnormal. One passes through a phase of illegal behaviour during childhood and early adolescence, while the other is more likely to develop into the habitual offender. The old lag, as we know, usually commits his offences alone, while environmental delinquents are invariably accompanied' (Mays, 1963, p. 226).

225

Sociology and the Stereotype of the Criminal

He supports his thesis thus:

'As R. S. Taylor (1960) showed in his study of detainees at Wandsworth, habitual criminals, who are by definition abnormal, are typically solitary offenders. Social avoidance, in fact, is one of their dominant characteristics' (ibid, p. 227).

To use the language of an earlier period, Mays appears to believe that the 'old lag' is possessed by a devil.

It does not appear to have occurred to these authors that they are describing and comparing two classes of persons; the first group being integrated in civil society with no experience of prison and the second group being those for whom prison is the norm, whose personality is the product of prison experience, and who enter civil society at rare intervals as strangers and remain for a short time. This is made clear in West's study *The Habitual Prisoner* in the table of 50 life histories given below (West, 1963, p. 120).

FIFTY RECIDIVISTS AT WANDSWORTH
Intervals at liberty between convictions

(Figures are given in months. Those fulfilling the criteria of a 'gap' are italicized. Gaps considered genuinely crime-free are marked with an asterisk.)

Case
number

1 1.2.3.6.0.3.20.0.4.1.9.9.*157**.15.0.5.2.2.1.2.0.2.1.1.0
   0.0.22.1.2.0.3.14.0.0.
2 21.4.*100**.25.42.9.10.27.
3 34.*73*.17.4.4.7.1.
4 2.96.1.2.5.1.3.5.1.2.0.9.2.6.10.0.
5 2.9.4.20.10.18.*73*.4.8.
6 35.2.5.7.3.5.10.10.12.10.7.22.11.*58**.51.
7 13.0.0.*106**.32.5.
8 27.6.*58*.7.
9 11.38.9.*58*.20.31.24.35.
10 31.17.*90*.*133*.42.*56*.7.
11 1.9.48.23.37.1.*75**.11.
12 26.1.27.31.6.*146**.0.9.5.24.
13 119.*54**.1.*112**.3.
14 9.21.5.*143*.8.16.*83*.46.14.13.16.
15 1.1.11.*87*.15.40.33.18.

226

Case
number

16 94.9.11.4.4.0.5.*79**.23.15.59.

17 130.11.4.2.*78**.3.

18 20.6.1.13.5.*66*.37.

19 13.*78**.26.5.18.83.

20 28.*54*.*121**.18.44.10.6.14.43.

21 36.7.2.29.10.14.13.23.29.10.27.12.*98*.30.0.0.5.

22 0.34.9.4.8.*79**.15.14.

23 11.2.30.*191*.23.

24 12.0.4.*114**.8.4.

25 52.13.*66**.5.0.0.6.

26 7.3.*67*.16.

27 54.*74**.6.

28 26.9.*105*.2.25.

29 15.*54**.3.32.0.4.2.2.2.1.1.*94**.2.1.3.0.3.0.1.1.1.2.2.

30 4.6.1.21.*61**.13.23.

31 6.4.5.*121**.19.2.0.8.15.47.1.

32 1.13.*70**.14.*68**.0.

33 81.8.*96**.28.7.

34 1.*59*.20.*118**.1.1.

35 5.4.9.16.2.0.11.*66*.10.17.11.12.7.*100**.7.0.3.

36 16.5.31.28.*95*.6.2.

37 0.*71*.21.12.*63*.*56*.21.11.*70*.5.8.17.5.

38 15.*92**.42.9.10.*71**.7.5.23.

39 4.2.5.2.2.2.2.1.15.7.24.5.0.33.9.*110**.*67**.80.

40 105.2.0.7.0.12.5.1.0.26.15.25.5.2.1.1.1.0.1.5.*103*.1.4.1
    1.5.2.

41 17.33.14.7.8.36.18.*61*.10.23.38.0.

42 8.2.3.0.1.3.4.3.8.*76**.15.5.30.4.18.5.

43 26.21.*71**.3.9.

44 30.*89*.6.

45 20.*93*.46.

46 16.14.8.2.*51**.5.6.4.1.15.26.34.1.

47 47.5.0.0.10.0.0.*59*.1.5.6.

48 6.43.32.11.19.0.7.*66*.17.25.65.

49 3.2.8.9.21.32.*51*.12.7.41.

50 1.8.3.0.16.*75**.3.8.

N.B.—Convictions as juveniles were not counted in this tabulation
and convictions for breach of probation were also discounted because
they referred to previous offences for which convictions were already
on record.

The evidence that persons who are convicted for one type of offence show a significant tendency to commit another offence of another type is often advanced as evidence of an inherent, generalized disposition to criminality.

The tendency to follow crimes of one type with offences of another has been demonstrated for sexual offences and for serious motoring offences.

For sexual offenders, the Cambridge investigation showed that out of a total of nearly 2,000 offenders, one in four had at least one other conviction for a non-sexual offence, mostly breaking or larceny, by the end of a four-year follow-up period from the date of their first conviction (Cambridge, 1957).

T. C. Willett found that in a sample of 653 'serious' motoring offences, more than one-fifth had a 'criminal record' for non-motoring offences (Willett, 1964).

Barbara Wootton, commenting on this argument on inherent criminality, says that 'persons known to the police are always likely suspects for any subsequent crime; and that one conviction, and still more one period of imprisonment is in itself only too likely to be criminogenic' (Wootton, 1963). It may be added that a 'known person' discovered committing an offence is more likely to be charged than an unknown person, and, if there is a choice of offence, to be charged with a serious rather than a lesser offence.

Underlying this discussion so far has been the assumption that, regardless of the intentions of those who maintain prisons, an objective consequence of prison is the production of men and women who are socialized to the life of the close society or 'prisonized'. This process results in their being so ill-adapted to life in civil society that they are vulnerable to re-imprisonment or may even positively seek prison as the only social and physical environment in which they can survive (Morris *et al.*, 1963, p. 70).

The discussion has dealt with two kinds of adaptation: that to the moral order of the prison – Clemmer's 'prisonization' – and that to the functional organization as described by Sykes. Both these authors also refer to the pathological consequences of these processes on individual capacity to adapt. Morris, in

developing these analyses, attempts a different appro
of classifying individuals by the form of their adaptatio
contrasts with Clemmer's approach, which is in terms of deg
of prisonization, and suggests that different patterns of adapt
tion may have different origins in, and consequences for, the
personalities of prisoners. Morris in addition describes the
general effects in reducing morale and intellectual capacity.

Morris, like Sykes, uses the typology of Merton presented in
'Social Structure and Anomie', but extends and develops it
(Merton, 1957, p. 139 *et seq.*). The patterns used are conformity,
innovation, ritualism, rebellion, retreatism, and manipulation.
Of these, conformity and ritualism tend to be functional for the
whole prison society, whereas rebellion and manipulation –
while they may provide the satisfaction of certain emotional
needs for the prisoners – tend to make the working of the prison
less smooth.

Morris sees rebellion and retreatism as having roots in mental
ill health and sees the prison system, including the reactions of
the prison staff, as likely to increase the disorder. He divides
ritualism into two forms, the ritualism of identity and the ritualism of dependency, and says that 'the dependent ritualist has
become wholly dependent upon the prison machine. He gradually loses all initiative, and outside prison is unable to adjust to
the demands of a competitive society, feeling only secure when
he is behind a prison wall' (Morris *et al.*, 1963, p. 173).

Reviewing this analysis he concludes:

'It is at the psychological level that imprisonment is a painful,
depriving and destructive experience. The important point here is
that while some prisoners actually experience a conscious sense of
pain and deprivation, there are others who are, as it were, anaes-
thetised to the pains of imprisonment by frequent exposure to it,
resulting in their being in an advanced stage of prisonization or
institutional neurosis. For these men the problems are serious in
that, unaware of the way in which imprisonment is progressively
reducing their chances of successful rehabilitation outside, they do
nothing to mobilise their resistance to it. What is even more
serious is that prison itself lacks both the facilities and the staff
resources either to successfully identify such individuals or to help
them.'

Q

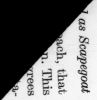

...eotype of the Criminal

...ates the scapegoat criminal that society
...pread emotional conflict which arises from

...to consider the psychological aspects of
...le more detail.

...F PRISON ON THE PERSONALITY
...F THE PRISONER

...account of the effects of imprisonment in
general has been given by A. J. W. Taylor, psychologist of the
Justice Department, New Zealand. He shows:

> 'The apparent consequences of confinement fit into three cate-
> gories:
> (1) changes due to initial adjustment to prison life;
> (2) changes due to losing touch with the outside world;
> (3) changes due to deterioration.
>
> These changes appear to be linked in progressive stages, and the
> longer a person is in prison the more likely is he to reach the third
> stage of deterioration. It is this third stage which is most serious;
> its symptoms are lack of interest, aims, ambitions, ideals, and
> emotional "flatness" and a lowered general efficiency. A person
> with these symptoms has insufficient resilience to meet the de-
> mands of everyday life, and is entirely dependent upon prison
> routines' (Taylor, 1960, p. 65).

Taylor describes the different individual responses, the
'normal criminal' who accepts the system, the prisoner who
represses his problems until he is free, and the others who 'find
the sequence of investigation, court appearance, remand, sentence, altogether too devastating and they crumble under the
combined weight of their guilt and the sentence of the court'.
The general responses of prisoners Taylor found to include 'dependence, unworthiness, boredom, despair, futility and apathy'.

In a review of the literature Taylor describes the origin and
effects of some of those categories, and it is notable that he relies
largely on prisoner-of-war studies: that is, studies in which the
returned prisoner is not a villain but a hero.

> 'Boredom, despair, futility and apathy are common feelings
> among prisoners. They are aware themselves of the symptoms of

230

withdrawal from life and in New Zealand prisoners use the term "boob happy" to describe this clinical state. The writer has been approached by inmates who feel that they are becoming dull automatons and with their emotional sensitivity blunted and their cognitive efficiency impaired by imprisonment. One recent admission described his fellow prisoners as "grey faces with grey suits in a grey world" and he took every opportunity of attending meetings conducted by outside speakers and of playing games with visiting teams "to see the sparkle in the eyes of citizens, because they *live*". If the withdrawal persists and intensifies it leads to personality deterioration that indicates a wastage of human material which, although an unintended by-product of a reformative policy, could be compared with the consequence of imprisonment when retribution was the paramount theme in penal treatment.

In all the literature about men in captivity one of the constantly recurring themes is that of personality deterioration. Fox says "It is the fight against the physical and mental deterioration almost inseparable from a long prison sentence that is the hardest part of the duty laid on the prison authorities."[1] Grünhut says that most prisoners suffer from mental vacuity, and that this is reflected in a dwindling memory, inability to concentrate, a strange obliviousness and a tendency to illusions and self deception.[2] The Royal Commission on Capital Punishment[3] was also concerned with evidence relating to deterioration and it seems clear that there is not experimental backing to support any of the widely different opinions that were given. Prisoners[4] writing of their own experience refer to "prison rot . . . mental inertia and inability to concentrate . . . being no longer capable of fending for themselves" and "living in the organic sense".

Further information came to hand during the First and Second World Wars and the Korean War, when, as a result of political or military activities, many people of many nations found themselves captive in prisoner of war camps, internment camps, concentration camps and camps for conscientious objectors.[5]

[1] Fox, L., *The Modern English Prison* (1934) Routledge, London.
[2] Grünhut, M., *Penal Reform: a Comparative Study* (1948) Oxford University Press.
[3] Report of the Royal Commission on Capital Punishment (1949-53). Cmd. 8932. H.M.S.O.
[4] Heckstall-Smith, A. *Eighteen Months* (1954) Wingate, London.
[5] See references in Taylor, A. J. W. 'Personality Deterioration and Imprisonment' 1957. Unpublished M.A. thesis, Victoria Univ.

231

One cannot assume that equal physical and psychological conditions obtained in different places of confinement, but nevertheless there appears to be a common syndrome of apathy, emotional flatness and loss of initiative in all situations. Captives and detainees recognize the syndrome and describe it in terms of "kriegie", "rice brain", "zombie", "flax happy", "stir crazy" and "barbed wire fever". Vischer[1] described the mental syndrome of the internee as "barbed wire disease or metapsychoses" – the main contributing causes of which were uncertainty of the future, loss of privacy, nostalgia, and the "constant menacing mockery of the barbed wire entanglements". Newman[2] compared the general reaction of prisoners of war to Caissons disease – the depressed and inadequate reaction leading to chronic apathy, loss of initiative, morale and personal drive that men make to normal situations after spending periods working below water in caissons. After eighteen months in solitary confinement as a suspected spy in France, Burney wrote: "I soon learned that variety is not the spice of life, but the very stuff of life. We need the constant ebb and flow of wavelets of sensation, thought, perception, action and emotion, lapping on the shore of consciousness, now here, now there, keeping even our isolation in the ocean of reality, so that we neither encroach nor are encroached upon . . . whatever we are, we have our shape and preserve it best in the experience of many things'[3] (Taylor, 1960, pp. 65, 67, 68, 69).

Taylor then goes on to discuss a subject rarely referred to in the literature: the effects of perceptual isolation. He quotes the work of Scott at McGill who showed, by experiment, that perceptual isolation produced similar symptoms of boredom, apathy, and the like, to those produced by prison, but in addition his subjects found themselves unable to perform familiar tasks or to concentrate in matters of importance to them. They became confused and lacked direction and drive (Scott, 1957).

Taylor comments: 'Perceptual isolation would be an even more important variable if it were linked also with the loss of ambition and normal motivation that is noted in some discharged prisoners' (Taylor, 1960, p. 68).

[1] Vischer, A. L. 'Report on "Barbed Wire Disease" ', *Lancet*, 12 July, 1919.
[2] Newman, P. H. 'The Prisoner of War Mentality", *Brit. med. J.* 1944, pp. 8-10.
[3] Burney, C. 'Solitary Confinement' (1952), Clarke and Cockerman, London.

THE PRISONER WHO IS A HERO

Even more remarkable is the fact that the experience of returned prisoners of war at the end of the Second World War should have been generally ignored.

In the latter stages of the war the needs of the repatriated prisoner of war began to be recognized by psychiatrists, psychologists, and sociologists working in the Army, and following a study of the nature of desocialization a pilot Civil Resettlement Unit was established early in 1945. After this experience some twenty C.R.U.s were established to

> 'act as bridges between the Army and civilian life, by providing a "community" in which there was considerable intercommunication between these two spheres. This community was "designed" along specifically psychological lines as a transitional society with the therapeutic aim of releasing those tensions which appeared to result primarily from P.O.W. experience, and of changing those attitudes which retarded the reassumption by the repatriate of a fully participant role in civilian life' (Curle, 1947, p. 42).

The Civil Resettlement Unit was based on an analysis of the functions of social structure, social roles, social relationships and culture in human adjustment and 'Resettlement was clearly recognized as a two-way process, calling for subtle emotional readjustment by all members of the reformed family and larger community' (ibid, p. 44).

The work of these units was assessed by making comparisons with control groups who had returned directly to civilian life. This established that there was a 'significantly higher proportion of well adjusted men in the sample who had attended a C.R.U.' (ibid, p. 240).

It would be unfair to assume that the Home Office are unaware of the nature of the problem of desocialization or that it is not conducting research into its nature.

A. Straker, Chief Psychologist at the Prison Department of the Home Office, reported in a paper to the British Association that:

> 'The study had revealed that a third of the first-offence group was convicted for further offences within a test two-year period. For

them the research findings suggested that, in so far as our prisons were failing in their work of social rehabilitation, it was partially because they were unable to prevent men from becoming increasingly isolated from society' (*Guardian*, 30-8-63).

One further matter which bears on the isolation of the prisoner must be described. It is the reception of the discharged prisoner in civil society.

Here again there is the same ambivalence found throughout the system. On the one hand there is a continuous process of expansion of humane provision, for example compulsory after-care through the probation service provided under the Criminal Justice Act, 1961, the work of the National Association of Discharged Prisoners' Aid Societies, the Central After-Care Association, and many other bodies. On the other hand there is the widespread fear of, and hostility to, the discharged prisoner which makes it difficult for him to find work and accommodation (Morris *et al.*, 1963, p. 303 *et seq.*).

The Report of the Prison Commissioners for 1960 has this to say about employment:

'Considerable publicity has recently been given in the Press and elsewhere to the difficulties of ex-prisoners in obtaining employment. While this should not be minimized, especially in the case of the ex-professional man, we are impressed by the number of firms and individual employers who accept the moral responsibility of finding – or making – employment for ex-prisoners, and of repeating the process despite the discouragements which may follow. Unfortunately, however, the attitude is still too prevalent which regards imprisonment as an automatic bar to employment irrespective of the relation of the past offence to the likely responsibilities of the job' (*Report on Prisons*, 1960, p. 31).

THE DISCHARGED PRISONER'S SOCIAL ISOLATION

The report for 1961 illustrates the effect of prison on employment prospects: 'The difficulty remains of placing men in competitive work after lengthy periods of being accustomed to the slower prison tempo' (*Report on Prisons*, 1961, pp. 31 and 32).

234

The same report describes both the problem of accommodation and the attempt being made to solve it.

'The problem of accommodation for a homeless man on release has now become critical and the list which the Division keeps of landladies in the London area who are prepared to accept the known ex-prisoner are regrettably small. Men are encouraged to find their own accommodation but at present-day prices they often find even the cost of a bed-sitting room without meals beyond their means. It has been estimated that there are well over 1,000 "sleeping rough" in London each night. Many are ex-prisoners, but by no means all are vagrants. This is a problem which appears to be increasing. The Division accordingly welcomes the formation of the Voluntary Hostels Conference which plans a Central Information Office to co-ordinate hostel accommodation, and circulate vacancies throughout Great Britain. It is hoped that membership of this Conference will assist the more effective planning of accommodation in advance and thus relieve the very real anxiety in many prisoners' minds as to where they are to sleep on their first night out of prison. On a more therapeutic level, the movement of establishing "halfway houses" where homeless ex-prisoners can develop new roots in a homely atmosphere, has flourished. Norman House and Langley House have each opened a second "home" and spontaneous new ventures have been established in Birmingham, Leicester and Liverpool. There is an increasing number of instances where the "house-parents" and the staff of the Division are working closely together and with individual clients. The Directory of such establishments, which we understand has been produced by the National Association of Discharged Prisoners' Aid Societies, is most welcome' (ibid, p. 31).

A case history illustrating the process of demoralization has been written by Tony Parker under the title of *The Unknown Citizen*. This describes the life of a petty thief trapped in the system of social isolation and habituation to prison life. The hero of the account is 'Charlie Smith', who by the age of 47 had served 26 years in prison for stealing property valued at less than £200, and who, being caught on the first day of his release attempting to steal from a mail bag, was sentenced to a further 10 years' preventive detention in order to 'protect society'. It is worth noting perhaps that apart from his 26 years in prison he had also spent several years in the Army before this, so that it might be argued that the process of desocialization had already been effected and that the army had adjusted him to prison life (Parker, 1963).

At the time of the preparation of this manuscript for the printer the third reading of the Criminal Justice Bill is taking place. This takes the policies of open prisons and parole a dramatic stage further. The aim of this Bill is, in the words of the Home Secretary, to 'empty the prisons', and it is expected that some 8,000 offenders in prison in 1967 could be released to attendance centres, treatment clinics, or hostels for homeless, rootless, or alcoholic offenders. Judgement, however, must be suspended until the policy has had time to be assessed.

There are two areas of doubt. The first is the ambivalence to which reference has already been made. At the same time as the movement to reduce the use of prisons reaches its climax, two new prisons have been built, prison security has been the subject of study by a committee headed by a distinguished naval officer, and overall security has been placed in the hands of a distinguished soldier. Secondly it may happen, as has already taken place with the open prison and parole, that the middle-class offender sentenced for the 'white-collar' offence will be more likely to escape prison than the working-class offender. The desocialized scapegoat may remain, but the social class range from which he will be drawn will be narrowed.

It is not only at this level that the attitudes of society add to the isolation of the prisoner. Two examples will suffice to show this:

In May 1963 the author was travelling from Liverpool, Lime Street, to Euston on an express, the 4.15 p.m., that stops at Crewe. The ticket collector rudely turned a passenger away and directed him to a stopping train, saying, 'We can't have chaps like you on the London train'. The ticket collector then explained to the writer that the man had been discharged from Walton Prison and was travelling with a warrant.

In January 1963 in the case of Faramus *v.* Film Artistes' Association the Court of Appeal ruled that 'Where the rules of a trade union provide that no person who has been convicted shall be eligible or retain membership of the union, the rule must be construed imperatively and not directively. The rule is absolute and the union has no power to retard.' The case of a

Mr Faramus is of interest. He was last convicted in 1940, joined the association in 1950, and was eventually elected to its executive committee. As the Association enforces a closed shop within fifty miles of Charing Cross, his ineligibility, discovered by chance in 1958, deprived him of any opportunity to work at his profession. Incidentally, the rule 4 (2) under which he was declared ineligible makes an exception for motoring offences, not punishable by imprisonment.

It should be added that no such rule exists in any of the major manual workers' unions.

Earlier, in a quotation from Howard, it was shown how the results of the Du Cane prison administration, the theories of Lombroso and others on criminal types, and the Victorian stereotype of the criminal were identical. Prison produced the criminal type, scientific theory identified him even to the pallor of his skin, and the public recognized him: the whole system was logical, watertight, and socially functional. The present system is more complex. There are powerful forces among the intellectual middle classes and among non-conformist religious groups, and even among a minority of social scientists, who would wish to modify or even abolish the prison system; on the other hand the majority of the general public – if public opinion polls are any guide – the popular press, many of the personnel of the prison service, and the majority in both Houses of Parliament, believe in punishment and social isolation. In such a system the change of prison conditions proceeds at a rate rapid enough to satisfy the pressures of reformers, while continuing to produce the stereotyped 'old lag', the 'abnormal', the 'psychologically motivated', the 'inner-directed' delinquent whose maladjustment is 'deepseated' and often 'intransigent to treatment' and who, in his turn, becomes the scapegoat needed by society and the data for the latter-day Lombrosos whose social function is to provide the 'scientific' explanations required by the culture.

REFORM AND THE SURVIVAL OF THE PRISON SYSTEM

Prison reform has one other function not yet fully discussed. Prison is based on the belief in the educative and deterrent properties of deprivation, so that the degree of deprivation is relative to the conditions in civil society. In the past in Britain, and at present in poor countries, this has presented difficulties, and the task of devising conditions worse than the norm has frequently taxed the ingenuity of administrators (Woodham Smith, 1961). In that there is a continuous process of improvement in living conditions outside prison and a tendency for conditions inside to remain unchanged or even in some cases to worsen, the function of prison reform may be simply to maintain the degree of *relative deprivation constant.*

This may be important to the survival of the prison system because it is observable that where the conditions and treatment of prisoners exceed certain limits, public interest is aroused, with political consequences (as in Kenya and Nyasaland). Thus prison reform may be seen as essential to the maintenance and survival of the prison system in a changing society.

CHAPTER EIGHT

The Stereotype of the Criminal and Sociology

Although this work is about crime, criminals, and social scientists, this is incidental rather than central to the argument. The main concern is to demonstrate the consequences in society and for sociologists of operating with a stereotype of the criminal rather than with a definition derived from an objective appraisal of the attributes of the variable with which the study is concerned. Such a definition must be an operational definition, that is, one that directs the investigator in his identification of his data.

In the history of social research, there is an outstanding example of the success of an inquiry of a systematic kind which achieved an identical aim for another 'outcaste' group, the poor. This was B. Seebohm Rowntree's *Poverty: a Study of Town Life* of 1899.

Up to the point at which this study was published, the stereotype of the poor was of persons who, if helped, would cease to make efforts to assist themselves, and, if given resources above the minimum of subsistence, would breed up to the point where hunger and pestilence reduced their numbers to the point where mere subsistence was possible. The diffusion of this stereotype throughout the middle and upper classes led to an impotence in social policy which cost literally between one and two million lives during the Irish Famine of the eighteen-forties and prevented all positive social reform except in the fields of public health and education, both only in part for altruistic reasons.

Rowntree, who followed Leibig, solved the problem of the stereotype by disregarding, in the second part of his study, the moralizing of his predecessors and defining the problem of poverty as one of the input-output ratio of energy. At that moment a scientific sociology was born and with it the Welfare State.

The writer, who served his apprenticeship with Rowntree, intends the present volume as another demonstration of the value of the scientific method in the study of society.

This work has attempted to examine concepts of crime and the criminal from the point of view of sociological theory. That is, it has attempted to account for the identification of certain behaviours for disapproval and certain persons for punishment.

The method owes much to Durkheim, but the argument has been confined to a single society rather than to 'Society' as a whole. Durkheim sought to establish a single causal factor in the 'collective conscience', whereas the writer has tried to take account of the multiplicity of social factors creating 'crime' while recognizing the importance of the degree to which social control is embodied in the sentiments of individuals. Central to the writer's approach is the notion of crime as a part of the conflict situation: a thesis antipathetic to the universalistic concept of Durkheim (Durkheim, 1947).

There are widely diffused beliefs about right and wrong, but the distribution of such beliefs and the differing forms of such beliefs await empirical investigation.

These essays make use of a variety of sources of data, newspaper reports, autobiographies, observation and discussion, to formulate hypotheses. It has been customary to dismiss such data with the pejorative adjective 'anecdotal', whereas studies which simply make unsupported assertions are acceptable and studies based on unstandardized interviews of unrepresentative samples of the population become 'scientific' by virtue of a few tables and percentages. Tom Harrisson, to whom the author is permanently indebted, pointed out long ago the rich variety of available social data as yet unexplored by sociologists. This work attempts to show the utility of such data. The end-products are hypotheses, stated formally in the introduction to this volume. These hypotheses can only be tested by researches on a scale and with efforts and expenditures comparable with work in physics. To pretend otherwise would be dishonest.

In the process of formulating these hypotheses the traditional methods of examining crime have been considered as a part of the culture whose social function is the creation and the maintenance of a stereotype. This is displayed in the selection of data, the variables observed, and the categories employed in classification.

It is modestly hoped that, if this demonstration has been successful, sociologists will turn away from the value assumptions implicit (or explicit) in their studies and from their avowed aim in social reform, and design their researches without reference to the pleasure or the pain they may give to priests or politicians. For, while it is understandable that social scientists in the employment of the State should ask the question 'It is commonly said that the British Police force is the best in the world, do you agree?' to please the Royal Commission on the Police (it did), it can hardly be argued that academic sociologists are under such duress (Appendix IV, Minutes of Evidence, Royal Commission on the Police, 1962, p. 7).

That there are pressures, both Shils and Kingsley Davis have made abundantly clear in their different ways, but the history of physics and economics and biology has shown that these can be resisted.

The central problem which lies below the surface in all discussions of crime concerns the moral order. In a complex society the rules are claimed to operate to the advantage of all, and, therefore, to demand general support. The possibility that an individual might profit by breaking the rules is justification of the use of force. The observation of the rule then becomes the best policy for society and for the individual. This simple model is inadequate to represent the real situation.

We begin in infancy by learning a substantially traditional, largely Christian, ethic, and to control the sexual impulse and defecation. This learning is not a conscious arrangement of means and ends for maximum satisfaction, but the acquisition of a complex of conditional responses, conscience, or the superego. These correspond to Durkheim's concept of the collective conscience and to the idea of the natural law. Behaviour which does not conform creates discomforting emotional and physical responses. In many situations the response is to the verbal

241

symbol for the nonconforming behaviour, so that changing the symbol may change the response. New conditional responses appear to be more difficult to learn in adult life.

The external moral order is learned later, and offers rewards or punishments for conformity or nonconformity but, unlike the internalized moral order with its automatic responses, the external order presents a third possibility, that of avoidance, of not being found out. In a literate society the conflict between the 'spirit of the law' and the 'word' opens up the possibility of avoidance of the kind much exploited in the medieval church.

Much of this social control derives from the organs of political power and is often the arbitrary imposition of the interests of groups with power, or of broad social classes, on the population as a whole or on other groups of classes. This process is masked by the substantial identity of those with social, political, ecohomic, and religious power and control of the ideology through education, religious teaching, and the means of mass communication.

The capacity of this group to change the designation of behaviours is very great. Crime can become virtue; criminals, heroes; enemies, allies; and friends, foes. The collective conscience becomes the product of political control, rather than its source.

Mass communications not only diffuse the ideology but undermine it, adding another factor to moral confusion. All infringements of the moral order are widely described, but those of persons of high status attract especial attention – a response to latent social conflict. The apparent indifference of the 'establishment' to morals deprives the moral order of its sacred and majestic quality.

The general form of the conflict of morals is well described by Garofalo in his *Criminalogia* of 1885 as the conflict between natural and positive crime, the distinction between acts prohibited because they are evil, and acts that are evil because they are prohibited. This is a formulation that is similar in conception to the distinction in Roman Law between jus gentium and jus civilis (De Quirós, 1911).

Nor is the examination of the role of class conflict new; it was brilliantly expounded by Joseph Kay in his essay on the 'Game

Laws' in *The Social Condition and Education of the People,* in
1850. This essay is important since it describes in a single passage
not only the social-class origin of a 'crime', but demonstrates the
identity of poaching and hunting when these are operationally
defined. He shows too the function of the judicial system in the
creation of the criminal.

'If detected, the young peasant, who is very often a man, who has
never committed any other crime or offence against the laws; who
has only yielded to the same kind of impulse as that which makes
his landlord love sport; who has, in short, only done that which we
should all do without the least remorse, were we in his position;
this poor fellow, who had no other amusement in which he could
indulge, and who has been goaded on by misery and destitution,
is caught by a gamekeeper, is carried off to the tribunal of the
petty sessions, where his own landlord, who is equally interested
in his punishment, for the sake of his own sport, is sitting as
judge! Before such an unfair tribunal the poor fellow is placed.
No jury is allowed him. He is tried, judged, condemned, and sentenced by the landlords themselves, and is by them sent off to the
county gaol, there to spend one, two, or six months, and often a
whole year, in company with felons and criminals of the worst
possible character. There he becomes inured to the contemplation
of vice of all kinds, and of all degrees. There he gradually loses all
horror of it; and thence he returns, hardened in villainy, and prepared for the commission of deeds, from which he would have
shrunk when he entered.

During the time of his incarceration, his poor wife and family
are driven to the workhouse in order to escape starvation; their
household goods are all sold up; their independence of character
is ruined; and the happiness of a whole family is often destroyed
for ever. This is no fanciful picture. It is an occurrence of every day
in the rural districts. About 5,000 such committals take place
every year in England and Wales!' (Kay, 1850, pp. 597, 598).

The part played by the ideology in the designation of crime is
a central element in Marx, especially where he discusses religion,
and it appears in an interesting form in Vaccaro, who regarded
the emergence of classes as the result of the evolutionary
struggle for existence in which the superior species subjugated
the inferior. De Quirós describes his argument thus:

243

'As a result of this struggle crime appears to Vaccaro as an act which the winners who constitute the ruling power consider dangerous to their own interests; the criminal appears as a rebel against the complicated system of domestication by which the winners try to develop only the aptitudes of the domesticated which they can better use for their ends; and punishment appears as one of the forces used by them, until, fear having taken root in the nervous cell, it sufficed to substitute the threat of physical pain for the permanent physical correction' (De Quirós, 1911, p. 62).

A theme in this essay is that of the contribution made by the sociologist and criminologist to the creation and maintenance of the stereotype of crime and the criminal. This stereotype asserts that crime is a distinctive kind of behaviour and that criminals are created by special physical, psychic, social, or environmental factors. Such theories are maintained and diffused by researches that are based on socially determined groups, generally chosen without controls, often by criteria which prejudge the issue.

The literature of crime and delinquency quoted in earlier chapters abounds with examples of the way in which authors prejudge their subjects and treat them as a class of 'unter-mensch' in much the same way as nineteenth-century sociologists, economists, and politicians regarded the poor, or early anthropologists and missionaries considered 'primitive' peoples. Criminals are described in a variety of pejorative terms – lads if they are young men, old lags if they are mature men – and there is no need to observe the normal canons of integrity in the interview: the subjects' mothers may be deceived with fairy stories about comparisons with young people in Australia, or subjects can be condemned as lying merely because a psychiatrist thinks so. The attitude system is identical with that of the police and prison officers except that the social scientists have a rich battery of hostile description derived from the 'technical' language of psychology and psychiatry.

The inevitable conclusions are substantially identical with those found in nineteenth-century criminology, with one exception. That is that criminologists no longer criticize society but identify themselves with the ideology of their own social stratum.

244

This essay has attempted to revive interest in the multifactor theory and to show the social factors to which 'criminal' behaviour is a response or an adaptation. Much of what has been written here derives from the writings of Ferri, who, in the last century, proposed a long series of measures designed to reduce crime and other forms of social-pathological behaviour. His method was to isolate the psychological, the environmental, and the social factors and to propose positive and preventive and corrective measures. Among his long list of reforms were free trade and the abolition of monopolies to reduce smuggling; the spread of the 'Malthusian Law' to reduce abortion and infanticide; measures to transform the status of the illegitimate child – again to reduce infanticide; the legalization of divorce to reduce bigamy and murder; and the control of offensive weapons, the widening of streets, and the improvement of lighting (De Quirós, 1911, pp. 27 and 28).

A discussion of two forms of symbiosis has been undertaken to show that crime is not a separate or aberrant form of behaviour: the symbiosis of criminal and victim and that of areas of social defect and specialized functional tracts of depravity, where the rich (nominally virtuous) and the poor (traditionally depraved) meet for their mutual exploitation.

This thesis has been illustrated by another nineteenth-century writer, Arthur Sherwell, and is well discussed by the Chicago urban sociologists.

The idea of the police as a crime-creating agency will not surprise students of social institutions, but the identification of the *corps d'élite* as a concept for the examination of institutional behaviour is perhaps new; it relates the two moral orders, natural and positive, to institutional private justice, examines the effects of the hierarchical division of labour and authority, and isolates the role of the symbolic system of communication.

The differential operation of the system of public justice as exemplified in the work of Sutherland and his school has been treated with curious ambivalence in British studies: it has been vigorously denied and, at the same time, expounded with particular reference to the motorist. Here it has been argued as a part of a general pattern of differential immunity expounded in topographic terms of social space. This differential immunity makes a substantial contribution to the popular stereotype of the criminal.

The demonstration, following the work of Alex Comfort, of the prevalence of 'pathological' behaviours that are approved provides data for the critical examination of the remnants of theories of atavism or degeneration and suggests a more productive use of persons with a special aptitude or a vocation for violence. Alternatively, the data could be employed, as Comfort has done, to criticize society.

There remains the problem of the social function of punishment and the theory of the criminal as scapegoat. This is not easy to demonstrate without recourse to concepts not subject to empirical verification. The theory has, nevertheless, a high degree of plausibility and many observations support the argument.

Here it may be interpolated that Christianity as an ethical system is heavily involved in the scapegoat culture. The expiation of sin by the sacrifice of the innocent person and later the innocent animals has a central role in Old Testament Judaism. The expulsion of the sacrificial animal, the scapegoat, into the desert is the analogy for all those punishments, deportation and transportation and now imprisonment, in which social separation and isolation are imposed. Finally, the crucifixion itself is the supreme case of the sacrifice of the innocent for the sins of a whole society, and the cross, a form of gallows, is the most widely diffused symbol in all Western culture. It is surely not implausible to see here one more ambivalence in the culture, the practice of the sacrifice of the scapegoat as solving the emotional maladjustment of the great mass of society and theories of crime and punishment as providing a 'rational' basis for the practice.

The present system of justice and punishment has the effect of making a small number of persons, drawn mainly from the poor, the ill-educated, and the unskilled, into designated criminals. In prison they become socially isolated and culturally disorientated and often deteriorate intellectually, and on release are more vulnerable to petty misdemeanour and to detection and arrest than any other group. Once caught in the system, their disorientation is progressive. The fact that the process that desocializes them is alleged to cure them provides the occasion for the increase of hostility with which they are regarded through time.

There is a widespread preoccupation in popular reading, in radio and television, and, in the cinema, with violence and the transgression of the mores. Matters of this kind are the major subject of our symbolic culture.

There is a widespread approval of punishment, including punishment by hanging, displayed in public opinion polls and in press reporting.

Many magistrates and judges, when passing sentence, refer to the outrage to popular sentiment of an offence, and act as though they believe the sentence will assuage the injury to the popular conscience. They pass sentences with wider aims than the punishment of the offender, to act as a deterrent, to prevent a process developing or a behaviour spreading, to make an example of: in other words, the prisoner receives more punishment than he deserves for the ends of society as a whole.

There is some evidence, therefore, that the identification and punishment of criminals do provide satisfaction for many people. What is not proved is that there is widespread guilt or aggression which is released or discharged when a criminal is punished. It would be possible to test such an hypothesis, but the results, if positive, might prove unacceptable.

If it was found that the punishment of offenders relieved guilt in others, and, if guilt acts to inhibit amoral or antisocial behaviour, it could be argued that punishment of scapegoats functions to allow crime in others and that, without such punishment, the general level of social behaviour would conform more closely to the mores. In effect, the function of punishment is to permit the continuance of a society in conflict with its own mores.

Punishment creates a confusion in the mores, since in most of its forms it is operationally identical with proscribed behaviour.

One last point remains. It has been argued that there is a real conflict between 'natural' and 'positive' law, and that what is described as crime, social pathology, or antisocial behaviour is an attempt to adapt to the situation in a complex society. The function of the social scientist is seen to be to improve 'positive' law and administration. Social adaptation does not, however, develop along a single path, and there is a long tradition of utopian socialism, political anarchism, pacifism, and humanism that has reasserted in a variety of contexts the importance of the natural law of pity and probity. This movement in the nineteenth century had many leading criminologists in its ranks. At present it is interesting that the Quakers, who opt out of the social competition of the affluent society and who have always maintained the moral identity of operationally identical behaviours, are leaders in this movement, and that political anarchism is now, as it was in the past, important in diffusing ideas which call into question the accepted system of beliefs about the criminal.

REFERENCES

ANDRY, R. G. (1960). *Delinquency and Parental Pathology. London.*

ANON (1965). *Mail Interception and Telephone Tapping in Britain.* London.

ARENS, R. and MEADOWS, A. (1962). 'Psycholinguistics and the Confession Dilemma', in *The Sociology of Punishment and Correction.* New York and London.

BALCHIN, NIGEL (1950). *The Anatomy of Villainy.* London.

BANTON, MICHAEL (1964). *The Policeman in the Community.* London and New York.

BERKOWITZ, L. (1962). *Aggression.* New York.

BRAITHWAITE, R. B. (1953). *Scientific Explanation.* London.

BURGESS, E. W. (1950). 'A Comment on Hartung, F. E., White Collar Offences in the Wholesale Meat Industry', *American Journal of Sociology*, Vol. LVI, July, p. 32.

BURT, L. (1959). *Commander Burt of Scotland Yard.* London.

CAMBRIDGE, Department of Criminal Science (1957). *Sexual Offences.* London.

CHRISTOPH, J. B. (1962). *Capital Punishment and British Politics.* London.

CLEMMER, DONALD (1958). *The Prison Community.* New York.

COMFORT, ALEX (1950). *Authority and Delinquency in the Modern State.* London.

CONE, T. E. (1961). 'Secular Acceleration of Height and Biologic Maturation in Children during the Past Century', *Journal of Pediatrics*, November, p. 740.

CURLE, ADAM (1947). 'Transitional Communities and Social Reconnection, *Human Relations*, Vol. I, No. 1. p. 42, and Vol. I, No. 2, p. 240.

DARBY, P. (1964). 'Legal Abortion', *New Society.* 13-8-64. London.

DAVIS, KINGSLEY (1959). *Human Society.* New York.

DE QUIRÓS, B. (1911). *Modern Theories of Criminality.* London.

DEMPSEY, JACK (1960). *Massacre in the Sun.* London.

DORS, DIANA (1960). *Swingin' Dors.* London.

DU CANN, C. G. L. (1960). *Miscarriages of Justice.* London.

DURKHEIM, EMILE (1938). *The Rules of Sociological Method.* Chicago.

249

DURKHEIM, E. (1947). *The Division of Labour in Society*. Glencoe, Ill.

ELLIS, HAVELOCK (1914). *The Criminal*. London
EYSENCK, H. S. (1964). *Crime and Personality*. London.

FIELD, THE (13-6-1963). London.
FOX, L. (1934). *The Modern English Prison*. London.
FREUD, S. (1913). *Totem and Taboo*. The Standard Edition of *The Complete Psychological Works of Sigmund Freud*, Vol. XIII. London and New York.
FRIEDMANN, W. (1959). *Law in a Changing Society*. London.

GIBBENS, T. C. N. and PRINCE, J. (1962). *Shoplifting*. London.
GIBBENS, T. C. N., MARRIAGE, A. and WALKER, A. (1963). *Psychiatric Studies of Borstal Lads*. Maudsley Monogr. No. 11, London.
GIBSON, E. and KLEIN, S. (1961). *Murder*. London.
GOFFMAN, ERVING (1961). *Asylums*. Chicago.
GRIGG, MARY (1965). *The Challenor Case*. Harmondsworth.
GRÜNHUT, M. (1948). *Penal Reform – a Comparative Study*. London.

HANNINGTON, WAL. (1936). *Unemployed Struggles* 1919-1936. London.
HARTUNG, F. E. (1950). 'White Collar Offences in the Wholesale Meat Industry in Detroit', *American Journal of Sociology*, Vol. LVI, July, p. 25.
HECKSTALL-SMITH, A. (1954). *Eighteen Months*. London.
HENDERSON, J. SCOTT (1953). *Report on an Enquiry into the Conviction of Timothy Evans, a Supplementary Report*. Cmnd. 8896.
HOOD, ROGER (1962). *Sentencing in Magistrates' Courts*. London.
HOWARD, D. L. (1960). *The English Prisons*. London.
HYDE, A. MONTGOMERY (1954). *The Trial of Christopher Craig and Derek William Bentley*. London.
HYDE, A. MONTGOMERY (1963). *Oscar Wilde, the Aftermath*. London.

INBAU, F. E. and REID, J. E. (1962). *Criminal Interrogation and Confessions*. Baltimore.
IRVING, C., HALL, R. and WALLINGTON, J. (1963). *Scandal '63*. London.

JAMES, A. E. (1965). Report on Detective Sergeant Harold Gordon Challenor. Cmnd. 2745. London.
JEHU, D. (1967). *Learning Theory and Social Work*. London.

KAY, JOSEPH (1850). *The Social Condition and Education of the People*. London.

KENNEDY, LUDOVIC (1964). *The Trial of Stephen Ward*. London.

KRASNER, LEONARD (1958). 'Studies of the Conditioning of Verbal Behaviour', *Psychological Bulletin*, Vol. 55, p. 160.

LAING, R. D. and ESTERSON, A. (1964). *Sanity, Madness, and the Family*, Vol. I. London

LAW REPORT, *The Times*, (14-11-63). Rowley v. Murphy.

LODGE, T. S. (1953). 'Sources and Nature of Statistical Information in Special Fields of Statistics, Criminal Statistics', *Journal of the Royal Statistical Society*, Part III, p. 292.

MACARTNEY, W. F. R. (1936). *The Walls have Mouths*. London.

MACHEN, E. W., JR. (1950). *The Law of Search and Seizure*. Chapel Hill.

MACK, J. (1964). 'Full-time Miscreants, Delinquent Neighbourhoods and Criminal Networks', *British Journal of Sociology*, Vol. XXIII, p. 38.

MARK, ROBERT (1965). 'The Rights of Wrong-doers', *The Guardian*, 18-5-65. London.

MARS-JONES, W. L. (1964). Report of Inquiry into the case of Halloran and Cox, and of Tisdall, Kingston, and Hill-Burton. Cmnd. 2526. London.

MARTIN, J. P. (1962). *Offenders as Employees*. London.

MAYS, J. B. (1954). *Growing up in the City*. Liverpool.

MAYS, J. B. (1963). 'Delinquency Areas – A Re-assessment', *British Journal of Criminology*, Vol. 3, No. 3, p. 219.

MEAD, G. H. (1918). 'The Psychology of Punitive Justice', *American Journal of Sociology*, Vol. XXIII, p. 586.

MERTON, R. K. (1957). 'Social Structure and Anomie', in *Social Theory and Social Structure*. Glencoe, Ill.

MORRIS, P. (1963). 'Staff Problems in a Maximum Security Prison', *Prison Service Journal*, Vol. 2, No. 6, p. 3.

MORRIS, T. (1958). *The Criminal Area*. London.

MORRIS, T. and BLOM-COOPER, L. (1964). *A Calendar of Murder*. London.

MORRIS, T. and MORRIS, P. with BARER, B. (1963). *Pentonville*. London.

MORRIS, T., MORRIS, P. and BIELY, B. (1961). 'It's the Prisoners who run this Prison', *Prison Service Journal*, Vol. I, No. 2.

MYRDAL, G. (1944). *An American Dilemma*. New York.

251

NEWMAN, U. J. (1962). 'Pleading Guilty for Considerations—a Study of Bargain Justice', in *The Sociology of Punishment and Correction*. New York and London.

PAKENHAM, LORD (1958). *Causes of Crime*. London.

PARKER, T. (1963). *The Unknown Citizen*. London.

PERKINS, R. M. (1940). 'The Law of Arrest', *Iowa Law Review*, Vol. XXV.

PHILLIPS, O. HOOD (1967). *Constitutional and Administrative Law*. London.

QUENNELL, P. (1960). *The Memoirs of William Hickey*. London

RICE-DAVIES, M. (1964). *The Mandy Report*. London.

RICHARDSON, S. A., DOHRENWEND, B. S. and KLEIN, D. (1965). *Interviewing, its Forms and Functions*. London.

ROLPH, C. A. (1962). *The Police and the Public*. London.

ROWNTREE, B. SEEBOHM (1899). *Poverty: a Study of Town Life*. London.

SARGANT, W. (1959). *Battle for the Mind*. London.

SCOTT, T. H. (1957) 'A Study in Perceptual Isolation', Unpublished Ph.D. thesis, McGill Univ. – Quoted by Taylor, A. J. W., *Journal of British Criminology*, Vol. I, p. 68.

SCHRAIN, G. H. (1964). 'Arson and Incendiarism', *The Insurance Monitor*, Vol. CXXV, No. 32, 6 August.

SEARS, R. R., MACCOBY, E. E. and LEVIN, H. (1957). *Patterns of Child Rearing*. Evanston, Ill.

SHARTLE, C. L. (1957). *Executive Performance and Leadership*. London.

SHERWELL, A. (1898). *Life in West London*. London.

SHILS, E. (1959). 'Social Inquiry and the Autonomy of the Individual', in *The Human Meaning of the Social Sciences*. Ed. D. Lerner. New York.

SHORT, J. F. and NYE, F. I. (1962). 'Reported Behaviour as a Criterion of Deviant Behaviour', in *The Sociology of Crime and Delinquency*. London and New York.

STINCHCOMBE, ARTHUR L. (1963). 'Institutions of Privacy in the Determination of Police Administrative Practice', *Amer. J. Sociol.*, Vol. LXIX, No. 2, p. 150.

STOTT, D. H. (1950). *Delinquency and Human Nature*. Dunfermline.

STREET, H. (1964). *Freedom, the Individual and the State*. London.

SUTHERLAND, EDWIN H. (1940). 'White Collar Criminality', *American Sociological Review*, Vol. 5, No. 1, February.

SUTHERLAND, EDWIN H. (1956). *The Professional Thief*. Chicago.

SUTHERLAND, EDWIN H. and CRESSEY, DONALD R. (1955). *Principles of Criminology*. New York.

SYKES, G. M. (1958). *The Society of Captives*. Princeton, N.J.

TAYLOR, A. J. W. (1957). 'Personality Deterioration and Imprisonment.' Unpublished M.A. thesis, Victoria University, referred to in Taylor (1960).

TAYLOR, A. J. W. (1960). 'The Effects of Imprisonment', *British Journal of Criminology*, Vol. I, No. 1.

THAW, L. (1963). 'No Ledgers for St. Michaels', *Aspect*, No. 7.

THORP, A. (1954). *Calling Scotland Yard*. London.

TUTTLE, E. O. (1961). *The Crusade Against Capital Punishment*. London.

VIDA-NAQUET, P. (1963). *Torture – Cancer of Democracy*. London.

VON HENTIG, HANS (1948). *The Criminal and His Victim*. New Haven, Conn.

WATSON, E. H. and LOWREY, G. H. (1962). *The Growth and Development of Children*, 4th ed. London.

WAUGH, ALEC (1928). *The Last Chukka*. London.

WEST, D. J. (1963). *The Habitual Prisoner*. London.

WILDE, O. (1891). 'The Soul of Man under Socialism', *Fortnightly Review*, Vol. 49, pp. 292-319.

WILDE, O. (1898). 'The Ballad of Reading Gaol'. London.

WILKINS, L. T. (1962). 'Problems in Prediction Methods', in *The Sociology of Crime and Delinquency*. London and New York.

WILKINS, L. T. (1965). 'A Behavioural Theory of Drug Taking', in *The Howard Journal of Penology and Crime Prevention*, Vol. II, 1962-65.

WILLETT, T. C. (1964). *Criminal on the Road*. London.

WOLFGANG, M. E. (1962). 'Victim-Precipitated Criminal Homicide', in M. E. Wolfgang, L. Savitz and N. Johnson: *The Sociology of Crime and Delinquency*. New York.

WOLFGANG, M. E. and FERRACUTI, F. (1967). *The Subculture of Violence*. London.

WOODHAM SMITH, C. (1961). *The Great Hunger*. London.

WOOTTON, BARBARA (1950). *Testament for Social Science*. London.

WOOTTON, BARBARA (1959). *Social Science and Social Pathology*. London.

WOOTTON, BARBARA (1963). *Crime and Criminal Law*. London.

YOUNG, A. (1965). 'Models for Planning Recruitment and Promotion of Staff', *British Journal of Industrial Relations*, Vol. III.

ZETTERBERG, H. L. (1927). *On Theory and Verification in Sociology.* New York.

ACTS OF PARLIAMENT

Air Force Act 1955 (3 and 4 Eliz. 2, c. 19), Sections 71 and 72.
Army Act 1955 (3 and 4 Eliz. 2, c. 18), Sections 71 and 72.
Auctions (Bidding Agreements) Act 1927 (17 and 18 Geo. 5, c. 12).
Criminal Justice Act 1967 (c. 80).
Criminal Law Amendment Act 1885 (48 and 49 Vict., c. 69).
Naval Discipline Act 1957 (5 and 6 Eliz. 2, c. 53).
Protection of Animals (Anaesthetics) Act 1964 (c. 39).
Street Offences Act 1959 (7 and 8 Eliz. 2, c. 57).

OFFICIAL REPORTS

Aviation Contracts (1964). First Report of the Inquiry into the Pricing of Ministry of Aviation Contracts. Cmnd. 2428. London.
Capital Punishment (1949-53). Royal Commission on, Cmd. 8932. London.
Criminal Statistics (1957). Cmnd. 529. London.
Electrical Equipment (1963). Report on the Supply of Electrical Equipment for Mechanically Propelled Land Vehicles. House of Commons Paper No. 21. London.
Homosexual Offences and Prostitution (1957). Report of the Committee on, Cmnd. 247. London.
Penal Practice in a Changing Society (Aspects of Future Development (England and Wales)) (1959). Cmnd. 645. London.
Police (1962). Royal Commission on the, Cmnd. 1728. London.
Prisons (1960), Report of the Commissioners of, Cmnd. 1467. London.
Prisons (1961), Report of the Commissioners of, Cmnd. 1798. London.
Report by J. Scott Henderson, Q.C. of an enquiry into certain matters arising out of the Deaths of Mrs Beryl Evans and of Geraldine Evans and out of the conviction of Timothy John Evans of the Murder of Geraldine Evans (1953). Cmd. 8896. London.
Supplementary Report by J. Scott Henderson, Q.C. (1953). Cmd. 8946. London.

Report by Mr A. E. James, Q.C. into the circumstances in which it was possible for Detective Sergeant Harold Gordon Challenor to continue on duty at a time when he appears to have been affected by the onset of mental illness (1965). Cmnd. 2745. London.

Report of Inquiry by Mr W. L. Mars-Jones, Q.C., into the Inquiries made, for the Information of the Secretary of State for the Home Department, into the Case of Thomas Halloran and Patrick Joseph Cox and the Case of Patrick Albert Tisdall, Thomas Alfred Kingston and Sidney Hill-Burton (1964). Cmnd. 2526. London.

Sheffield Police Inquiry (1963). Cmnd. 2176. London.